# OXFORD HISTORICAL SERIES

*Editors*

V. H. GALBRAITH  J. S. WATSON  R. B. WERNHAM

BRITISH SERIES

# NOTE

*This Series comprises carefully selected studies which have been submitted, or are based upon theses submitted, for higher degrees in this University. In 1948 a new General Series was added to a British Series. The British Series is a collection of works which advance knowledge of the structural development, whether political, ecclesiastical, or economic, of British Society. The General Series comprises works on any aspect of non-British history, and also works on British history which lie outside the scope of the British Series.*

## BRITISH SERIES

*Public Order and Popular Disturbances, 1660–1714*
By M. BELOFF. 1938.

*The Corporation of Leicester*
By R. W. GREAVES. 1939.

*English Diplomatic Administration, 1259–1339*
By G. P. CUTTINO. 1940.

*The Social Ideas of Religious Leaders, 1660–1688*
By R. B. SCHLATTER. 1940.

*Northamptonshire County Elections and Electioneering, 1695–1832.* By ERIC G. FORRESTER. 1941.

*The Wiltshire Woollen Industry in the 16th and 17th Centuries.* By G. D. RAMSAY. 1943. *Out of print.*

*Elizabeth's Army.* By C. G. CRUICKSHANK. 1946.

*The English Lands of the Abbey of Bec*
By M. MORGAN. 1946.

*The Economic Development of some Leicestershire Estates.* By R. H. HILTON. 1947.

*The Oxfordshire Election of 1754.*
By R. J. ROBSON. 1949.

*Durham Jurisdictional Peculiars.*
By FRANK BARLOW. 1950.

## GENERAL SERIES

*Canonization and Authority in the Western Church*
By E. W. KEMP. 1948.

# MEDIEVAL ECCLESIASTICAL COURTS IN THE DIOCESE OF CANTERBURY

By

BRIAN L. WOODCOCK

Late Lecturer in History, University of Glasgow

OXFORD UNIVERSITY PRESS

LONDON: GEOFFREY CUMBERLEGE

1952

*Oxford University Press, Amen House, London E.C.4*

GLASGOW NEW YORK TORONTO MELBOURNE WELLINGTON
BOMBAY CALCUTTA MADRAS CAPE TOWN

*Geoffrey Cumberlege, Publisher to the University*

PRINTED IN GREAT BRITAIN

BRIAN LINDSAY WOODCOCK was born in London on 31 May 1920. He attended the City of London School where he was awarded a Skinners' Exhibition. He went up to Balliol College in 1939 as a commoner. He joined the Army in 1940. After four years with the Royal Signals, including active service in Normandy and Germany, he returned to Oxford in 1945 to resume his studies. In 1947 he won the Roger Hall Prize at Balliol and took a first class in the School of Modern History. In 1948 he was given an Honorary War Memorial Studentship, but in the autumn went to Glasgow, where he had been appointed an assistant in the Department of History in the University. In 1949 he was made a Lecturer. In March 1950 he was struck down by a serious illness and was not fit to do any work until January 1951. His recovery seemed to be complete, but in the summer heart trouble caused a relapse. He died on 28 July 1951, a few weeks after his marriage to Miss Audrey Murray.

Such is the brief story of the author of this study on pre-Reformation Church Courts in the Diocese of Canterbury. Woodcock began work on it in 1947 as a dissertation for the degree of Bachelor of Letters at Oxford. He proceeded to the degree in 1950, and revised his study after his illness. The book is based upon original work in the archives of the Dean and Chapter in Canterbury Cathedral. Since Dr. Churchill, in her important treatise on Canterbury Administration (1933), showed how much could be done in the neglected field of ecclesiastical jurisdiction, and the Librarian of the Dean and Chapter, the late W. P. Blore, in his self-effacing and generous way, revealed to his fellow scholars the wealth of unexplored material at Canterbury, much fine work has been done, and is now being done, on the ecclesiastical archives of Canterbury, just as the devoted labours of the late Canon C. W. Foster at Lincoln and the numerous writings of Professor Hamilton Thompson broke the ice which for so long had locked up the secrets of diocesan and cathedral muniments elsewhere. Woodcock's book, none the less, is the work of a pioneer, for it opens vistas which historical scholars, including Maitland, had feared to be closed. It is a very remarkable outcome of three years' study, and justifies the insight of his supervisor, Miss Kathleen Major, who suggested the subject to him. His survey of the material available at Canterbury, and his scholarly, though necessarily tentative, illustration of the uses to which it can be put, reveal unexpected possibilities of insight into the daily lives of men and women in a pre-Reformation diocese as subjects of an active jurisdiction, parallel to that of the common law. That this jurisdiction existed we already knew, but the prospect of seeing it at work is exciting.

F. M. P.

OXFORD
*September* 1951

# ACKNOWLEDGEMENTS

My husband did not have an opportunity of examining this work in proof. It is very likely in consequence that there are errors now remaining which he would have wished to be rectified; for these I must take responsibility. I have added only one footnote, the substance of which I know he wished to be included.

He would have wanted to make grateful acknowledgement for assistance at all stages of this work, first and in particular to Miss Kathleen Major, who supervised the preparation of his thesis, and has been most generous in encouragement, assistance, and advice; and also to Sir Maurice Powicke, Professor V. H. Galbraith, and Professor Norma Adams for help and suggestions. Our friend Mr. W. Urry, Archivist to the Dean and Chapter of Canterbury, makes work on the documents in his care congenial as well as fruitful, and has given much help; and the gratitude of all who work on ecclesiastical court material in Canterbury must always be extended to the late Mr. W. P. Blore, formerly honorary Librarian to the Dean and Chapter, some of whose transcriptions have been used in this volume. Mr. Blore's work was always at the service of others. Acknowledgement and thanks for access to archives are due primarily to the Dean and Chapter of Canterbury and to the Kent County Record Office at Maidstone. Extracts from *Archaeologia Cantiana* are reproduced by permission of the Kent Archaeological Society.

I must add my own grateful thanks for assistance with proofs, and the many queries arising from them, to many of those already mentioned, but also to Mr. R. W. Southern, and in particular to Dr. E. L. G. Stones, who has most kindly put his time, experience, and meticulous care at my disposal.

There are various scholars and friends not mentioned here by name who will, I hope, understand that their assistance has been appreciated. Finally, my husband would have particularly desired me to express his gratitude to his mother, whose patient and accurate preparation of typescript greatly eased his labour.

A. M. W.

# CONTENTS

ABBREVIATIONS      x

MAP OF DIOCESE OF CANTERBURY      xii

INTRODUCTION      I

## PART I

## THE JURISDICTIONS

I.  (i)  Canterbury Diocesan Jurisdiction      6
  (ii)  Sede Vacante Jurisdiction      15
 (iii)  The Archdeaconry of Canterbury      19
 (iv)  The Exempt Parishes      21
  (v)  Relations between the Jurisdictions      26

## PART II

## PROCEDURE AND PRACTICE OF THE COURTS

II.  TYPES OF BUSINESS AND SESSIONS OF THE COURTS      30

III.  THE PERSONNEL AND THEIR DUTIES      37

IV.  PRACTICE OF THE COURTS. INSTANCE      50

V.  PRACTICE OF THE COURTS. APPEALS IN INSTANCE CASES      63

VI.  PRACTICE OF THE COURTS. EX OFFICIO      68

VII.  PRACTICE OF THE COURTS. PROBATE      72

VIII.  FINANCIAL ADMINISTRATION      75

IX.  NUMBERS AND TYPES OF CASE      79

CHART illustrating amount of 'Instance' business handled by the Consistory Court, 1373–1535      84

X.  THE ENFORCEMENT OF DISCIPLINE      93

XI.  THE COURTS AND SOCIETY      103

# CONTENTS

## APPENDIX

| | |
|---|---|
| I. Lists of Officers of the Courts | 113 |
| II. Commission of Registrar of Consistory Court | 123 |
| III. *Sede Vacante* Commission of Apparitor General of City and Diocese | 124 |
| IV. Disposal of Instance Cases: Consistory Court | 125 |
| V. *Acta* and Bill of Costs | 125 |
| VI. Documents in Tuitorial Appeal | 126 |
| VII. A General *Provocatio* | 131 |
| VIII. Instructions for Ex Officio Citation | 133 |
| IX. Exercise of the Prerogative Jurisdiction | 133 |
| X. Documents in Defamation Suit | 134 |
| XI. An Expense Account | 135 |
| BIBLIOGRAPHY | 138 |
| INDEX | 147 |

# ABBREVIATIONS

| | |
|---|---|
| *Arch. Cant.* | *Archaeologia Cantiana.* |
| *B.I.H.R.* | *Bulletin of the Institute of Historical Research.* |
| Bracton | Bracton, *De Legibus et Consuetudinibus Angliae.* |
| *Chichele* (C. Y. Soc.) | *Register of Archbishop Chichele*, Canterbury and York Society, ed. E. F. Jacob. |
| Churchill | I. J. Churchill, *Canterbury Administration.* |
| *C.P.L.* | *Calendar of Papal Letters.* |
| *C.P.R.* | *Calendar of Patent Rolls.* |
| E.E.T.S. | Early English Text Society. |
| *E.H.R.* | *English Historical Review.* |
| Fournier | P. Fournier, *Les Officialités au Moyen Age.* |
| Gibson | E. Gibson, *Codex Iuris Ecclesiastici Anglicani* (Oxford, 1761). |
| H.M.C. | Historical Manuscripts Commission. |
| Holdsworth | W. S. Holdsworth, *History of the English Law.* |
| Le Neve | J. Le Neve, *Fasti Ecclesiae Anglicanae*, &c. (Oxford, 1854). |
| *Lib. Arch. El.* | C. L. Feltoe and E. H. Minns, *Vetus Liber Archidiaconi Eliensis*, Cambridge Antiquarian Society, No. XLVIII. |
| *L. P. Henry VIII.* | *Calendar of Letters and Papers, Foreign and Domestic, Henry VIII* (1864–1932). |
| Lyndwood | W. Lyndwood, *Provinciale* (Oxford, 1679). |
| Phillimore | R. Phillimore, *Ecclesiastical Law of the Church of England* (1895). |
| P.R.O. | Public Record Office. |
| *Reg. Epp. Jo. Peckham.* | *Registrum Epistolarum Johannis Peckham, Archiepiscopi Cantuariensis*, Rolls Series, ed. C. T. Martin. |
| *Rot. Parl.* | *Rotuli Parliamentorum* (1771–83). |
| R.S. | Rolls Series. |
| Smith | R. A. L. Smith, *Canterbury Cathedral Priory.* |
| Somner | W. Somner, *Antiquities of Canterbury*, ed. N. Battely (1703). |
| *T.R.Hist.S.* | *Transactions of the Royal Historical Society.* |
| *V.C.H.* | *Victoria County History.* |
| Wilkins | *Concilia Magnae Britanniae et Hiberniae*, ed. D. Wilkins (London, 1737). |
| *Winchelsey* (C. Y. Soc.) | *Register of Archbishop Winchelsey*, Canterbury and York Society, ed. R. Graham. |

## ABBREVIATIONS RELATING TO MSS. SOURCES

*(Dean and Chapter Library, Canterbury, unless otherwise noted)*

| | |
|---|---|
| C. Ant. | Chartae Antiquae. |
| Ch. Ch. Letters | Christ Church Letters. |
| E. S. Roll | Ecclesiastical Suit Roll. |
| Lit. MS. | Literary MS. |
| MS. | Manuscript (not otherwise designated). |
| P.R.C. | Probate Registry Collection at Kent County Record Office, Maidstone. |
| Reg. | Register, unless otherwise designated Lambeth or Maidstone, in the Dean and Chapter Library, Canterbury. |
| S.V. 1; 2; 3. | Sede Vacante Scrapbooks 1, 2, 3. |

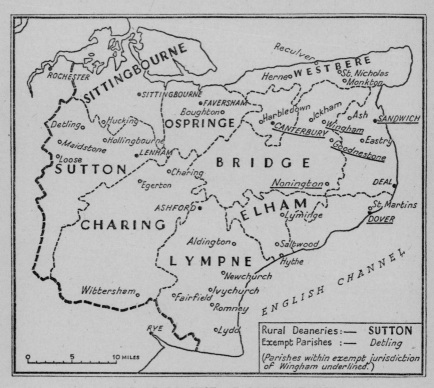

MAP OF DIOCESE OF CANTERBURY

For list of exempt churches see Somner, Appendix to Supplement, p. 57.

# INTRODUCTION

THE character and scope of ecclesiastical jurisdiction in England during the Middle Ages has largely been derived from studies in the Canon Law, collections of Provincial Constitutions, Bishops' Registers, and the printed records of episcopal visitations. The organization and practice of the Courts Christian, or ecclesiastical courts, which by their ubiquity and continuous session bore the greater burden of the enforcement of canonical discipline and the work of settling pleas answerable *in foro ecclesiastico*, have still to be investigated. By analogy, our knowledge of the history of the Common Law in England, if still restricted to similar evidences upon which our knowledge of the operation of ecclesiastical jurisdiction is based, would extend little farther than the information which could be gleaned from Bracton and Fleta and the printed records of the general eyres. Little would be known about the practice of the central courts or of the local courts, whether communal or franchisal.

This preliminary study of the operation of the courts within the diocese of Canterbury may, I hope, shed a little light on the actual organization and practice of the Courts Christian in England before the Reformation. A knowledge of the working and routine of these courts should provide keys to open many doors: the incidence and character of tithe disputes; the practice of ecclesiastical judges in matrimonial causes; the duties of churchwardens; the work of probate; the procedure in cases of defamation and perjury; the relations of the courts with the Common Law courts and the secular power; and many other aspects of ecclesiastical jurisdiction which the records of these courts illuminate.

In 1898 the late F. W. Maitland complained of the lack of material which might be employed for the reconstruction of the history and organization of ecclesiastical courts. 'As yet', he wrote, 'very few attempts have been made to put into print the records out of which that history must be wrung.'[1] Little has been achieved since. In the main we still have

[1] F. W. Maitland, *Roman Canon Law in the Church of England*, p. 130.

to rely for our knowledge of these courts upon the report Stubbs drew up for the Royal Commission of 1883[1] and upon reference books on Ecclesiastical Law.[2] The two main reasons for the comparative lack of progress in this field are: first, the inaccessibility of ecclesiastical court records;[3] and secondly, the difficulty of interpreting an often singularly repellent and seemingly intractable bulk of material. It is to be hoped that the forthcoming report on ecclesiastical archives to be drawn up under the auspices of the Pilgrim Trust will help to remedy problems of accessibility and provide a nation-wide survey of ecclesiastical court records; while increasing familiarity with the organization and business routine of the courts will assist archivists and editors.

This present study is restricted to a survey of the two Canterbury diocesan courts, the Consistory Court and the Archdeacon's Court, in pre-Reformation times. It is divided into two parts. Part I is devoted to a brief account of the development of the jurisdictions and their relationships. Part II contains a description of the organization and procedure of the courts. The records of the Canterbury courts provide suitable material for a preliminary study of this kind because of their comparative accessibility, the presence of many pre-Reformation Act books, and by the presence of much vital accessory material relating to the courts contained in the archives of the prior and chapter of the monastery of Christchurch which are now in the possession of the Dean and Chapter of Canterbury.

In 1928–9 a great quantity of court records belonging to the diocesan Consistory Court and the Court of the Archdeacon of Canterbury was transferred from the Diocesan

---

[1] Report on Ecclesiastical Courts, 1883, Historical Appendix No. 1 to vol. i (Parliamentary Papers, 1883, vol. xxiv).
[2] See Bibliography, pp. 143–4.
[3] For a vehement American view upon the inaccessibility of these records cf. M. Knappen, Tudor Puritanism, p. 517: 'The Records of Ecclesiastical Courts are as yet largely unworked. Guarded by prohibitive fees and scattered about in every conceivable place from the basement of Somerset House to the attic of the provincial lawyer who acts as diocesan chancellor, they rouse unprintable thoughts of envy and despair.' Even before Mr. Knappen wrote (1939), classification of accessible diocesan records has been in progress at the Diocesan Archives, York; the Record Office, Lincoln; the Museum, Leicester; the Essex County Record Office; and at the Bodleian Library, Oxford.

Registry store over the Christchurch Gate to the Dean and Chapter Library, where it remained for many years inadequately catalogued and inadequately described. Another collection of Probate Act books, Wills and Registers of Wills, together with material relating to the same courts, once contained in the Canterbury Probate Registry, is now deposited in the Kent County Record Office at Maidstone.

The mere bulk of these two collections is disheartening. Some three hundred Act books survive at Canterbury alone. About forty Act books survive from the period preceding the year 1535. The earliest surviving Consistory Court Act book dates from 1364 and the earliest Archdeaconry Court Act book from 1476, but evidence of the operation of the courts in the late thirteenth century is contained in the archives of the prior and chapter of Christchurch surviving from those periods when the courts were under the supervision or control of commissaries of the prior and chapter during vacancies of the archiepiscopal see. All this material, together with information contained in the series of Archbishops' Registers at Lambeth, provides adequate evidence of the operation and procedure of the two courts in the three centuries preceding the Reformation. It must be emphasized that the limitation of date is imposed from without and is not intrinsic to the records themselves. The Reformation caused a certain confusion and lowering of business standards but caused no break in the continuity of the administration of the courts.

The limitations of this study preclude any detailed comparison between the working of the courts within the diocese of Canterbury and courts in other dioceses. It is obvious, however, that the Canterbury courts are unique in so far as their jurisdictions were subordinated to the archbishop of Canterbury and not merely to a bishop as 'Ordinary' within his own diocese. Their officers stood in a more direct relationship to the archbishop than the majority of ecclesiastical judges in the rest of the kingdom. Another general point of comparison is due to the comparatively small size of the diocese of Canterbury, covering as it did only the eastern half of Kent. In a diocese as large as that of Lincoln, covering several counties, there were not only several archdeacons' courts, but also a number of courts of commissaries of the bishop within the various archdeaconries, as well as the Consistory Court of the bishop at Lincoln. Within the diocese of Canterbury, apart from certain exempt jurisdictions, there were only two courts—the Consistory Court and the Archdeacon's Court—and the relationship between them was different from that prevailing elsewhere.[1] With regard to procedure or legal practice, however, a comparison with other courts should not reveal many differences, for all Courts Christian were subject to the rules of a universal Canon Law and staffed by professional judges who moved from one court to another in the course of their careers;[2] but no adequate basis exists for the correlation of the practice of particular courts with the injunctions of the Canon Law. The collections of English Provincial Constitutions and even Lyndwood's gloss provide but meagre material for an effective comparison, and as yet few attempts have been made to correlate or edit medieval manuscripts in English libraries dealing more specifically with the practice and processes of the ecclesiastical courts.[3] Apart from references in particular details, the whole emphasis of this study has been placed upon the actual working and business routine of the courts.

The limitations of this study also preclude excursions into those fields of general ecclesiastical activities and institutions which the court records so profusely illustrate. The temptation to produce a hasty anthology of illustrations of the general ecclesiastical and social background is very great, for the custom of the ecclesiastical lawyer in writing down the depositions of witnesses has meant that the *acta* of the ecclesiastical courts contain intimate, vivid, and piquant revelations of the lives, characters, and opinions of many ranks and conditions of men. This type of historical material can only be given its full value once the frame in which it is set is thoroughly delineated and the administrative and judicial contexts adequately elucidated. The full record of a tithe dispute may be scattered in any number of different Act books

---

[1] *Infra*, p. 13.
[2] *Infra*, pp. 37–38.
[3] Dr. L. Warhmund printed some of the more general treatises in *Quellen zur Geschichte des römisch-kanonischen Processes im Mittelalter* (Innsbruck, 1907–28).

and loose papers which frequently defy rapid or logical cross reference. The arrangement and the use of this material can only follow the preliminary reconstruction of the business routine of the court or courts concerned. This study can only incidentally indicate the wealth of material to be found in the court records.[1]

[1] *Infra*, pp. 139–40, for remarks on arrangement and classification of ecclesiastical court records.

# PART ONE

## I

## THE JURISDICTIONS

### (i) CANTERBURY DIOCESAN JURISDICTION.[1]

IT is wise to assume, in studying the growth of medieval institutions and jurisdictions, a progress from the less formal and ill defined to the more formal and well defined. The evolution of the courts exercising the jurisdiction of the archbishops of Canterbury does not differ in this respect from the evolution of the king's Courts of Law. Indeed, the process of definition of both lay and ecclesiastical jurisdictions was roughly contemporaneous. It is in the second half of the thirteenth century that the archbishops of Canterbury were finally equipped with a provincial court operating in London, the Court of Canterbury, a peripatetic Court of Audience attendant upon their own person or household, and a Consistory Court exercising purely diocesan jurisdiction within their own see of Canterbury. This proliferation and definition of courts was caused by the great increase in the provincial appeal business of the archbishop and the substitution of regular court machinery to replace the older system of appointing judges delegate to hear cases of appeal from inferior jurisdictions. The delimitation of the archbishop's diocesan jurisdiction and the evolution of the archbishop's 'Consistory Court' at Canterbury as a purely diocesan court was a residue of the process of obtaining well-defined courts of jurisdiction on the provincial level.

The detailed history of the evolution of these various courts is difficult to unravel, partly because of the loose termi-

---

[1] For a detailed survey of the administration of the archbishops of Canterbury the reader is referred to the great pioneer work of Miss Irene Churchill, *Canterbury Administration*. This, and Miss Marjorie Morgan's article, 'Early Canterbury Jurisdiction', *E.H.R.*, vol. lx (1945), pp. 392–9, form the base for this chapter, which is mainly concerned with the further elucidation of the history of the archbishop's diocesan jurisdiction.

nology employed in a period of rapidly evolving jurisdictions, but largely because of the unsatisfactory nature of the surviving material. To ease the difficulties of terminology the following terms are employed in this study:

'CURIA CANTUARIENSIS' is employed to denote the jurisdiction of the archbishop over all his province, in his position as metropolitan, irrespective of particular court apparatus. It is used for describing the archbishop's jurisdiction in the period before the full delimitation of his various courts.

THE COURT OF CANTERBURY is employed to denote the actual court apparatus which dealt with the provincial appeal business of the archbishop.

From the end of the thirteenth century this court sat in the church of St. Mary de Arcubus (Bow Church) in the archbishop's exempt deanery of the Arches within the city of London. The archbishop's Official presided over its sessions. He frequently combined his office with that of dean of the Arches. In modern times the court is officially known as the *Court of Arches*.

'CONSISTORY COURT' is employed to describe the court apparatus at Canterbury irrespective of the jurisdiction exercised by it.

CONSISTORY COURT is employed to denote the diocesan court of the archbishop. The judge of this court was the archbishop's 'commissary general of Canterbury'.

It would be dangerous to assume that any mention of the archbishop's 'Consistory Court' at Canterbury before *c.* 1278 indicates that this was the same institution as that presided over at a later period by the commissary general of Canterbury and which served the archbishop as a forum for the conduct of diocesan litigation. It is highly probable that in the period before the establishment of the Court of Canterbury in London the undifferentiated jurisdiction of the archbishop was exercised through the medium of one court sitting in the cathedral at Canterbury, and this may well have been termed his 'Consistory Court'. That this may be so is indicated by the apparent absence of the officer known as the 'commissary general of Canterbury' or as 'commissary general of the city and diocese of Canterbury', who presided over the sessions of the later diocesan Consistory Court, and by the evidence which may be gleaned concerning the establishment of the Court of Canterbury in London.

The title 'commissary general' in itself is a vague term. At an early period when jurisdiction was ill defined and persons were frequently delegated to deal with specific cases coming within the cognizance of the archbishop, the term 'commissary' was probably often employed to denote such persons; but the fuller titles, 'commissary general of the city and diocese of Canterbury' or 'commissary general of Canterbury', seem to indicate a person whose authority is exercised over a particular area. There is no evidence of the existence of an officer bearing these more elaborate titles or their equivalent before 1278–9, when Robert de Seleseya, or Celeseye (Selsey), appears as the commissary of the prior and chapter of Christchurch dealing with business arising within the city and diocese of Canterbury and the archbishop's exempt deaneries during the vacancy preceding the election of Archbishop Pecham.[1] This commissary, Miss Morgan hints, was a predecessor of Master Martin de Hampton, the commissary general of Archbishop Pecham, the first for whom a commission of appointment survives.[2]

Miss Churchill perhaps exaggerates the antiquity of the office of commissary general of Canterbury when, in reference to Master Martin's commission, she claims it to be an office 'well established, whose general sphere was known and understood'.[3] She found a predecessor for M. Martin de Hampton in a certain John de Ravingham,[4] and although the latter may be identified with a John de Ravenigham who appears as a proctor in the rolls of the 'Curia Cantuariensis' of 1272[5] and as presiding judge of the 'Consistory Court' c. 1279,[6] there is no evidence of any predecessor to the Robert

[1] e.g. S.V. 1, p. 98. Two certificates of citation from the deanery of Bocking, dated 20 July 1278 and 7 Feb. 1278/9. They were addressed to 'venerando discrecionis viro fratri Roberto de Celeseye Commissario dominorum prioris et capituli ecclesie Christi Cant' iurisdiccione archiepiscopali ecclesiarum et decanatuum civitatis et diocesis Cant' et extra exemptarum sede vacante'.

[2] M. Morgan, 'Early Canterbury Jurisdiction', E.H.R., vol. lx (1945), p. 397. For text of commission, see Churchill, vol. ii, p. 13.

[3] Churchill, vol. i, p. 54.  [4] Ibid.

[5] e.g. E.S. Roll No. 21, 'Acta' from 26 Mar. 1272.

[6] S.V. 3, p. 7. Fragmentary deposition in a matrimonial suit dated 1294 wherein it is alleged that he had ordered the marriage of the parties sixteen years previously.

de Seleseya of 1278. A certain Henry of Depham appears as 'commissary general' of the Official in the rolls of the 'Curia Cantuariensis' which survive from the vacancy of 1270–3, but he is never described as 'commissary general of Canterbury' and is never found dealing with first-instance diocesan cases.[1]

None of the extensive administrative records of the prior and chapter of Christchurch contains references to a 'commissary general of Canterbury' before 1278. Citations and mandates connected with suits in which the prior and chapter were involved were addressed either to the archbishop's Official or to the dean of Christianity at Canterbury,[2] never to the commissary general of Canterbury, who is certainly found dealing with this business of citation and delivery of mandates at a later period.[3] The continuator of Gervase makes no mention of the commissary general in an account of many events of local interest.[4] The existing evidence seems to suggest that there was no such officer before 1278; nor would the need have arisen for a diocesan commissary until the archbishop's Official was permanently occupied with the business of presiding over the sessions of the Court of Canterbury in London. Before this court was permanently established within the deanery of the Arches, the Official could still exercise a close supervision of affairs within the diocese. In the event, it would appear, even then, that the Officials only reluctantly relinquished their supervision of diocesan affairs, and that the direct appointment of the commissaries general of Canterbury by the archbishops was preceded for a time by their appointment by the Officials. At least the early commissaries of the prior and chapter were considered as deputies of the Official during the periods when the archiepiscopal see was vacant. In 1278–9 Robert de Seleseya sometimes describes himself as 'gerens vices dominorum Prioris et capituli ecclesie Xpi Cant' et eorundem Officialis

---

[1] E.S. Rolls *passim*; cf. M. Morgan, 'Early Canterbury Jurisdiction', *E.H.R.*, vol. lx (1945), p. 398.
[2] e.g. in the many documents under the general heading C.Ant. D. which relate to the prolonged dispute between the prior of Christchurch and the monastery of St. Martin's, Dover.
[3] Cf. Churchill, vol. i, chap. 1.
[4] Gervase, *Opera* (R.S.), vol. ii.

commissarius'.[1] At the beginning of the vacancy of 1292–4, the Official of the prior and chapter, John de Selveston, issued a commission to Richard de Clyve, appointing him commissary, 'Quia excercicio iurisdiccionis in civitate et Dyocesi Cant' intendere non poterimus arduis frequencius negotiis prepediti ...', to exercise the diocesan jurisdiction 'quotiens nos abesse contigerit'.[2] This may have been presumption on the part of this Official, but it may reflect an earlier custom. The prior and chapter had on this same occasion already directly commissioned Richard de Clyve to be their commissary,[3] and alongside the crossed-out copy of the Official's commission in their register is written: 'Ista commissio fuit ab omnibus in capitulo reprobata'.[4] Apparently the prior and chapter preferred to delegate their authority directly. The archbishops did likewise. Archbishop Pecham had already directly appointed Master Martin de Hampton in 1282.[5] In so far as the available evidence allows, it is probable that the exercise of the archbishop's diocesan jurisdiction by a separate commissary general began within a few years of 1278. This accords well with the evidence which suggests that it was just at this period that the Court of Canterbury was permanently established in London.

Miss Morgan has traced the development of the archbishop's provincial jurisdiction.[6] She found that in regard to the hearing of appeals 'a thorough formalization of business took place at Canterbury during the primacy of Boniface of Savoy' (1245–70) and that the older custom of 'delegating the settlement of provincial cases to some local dignitary had given way to a new practice of hearing the routine in a central court held at Canterbury and presided over by the Official of Canterbury or his commissary'. She also decides, however, that some time before the end of the thirteenth century the Court of Canterbury in London 'had supplanted the Court at Canterbury for routine provincial business'.[7]

---

[1] e.g. S.V. 2, p. 168. Issue of *provocatio* against usurpation of jurisdiction by the archdeacon dated 12 June 1278. (*Infra*, pp. 66–67 for description of *provocationes*.)
[2] Reg. Q, f. 3. Commission dated 4 Jan. 1292/3.
[3] Churchill, vol. ii, p. 13. Commission dated 14 Dec. 1292.
[4] Reg. Q, f. 3.            [5] Churchill, vol. ii, p. 13.
[6] M. Morgan, 'Early Canterbury Jurisdiction', *E.H.R.*, vol. lx (1945), pp. 392–9.
[7] Ibid., p. 397.

The problem of the date of the transfer of the hearing of provincial business to London is a vexed one. The earliest surviving regulations for the admission of proctors and advocates of the Court of Canterbury are contained in a letter of Archbishop Kilwardby (1272–8) which he sent to the dean of Arches, who may have already been used to conducting provincial business on the archbishop's behalf.[1] Against this there is evidence to show that during the vacancy of 1270–3 this business was conducted at Canterbury by commissaries of the prior and chapter of Christchurch. Nine rolls of the 'Curia Cantuariensis' survive from this period in the Dean and Chapter Library. They contain *acta* of cases heard at Canterbury.[2] Local Canterbury men or agents of the prior and chapter were engaged as proctors on this occasion, for on the dorse of one roll appear the names of nine 'notariorum capituli ecclesie Xpi Cant' iuratorum sede vacante', some of whom frequently appear elsewhere as conducting the business of the monastery.[3] This Sede Vacante material, however, does not necessarily indicate that this was the last occasion in which the business of the 'Curia Cantuariensis' was conducted at Canterbury. It is possible that Archbishop Boniface may have already commissioned the dean of the Arches to deal with such business and that the prior and chapter of Christchurch may have insisted that it should be conducted at Canterbury for the duration of the vacancy. Unfortunately no evidence of the conduct of provincial business survives for the vacancy of 1278–9, but it appears that during the primacy of Pecham (1279–92)[4] and certainly during the vacancy that followed his death, 1292–4, the provincial appeal business was being conducted in London.[5] There is no indication that it was ever conducted at Canterbury again, even during periods when the archiepiscopal see was vacant. The year 1279 may therefore be provisionally allotted as a

[1] Cf. Churchill, vol. i, p. 426; for text, Wilkins, vol. ii, pp. 37 et seq.

[2] E.S. Rolls Nos. 14, 15, 18, 20, 21, 22, 39, 208, 222.

[3] William de Essexia, Henry de Berrewic, John de Beccles appear many times in contemporary Ch.Ch. registers as agents of the prior and chapter. The six others are Richard le Doul de Cant', John de Cambio de Cant', Michael de Lenna, Winfred de Sco. Martino, John de Furneus, William Freysel.

[4] Cf. Churchill, vol. i, pp. 424–69.

[5] E.S. Rolls and Sede Vacante material *passim*.

limiting date to the permanent establishment of the Court of
Canterbury in London.

Whether the establishment of this court was five or ten
years earlier than 1279, it involved the abandonment of the
apparatus of the 'Consistory Court' at Canterbury, in so far
as provincial business was concerned. The latter court was,
however, still suitable for the hearing of first-instance diocesan cases. It would appear that its position as the diocesan
court of the archbishop took a few years to be strictly defined.
Its judges, the commissaries general of Canterbury, now the
chief administrative agents of the archbishops within the diocese, still possessed a certain measure of control over the
archbishop's exempt deaneries outside the diocesan bound-
aries.[1] During the 1278–9 vacancy Robert de Seleseya, the
diocesan commissary of the prior and chapter of Christchurch, received certificates of citations of persons required
to attend the 'Consistory Court' from within these deaneries.[2]
Master Martin de Hampton, the commissary general of
Archbishop Pecham, possessed certain powers within these
same jurisdictions;[3] but after 1292 there is no evidence,
either from the *acta* of the Consistory Court for the vacancy
of 1292–4, or from the later fourteenth- and fifteenth-century
Act books, to suggest that this extended jurisdiction over the
exempt deaneries was maintained. Appeal cases arising within
these jurisdictions were heard at the Court of Canterbury or
in the Court of Audience.[4]

The subordinate status of the 'Consistory Court' at Canterbury was soon recognized in the matter of appellate jurisdiction. At least as early as 1288, a regular avenue of appeal
from the 'Consistory Court' to the Court of Canterbury had
been established, for in that year an appeal was made in a
matrimonial suit against a sentence published by the commissary, Master Martin de Hampton. In 1294 Richard de
Clyve, the commissary of the prior and chapter of Christchurch, received the 'remission' of this same suit from the
Court of Canterbury.[5] The *acta* of numerous cases of appeal

[1] For a description of these deaneries see Churchill, vol. i, pp. 62–81.
[2] *Supra*, p. 8 and n. 4.       [3] Cf. Churchill, vol. i, p. 56.       [4] Ibid., p. 80.
[5] S.V. 3, p. 66. Remission in matrimonial suit 'Muriel of Dunham *v.* John
Burnoth of Chartham', dated 22 July 1294. E.S. Roll No. 49 contains depositions
of witnesses in this suit.

from the Consistory Court to the Court of Canterbury survive among the Sede Vacante material of the period 1292–4.

Another fact which tends to support the thesis of a late
definition of the archbishop's diocesan jurisdiction is the
absence of any avenue of appeal between the Court of the
Archdeacon of Canterbury and the Consistory Court. In
later medieval and modern times appeals lay from the Court
of the Archdeacon to the Court of Canterbury or to the Court
of Audience, never to the Consistory Court at Canterbury.
In other dioceses the archdeacons' courts were subordinate
in this respect to the consistory courts of the bishops.[1] That
no such appellate jurisdiction was exercised by the Consistory
Court at Canterbury may have been due to the privileged
position of the archdeacon of Canterbury as coadjutor to the
archbishop[2] but was probably due in part to the late definition
of the archbishop's diocesan jurisdiction. The diocesan Consistory Court came, as it were, to be set alongside an older
channel of appeal from the archdeacon's jurisdiction to the
'Curia Cantuariensis'. Even though the 'Consistory Court'
at Canterbury had come to deal exclusively with diocesan
business, plaintiffs and defendants in the Archdeacon's Court
continued to enjoy the right of appeal to the highest courts of
the archbishop. This privileged position of archbishops'
archdeacons in the matter of appeals was recognized in the
1533 Act in Restraint of Appeals.[3]

Evidence concerning the operation of the 'Consistory
Court' at Canterbury before the year 1300 is limited to
(i) a description of the court in the year 1259; (ii) documents
surviving from the vacancy of 1278–9; (iii) rolls and documents surviving from the vacancy of 1292–4.[4] The description of the 'Consistory Court' and its personnel is contained
in the 'Boniface Roll'[5] which records a dispute between the
monks of Christchurch and Archbishop Boniface. The monks
were refusing to admit the claim that the archbishop could
cite them to appear before him outside the monastic precincts
to answer various charges he had prepared against some of

---

[1] Cf. Constitutions of Clarendon, c. 4.
[2] For description of powers of the archdeacon of Canterbury, see Churchill,
vol. i, pp. 43–53.  [3] 24 Hen. VIII, c. 12.
[4] Infra, pp. 138–42 for description of MSS. sources.  [5] C.Ant. A 7b.

their number. At one stage in a long dispute they decided to
appeal to Rome. They published the appeal 'coram consistorio capituli . . . domini Archiepiscopi' in the cathedral.
The account of this event includes a long list of officers and
other persons who were present on that occasion. The presiding judge was a certain Walter de Achiryse (Acrise) *gerente
vices officialis curie Cant'*. The account also lists a *notarius
consistorii*; perhaps the registrar; four *clerici consistorii*, who
were probably proctors; a *preco* or crier; and a number of
persons who were probably parties to suits pending in the
court on that particular day.[1]

Unfortunately no indication is given of the scope of the
jurisdiction exercised through the medium of this 'Consistory Court' apart from the description of the judge as the
deputy of the Official 'Curie Cantuariensis'. It is possible that
it is the still undifferentiated jurisdiction of the archbishop as
metropolitan. The Official, Hugh de Mortimer, is found
from the same account to be attending the archbishop in
person at his manor of Teynham.

The rolls and documents which survive from the vacancy
of 1278–9 are exclusively of a non-provincial and mainly
diocesan character. This is in itself not a decisive indication
that the 'Consistory Court' was restricted to that type of
business, but it would appear from the existence of two sets
of officers that provincial and diocesan business were now
distinct. While R. de Stratford was appointed Official of the
Court of Canterbury,[2] Robert de Seleseya is found acting as
the commissary of the prior and chapter of Christchurch for
the conduct of business arising within the diocese and exempt
deaneries.[3] The rolls and documents surviving from the
vacancy of 1292–4 show quite clearly that during this
vacancy the prior and chapter appointed officers to supervise
two distinct jurisdictions through the medium of two distinct
courts. Master John de Selveston, their Official, presided
over the Court of Canterbury in London, while Richard de
Clyve, as commissary for the diocese, presided over the Consistory Court at Canterbury.[4]

---

[1] For names of the officers of the court see Appendix No. I.
[2] Reg. I, f. 150b.                                    [3] *Infra*, p. 8 and n. 1.
[4] By the composition of 1278, regarding the conduct of *sede vacante* jurisdiction

## (ii) SEDE VACANTE JURISDICTION

It is unfortunate that our knowledge of early Canterbury jurisdiction is so largely confined to the evidence of material surviving from periods when the archiepiscopal see was vacant, for *sede vacante* jurisdiction was itself subject to delimitation during the thirteenth century. The disputes which arose between conflicting claimants for the exercise of this jurisdiction seriously jeopardized its effective operation in the two vacancies 1278–9 and 1292–4.

During the thirteenth century there were three claimants for the exercise of Canterbury jurisdiction on the death or resignation of an archbishop: the bishops of the province; the prior and chapter of Christchurch; and the archdeacon of Canterbury. The disputes arising between the first two are well known. They were resolved by the settlement of 1278, when it was arranged that the bishop of London should choose the Official of Canterbury from two persons to be nominated by the prior and chapter; the Official then to be formally appointed by the prior and chapter. The nomination of the two persons for election by the bishop of London was to be made within a month. During this preliminary period the prior and chapter could conduct provincial business without interference.[1]

The conflict between the prior and chapter and the archdeacons has never been described in any detail. It was waged on the diocesan rather than the provincial level. It would appear that during the vacancies of 1240–5 and 1270–3 the archdeacons exercised wide powers, but after their conflicts with the prior and chapter during the vacancies of 1278–9 and 1292–4 the monks of Christchurch (latterly under the energetic leadership of Prior Henry of Eastry) virtually

drawn up between the bishops of the province of Canterbury and the prior and chapter of Christchurch, the prior and chapter were allowed a month's grace after the death or resignation of an archbishop before they nominated two persons to be presented to the bishop of London for the latter to choose one as Official of Canterbury. During this month the prior and chapter could appoint a person to transact both provincial and diocesan business. They did so in 1292 and during later vacancies (cf. Churchill, vol. i, pp. 554–6), but there is no evidence to suggest that the sessions of the Court of Canterbury were transferred to Canterbury during these very brief periods.

[1] See Churchill, vol. i, p. 555, and pp. 551–70 for discussion of *sede vacante* jurisdiction in general.

excluded the archdeacons from the conduct of the *sede vacante* jurisdiction within the diocese. The archdeacons during these last two vacancies seem to have based their claims on purely temporary settlements made between their predecessors and the prior and chapter during the two previous vacancies. In 1241, after the death of Archbishop Edmund Rich, the prior and chapter came to an agreement with the formidable Archdeacon Simon Langton, the brother of Archbishop Stephen Langton. For the duration of this vacancy Simon Langton was granted the powers of institution within and without the diocese, collation to vacant benefices, the cognition of matrimonial causes, and the right to signify excommunicates to Chancery.[1] This grant of *sede vacante* powers was to operate in Simon's lifetime and was therefore temporary in character, but it probably represented the basis for the archdeacons' claims during the remaining vacancies of the thirteenth century. The exercise of the *sede vacante* jurisdiction within the diocese was probably made all the easier for the earlier archdeacons by the absence of any well-defined diocesan jurisdiction, but after *c.* 1270 with the evolution of the office of commissary general this would have become more difficult.

Little is known of the archdeacon's claims in the vacancy of 1270–3. Hugh de Mortimer (lately Official of the 'Curia Cantuariensis') was allowed to attend to diocesan business.[2] On a writ of signification he described himself as 'Archidiaconus Cant', Custos Spiritualitatis'. Unfortunately this is the only scrap of business of a diocesan nature that has been found for this vacancy;[3] in all probability he may have claimed and exercised the same rights as Simon Langton. His successors were not so fortunate, for they had to contend with commissaries eager to enforce the claims of the prior and chapter. Robert de Seleseya in 1278–9, and Richard de Clyve in 1292–4, the diocesan commissaries of the prior and chapter, launched fierce attacks upon the archdeacon and the clergy who supported him in his refusal to recognize their jurisdiction. The material contained in the Sede Vacante Scrap-

---

[1] Somner, Part 1, Appendix, p. 67, Transcript No. LXII; cf. Churchill, vol. i, p. 44 and pp. 551–2.                                              [2] Ibid., p. 552.
[3] P.R.O. Significations File 1, No. 56, dated 11 Nov. 1271.

books bears witness to the determination of both these commissaries in the task of reducing the offending clergy to obedience. In 1278 the archdeacon and his commissaries were excommunicated.[1] In 1292–4 the Official of the archdeacon and many of the rural deans conducted a campaign of disobedience;[2] and in return deans and clergy were suspended and excommunicated.[3] Inductions were effected 'in default of the archdeacon';[4] while visitations were conducted with great vigour in parishes normally subject to the archdeacon.[5] On the whole the prior and chapter seem to have met with considerable success in enforcing their own *sede vacante* claims. Rural deans continued to certify citations, although perhaps grudgingly. The dean of Charing, in particular, addressed Richard de Clyve as one 'qui se gerit pro Commissario Cant' sede vacante'[6] and returned many certificated 'salvo iure Archidiaconi'.[7]

Both the archdeacon and some of his supporters appealed to the Court of Canterbury and to Rome. After the 1278–9 vacancy the vicar of Lympne, one of the clergy excommunicated by Robert de Seleseya, appealed to Rome against the actions of the latter, claiming that 'nullam habebat jurisdiccionem ordinariam seu eciam delegatam'.[8] Robert de Gernemuth (Yarmouth), then archdeacon, died while his own appeal at Rome was still *sub judice*.[9] His successor Richard de Ferringes took up the cause. The events of the vacancy of 1292–4 added fuel to the flames. Judges delegate were appointed to deal with the case in England, but the dispute

---

[1] Reg. Q, f. 150b.

[2] Shadwell MS. 4. Citation of William, the archdeacon's Official, to answer articles brought against him, dated 23 Mar. 1293/4.

[3] S.V. 1, p. 3. Suspension of dean of Sandwich. E.S. Roll No. 134 for excommunications of deans of Elham and Bridge; cf. Reg. Q, f. 17b.

[4] e.g. S.V. 1, p. 10. Induction to Barfreston dated 29 Oct. 1293.

[5] Visitation Rolls III *passim*. Some of these have been printed by C. E. Woodruff in *Archaelogia Cantiana*, vol. xxxii, pp. 143–80; cf. particularly Roll 7 (p. 159) for attached list of excommunicates.

[6] e.g. S.V. 3, p. 65. Certificate of citation.

[7] Ibid., Certificates, pp. 52, 60, 65.

[8] Ch.Ch. Letters, vol. ii, No. 316. A letter addressed to judges delegate in England from James, canon of Bologna, auditor at the papal curia, dated at Rome 23 Mar. 1279/80 (noticed by R. L. Poole in H.M.C. Reports, *Various Collections*, i, p. 243).

[9] C.Ant. C 1285. Letter dated 5 Apr. 1280 from the advocate of the prior and chapter promising to carry on the case if the next archdeacon prosecuted the appeal.

lapsed upon the election of Richard to the see of Dublin in
1298.[1] A faint repercussion was felt in 1326, when an
absentee archdeacon, Simon Barjona, put forward his claims
to Archbishop Walter Reynolds. The prior of Christchurch,
Henry of Eastry, looking back upon his triumphant upholding of his rights in 1292–4, could well minimize the whole
affair. He informed Reynolds that 'querela Archidiaconi . . .
est modicum ponderanda quia videtur quod querit nodum in
scirpo et occasionem ubi nulla subest causa'.[2]

The *sede vacante* conflicts were probably one of the main
incentives for the compilation of the registers which still
survive at Canterbury. Register Q, in particular, is virtually
a handbook on the conduct of vacancy jurisdiction. The procedure to be followed upon the demise of an archbishop is
clearly set forth. The register contains a description of the
appointment of the diocesan commissary Robert de Clyve
and his preliminary activities at the beginning of the vacancy
1292–4, a description probably compiled from the material
which still survives in the Sede Vacante Scrapbooks and
Chartae Antiquae.[3]

The procedure followed in the appointment of officers to
conduct the *sede vacante* jurisdiction varied from one vacancy
to another. At the commencement of the vacancy of 1292–4
Archbishop Pecham's commissary Master Martin de Hampton ceased to act, but he continued to be employed as an
agent of Richard de Clyve, the commissary appointed for the
duration of the vacancy,[4] and resumed his office upon the
election of Archbishop Winchelsey. The prior and chapter
did not always appoint a new commissary of their own in this
way. Sometimes they issued a *sede vacante* commission to the
person who had acted as commissary general *sede plena* and
occasionally appointed a colleague to assist him. This latter
was a frequent practice during the fifteenth century and
entailed no interruption in the sessions of the Consistory
Court.[5] During vacancies of the archiepiscopal see the prior

---

[1] Some twenty documents in this suit survive among the Chartae Antiquae.
[2] Reg. L, f. 145*b*, dated 6 Apr. 1326; cf. H.M.C. Report, no. 9, p. 95.
[3] Reg. Q, f. 3.
[4] S.V. 3, p. 88. Mandate for inquisition, dated 30 Sept. 1293.
[5] Commissaries *sede vacante* are noted in the list of commissaries general in
Appendix No. I.

and chapter appointed those officers who would normally be appointed by the archbishop *sede plena*; during the vacancy of 1500–1, for example, John Taylor, the diocesan apparitor general, received his commission from the prior and chapter.[1]

## (iii) THE ARCHDEACONRY OF CANTERBURY

The evolution of this jurisdiction does not present as many problems as that of the jurisdiction of the commissary general. The earliest surviving court *acta* date from 1292,[2] but it is probable that some organization for the exercise of the archdeacon's jurisdiction had existed from the date of Lanfranc's grant to Archdeacon Valerius. According to the account contained in the 'Black Book of the Archdeacon', Lanfranc gave his archdeacon all jurisdiction in the city and diocese of Canterbury excepting churches in the archbishop's patronage (the 'exempt parishes') and the hearing of matrimonial causes.[3]

The deputy, the vice-archdeacon or, later, the Official of the archdeacon appears by the end of the twelfth century. A certain Robert, vice-archdeacon of Canterbury, appears in 1168.[4] The Ralph who figures as *quondam vice archidiaconus* in a Christchurch rental *c.* 1200[5] was probably a predecessor to Master Everard who appears as vice-archdeacon in 1195×1200.[4] By 1239 a 'J. de Londiniis' is designated 'Official' of the archdeacon,[6] and the 'Boniface Roll' provides a glimpse of Master Omer as the archdeacon's Official in 1259.[7] The Official remained the effective president of the Archdeacon's Court from the end of the thirteenth century.

The scope of the archdeacon's jurisdiction during the twelfth and most of the thirteenth centuries must remain obscure in default of records. Whether the grants of Archbishops Richard and Stephen Langton merely confirmed, or

---

1 Reg. R, f. 41*b*. Commission dated 20 Sept. 1500.
2 E.S. Roll No. 89. Copy of Consistory Court *acta* which contains description of proceedings in the Archdeacon's Court; cf. S.V. 1, p. 40.
3 Churchill, vol. i, p. 43.
4 C. R. Cheney, *English Bishops' Chanceries 1100–1250*, pp. 132, 143; cf. ibid., pp. 143–6 for discussion of vice-archdeacons.
5 Lit. MS. B 7, f. 7*b*, a reference provided by Mr. W. Urry.
6 Gervase, *Opera* (R.S.), vol. ii, p. 167.
7 C. Ant. A 7*b*; for list of Officials, see Appendix No. I.

improved upon, the extent of his powers cannot be ascertained. Stephen Langton's grants of 1227 to his brother Simon certainly specified the right of appointing the rural deans and the return of two parishes, Hackington and Teynham, which previous archbishops, Baldwin and Hubert Walter, had reserved as part of the plans for erecting their famous collegiate church. It is doubtful, however, whether the archdeacons ever acquired, *sede plena*, jurisdiction within the exempt parishes, or in the matter of matrimonial litigation.[1] These remained reserved to become the main elements of the later jurisdiction of the commissaries general.[2]

After the appointment of Archdeacon Ferringes to the see of Dublin in 1298, the personal influence of the archdeacon declined. The majority of the fourteenth-century archdeacons were papal nominees, many of whom never set foot in England.[3] In theory their Officials possessed extensive powers as vicegerents, but in practice, the holders of the Officiality tended to become subordinate to the archbishops and their commissaries general. As men of lesser rank, unwilling to risk their careers, they respected the favour of the archbishop rather than that of an absentee archdeacon. They were bound by their oaths of obedience to the archbishop or to the prior and chapter of Canterbury.[4] Evidence is lacking as to the measure of control these archdeacons retained over the appointment and conduct of their deputies. One, however, had little confidence in the ability of his Official to handle cases in which his own and his tenants' interests were at stake. In 1308 Bernard Etil de la Breto commissioned his proctor in England to remove such cases from the cognizance of the Official.[5] In the fifteenth and early sixteenth centuries the archdeacons were the clients or relations of the archbishops, and there is no evidence to suggest that any of them personally interested themselves in the running of their court. The Officials of this period probably regarded their office as a stepping-stone to higher positions within the

---

[1] Cf. Churchill, vol. i, pp. 43–53.  [2] *Infra*, p. 82.
[3] Cf. the unsatisfactory list in Le Neve, vol. i, pp. 39–42.
[4] Cf. Churchill, vol. i, p. 50; cf. Reg. G, f. 128*b*, and Reg. Q, f. 205, for oaths taken *sede vacante*.
[5] Bernard was appointed 20 Nov. 1305; cf. Le Neve, vol. i, p. 39; cf. Reg. I, f. 287*b* for the *Revocatio causarum a iudice suspecto*, dated 28 June 1308.

hierarchy of ecclesiastical jurisdiction. Four Officials are found acting as commissaries general of Canterbury at later stages in their careers.[1]

When the archdeaconry fell vacant the jurisdiction of the Official lapsed, and he was either replaced by the commissary general or confirmed in office for the duration of the vacancy. The spiritualities of the archdeaconry were at the disposal of the archbishop in either case. In 1323 Archbishop Reynolds appointed Master Robert de Malling, then commissary general, to exercise jurisdiction within the vacant archdeaconry. Robert's successor, Thomas de Chartham, was instructed to hand over the rolls of the court to the incoming Official upon the termination of the vacancy.[2] In the vacancy of 1374 the commissary general, Robert de Bourne, was actually commissioned as Official.[2] During the vacancy caused by the deprivation of Aymer de la Roche in 1379, William de Malberthorp, the commissary general, was instructed to exercise the archidiaconal jurisdiction if the Official, John de Petham, refused to act.[3] As the latter is still found as Official in 1383,[4] it is probable that he did not support the lost cause of his superior.

## (iv) THE EXEMPT PARISHES

Many parishes in the diocese of Canterbury were exempt from the jurisdiction of the archdeacon throughout the Middle Ages.[5] In some of these parishes the rectors had been granted, or had acquired, autonomous powers which virtually made them petty 'archdeacons'. The early history of the exempt parishes is not very clear, but it appears that most of them either contained archiepiscopal manors, as at Charing or Saltwood, or possessed revenues which provided suitable incomes for officers in the archbishop's administration. All were in the archbishop's collation. The 'Black Book of the Archdeacon', compiled at the beginning of the fourteenth century, indicates that there were then some twenty-five churches and chapels which had been at some time or

---

[1] For references see Appendix No. I.  [2] Churchill, vol. i, p. 49.
[3] Ibid., p. 51.  [4] Ibid., vol. ii, p. 229 n.
[5] For list of exempt parishes see Somner, Appendix to Supplement, p. 57. For an account of the exempt parishes see Churchill, vol. i, pp. 83–94.

other allotted to the archbishop and had remained exempt
from the jurisdiction of the archdeacon. During the thirteenth and fourteenth centuries the number of autonomous
rectors and the extent of their jurisdictions varied from time
to time, dependent upon grants and revocations of individual
archbishops. Miss Churchill's account of these autonomous
'exempts' can be supplemented at many points from the
Sede Vacante Scrapbooks and Registers.

The exempt rectors put up a tenacious resistance to the
*sede vacante* claims of the prior and chapter, and the latter
were involved in litigation with many of them, both in the
Court of Canterbury and at Rome, an additional embarrass-
ment to the current conflict with the archdeacon and his
supporters among the non-exempt clergy.[1] The spirited
independence of these rectors can be seen not only in Anselm
of Eastry's excommunication of the prior and chapter during
a tithe dispute in 1285,[2] but also in a letter written by the
rector of Adisham to Richard de Clyve, commissary of the
prior and chapter during the vacancy of 1292–4. The latter
had summoned him to answer for certain irregularities in the
conduct of his jurisdiction. The rector replied: '. . . Et ut
scitis ecclesiasticus tunc ordo confunditur si unicuique sua
iura non serventur, cum ad rectores ecclesiarum exemptarum
omnimodo iurisdictio pertineat, rogo quod ad alia quedam
notoria manus vestras non extendatis; solum enim illa visita-
tionem Archiepiscopalem contingunt . . .', and he finished:
'valete in Xpo et glorioso Marture Thoma patrono nostro.
Sufficiat vobis pro iuris vestri observatione quod factum est
ne forte sanguinem eliciatis si nimis eniungatis'. Such was
the voice of ecclesiastical feudalism.

The main charges brought against the rectors of these
'exempts' are contained in a memorandum drawn up by the
prior and chapter probably as a result of their experiences
during the same vacancy.[3] The prior and chapter asserted

---

[1] Sede Vacante Scrapbooks *passim*. In the vacancy of 1292–4 the prior and chapter were involved in suits at the Curia with the rectors of Woodchurch, Maidstone,
Saltwood, and Charing.

[2] S.V. 2, p. 210, dated 19 Mar. 1284/5.

[3] S.V. 3, p. 47. Unfortunately only the inadequate transcript of J. Brigstock
Sheppard remains. The original has been rendered completely illegible by the
application of chemicals.

that the rectors had usurped the archbishop's jurisdiction in matrimonial suits; that their vicars or curates were too ignorant of the law, endangered the souls of their parishioners, and caused loss to the Consistory Court; that the rectors exacted arbitrary payments for probate of wills; and that many of them, in receipt of only temporary grants of jurisdiction from the archbishop, claimed the exercise of jurisdiction as a customary right. Archbishops Pecham and Winchelsey did not favour the independence of many of these rectors. In 1279 Pecham wrote to the prior supporting him in his late attempts to exercise his vacancy jurisdiction in the exempt parishes[1] and in the following year restricted the rectors' powers. They were to enjoy their rights of jurisdiction in testamentary and matrimonial cases, but only when they were resident or in his service. Vicars of appropriated churches were allowed testamentary jurisdiction, but only the preliminary hearings of matrimonial cases.[2] It is probable that the need for closer supervision of the activities of these rectors contributed to the rise of the office of commissary general. In the fourteenth century the Consistory Court took over an increasing proportion of their business as their autonomous jurisdictions gradually lapsed.[3]

Archbishop Winchelsey's conflict with the abbey of St. Augustine probably did not make him feel predisposed to the general principle of exempt jurisdiction. In the years 1299 to 1303 the attempt of the abbot of St. Augustine's to erect a large exempt jurisdiction over some forty parishes within the diocese of Canterbury presented the archbishop with a far weightier problem than the pretensions of individual rectors.[4] If the abbot of St. Augustine's had won this conflict the diocese of Canterbury would have been cut in two, and St. Augustine's would have acquired a larger 'enceinte' of dependent churches than that possessed by the abbey of St. Albans.[5] The abbot planned to erect three rural deaneries. These were Sturry, containing sixteen churches;

[1] Reg. Epp. Jo. Peckham (R.S.), vol. i, p. 33, letter dated 4 Aug.
[2] Churchill, vol. i, p. 85      [3] Infra, p. 25.
[4] Details of the conflict can be found in Winchelsey (C.Y. Soc.) and in A. H. Davis, Chronicle of St. Augustine's Abbey (W. Thorne).
[5] For the subject of monastic 'peculiars' see M. D. Knowles, The Monastic Order in England, pp. 600–6.

Minster in Thanet, containing eight churches; and Lenham, containing fifteen churches; the whole to be under a commissary general responsible to the abbot. William, the almoner, was appointed to this office,[1] but it is doubtful whether he was ever allowed to exercise this new jurisdiction. After three years of confusion the scheme was finally quashed by the terms of the Bull which Winchelsey obtained from the Pope in 1303.[2]

By the end of the primacy of Archbishop Reynolds (1313–28) ten rectors and one vicar retained their autonomous jurisdictions. They were the rectors of Maidstone; Saltwood; Charing; Pagham; Ickham; Deal; Reculver; St. Alphege, Canterbury; St. Martin's, Canterbury; Monkton in Thanet; and the vicar of Lyminge. During the fourteenth century the archbishops continued to issue commissions for the exercise of this type of jurisdiction, but on a strictly temporary basis.[3] Many of these commissions survive in the Archbishops' Registers, and more can be found in the Sede Vacante Registers.[4] It was the policy of the archbishops to collate reliable persons in their administration to such rectories. Many Officials of the archdeacon and many of the commissaries general are found beneficed in this way.[5]

None of the records of these autonomous jurisdictions survive, though their existence is sometimes noted in the Archbishops' Registers, and suits originally heard by exempt rectors have left traces among the surviving documents of the Consistory Court. In 1294 the commissary received an inhibition in a matrimonial suit from the Court of Canterbury which indicates that the suit had been heard originally by Anselm the rector of Eastry.[6] In the same year the commissary, Richard de Clyve, inhibited a case which was being heard by the rector of Maidstone. He ordered the 'process' of the case to be dispatched to Canterbury, but later remitted the case to the rector.[7] While a rectory was vacant the com-

---

[1] A. H. Davis, *Chronicle of St. Augustine's Abbey*, pp. 342–3.
[2] *Winchelsey* (C.Y. Soc.), p. 471.     [3] Churchill, vol. i, pp. 86–87.
[4] See Churchill, vol. ii, pp. 27–30, for transcripts of commissions contained in the Archbishops' Registers.
[5] For lists of these officers see Appendix No. I.
[6] S.V. 3, p. 66, dated 16 Oct. 1294.
[7] S.V. 3, pp. 71–72. Inhibition dated 5 Oct. 1294.

missary general held the rolls and conducted the business arising in the parish. In 1321–2, for example, the commissary general was instructed to hand over the seal and rolls of court to the rector of Monkton upon the renewal of a grant of jurisdiction.[1]

It cannot be definitely established when any of these autonomous jurisdictions finally lapsed, but no commissions are found after the primacy of Archbishop Sudbury (1375–81).[2] One autonomous jurisdiction survived until 1547, but this was a special case. The provosts of the college of Wingham exercised ordinary jurisdiction over a small area around Wingham. Pecham had founded the college in 1287 and assigned to it the churches of Wingham (already an autonomous 'exempt'), Ash, Nonington, and Goodnestone.[3] The provost appointed his own Official. At the beginning of the sixteenth century the Official of the archdeacon is found holding the office, but the jurisdiction remained distinct. In 1509 Nicholas Hillyngton, the archdeacon's Official, came into the Consistory Court at Canterbury and claimed cognizance of a case in his capacity as 'Officialis exempte jurisdiccionis de Wingham'.[4] The college was suppressed in 1547.[5] A fine Register of Wills (1471–1546) is the only record of this jurisdiction which survives.[6]

The commissary general, alone, exercised jurisdiction over the exempt parishes as a whole. These parishes were scattered from one end of the diocese to the other, with the exception of a compact group in the Romney Marsh region. Here an 'exempt' rural deanery was formed. The only evidence for its existence is provided by an entry in a *Liber Correctionum* of 1474, where a certain 'Dompnus Thomas' is reported as having retained the seal *decanatus exempt' jurisdictionis in Marisco* without due authority.[7] Perhaps the 'dean' acted as a general agent of the commissary general and as a 'keeper of the pleas' during the intervals between the sessions of the Consistory Court at Hythe and Romney.[8]

[1] Churchill, vol. i, p. 86; transcript, ibid., vol. ii, p. 27.
[2] Ibid., vol. i, p. 93.                    [3] *V.C.H. Kent*, vol. ii, p. 234.
[4] Y. 2. 5, f. 8b, under date 8 Oct. 1509. Matrimonial suit 'Laurence Omer *v.* Christine Payne', both of Ash.                    [5] *V.C.H. Kent*, vol. ii, p. 235.
[6] Maidstone, P.R.C. 33. 1.                    [7] Y. 1. 11, f. 351, under date 19 Dec.
[8] *Infra*, pp. 31–34 for description of sessions of the court.

## (v) RELATIONS BETWEEN THE JURISDICTIONS

The relations between the jurisdictions of the commissary general and the archdeacon were complex. They can only be examined in detail from the end of the fourteenth century onwards. The commissary general exercised the sole ordinary jurisdiction within the exempt parishes in matters of correction and probate of wills. The archdeacon had no jurisdiction within these parishes whatsoever. Trespassers within this special preserve were punished. In 1471 'Dominus' William, incumbent of Crundale, was cited to appear in the Consistory Court for having cited inhabitants of the exempt parish of Godmersham to appear in the Archdeacon's Court. He proved, however, that they lived not in Godmersham but in Crundale.[1] The archdeacon's Official, on his part, apparently claimed that he could cite such inhabitants of exempt parishes if they had performed acts outside those parishes. In 1509 the Official summoned John Austyn of the exempt parish of Smeeth to answer as defendant in a perjury suit 'ratione contractus in parochia de Petham'.[2]

Outside the exempt parishes the two jurisdictions were concurrent except in the matters of matrimonial litigation, visitations, and probate. Matrimonial suits were reserved for the commissary general as the officer of the archbishop.[3] Visitations of a routine character were carried out by the archdeacon's Official, who generally 'visited' the deaneries once or twice a year.[4] There is no evidence that the commissary general 'visited' the non-exempt parishes unless specifically delegated to do so by the archbishop.[5] In matters of probate the commissary general proved wills and granted letters of administration within the exempt parishes; the archdeacon's Official in the non-exempt parishes, except in periods when the archdeaconry was vacant, and in cases where persons died leaving *bona notabilia* in two or more

[1] Y. 1. 11, f. 136, under date 16 Sept.
[2] Y. 4. 3, f. 220, under date 12 Oct. Perjury suit 'John Godfrey *v.* John Austyn'.
[3] *Infra*, p. 82.
[4] Archdeaconry Visitation books survive from 1498 onwards; for list and note of portions printed in *Archaeologia Cantiana, infra*, p. 142.
[5] Usually at times of archiepiscopal visitations. See Churchill, vol. i, pp. 131–49, for descriptions of archiepiscopal visitations of the diocese and delegations of authority to the commissary general.

dioceses. In this latter the commissary general exercised the archbishop's prerogative jurisdiction in so far as the deceased had left goods within the diocese of Canterbury.[1] In the remaining spheres of Instance and Ex Officio business ('civil' and 'criminal' jurisdiction) the commissary general and the archdeacon's Official exercised identical powers. Persons living in non-exempt parishes were cited to appear in either court.

It might be surmised that such concurrency of jurisdiction would have resulted in friction between the personnel of the courts and confusion for their clients, but business was transacted in such a manner that trouble was avoided. A person prosecuting another *ad instantiam partis* was hardly likely to have him cited in both courts at once. In matters of correction the condemnation of a person in both courts for the same offence was avoided by the employment of 'letters of correction' or 'letters of purgation'. Although persons might be cited twice, they were safe from a second condemnation if they could show that they had already been corrected once. Exhibition of letters of correction is often noted in the Ex Officio Act books,[2] but despite this there were probably some unfortunates who found themselves convicted in both courts for the same offence, like the people in Chaucer's *Friar's Tale*.[3]

Expediency seems to have been the main element in determining the plaintiffs' choice of court in Instance business. The two main courts, the Consistory Court and the Archdeacon's Court, sat at different times and went 'on circuit' in different parts of the diocese. The plaintiff would resort to that court which seemed most convenient. In cases where the defendant lived in an exempt parish, however, the plaintiff had of necessity to resort to the Consistory Court. Apart from the power of citing persons living in exempt

[1] *Infra*, pp. 73–74 for discussion of this prerogative jurisdiction.
[2] e.g. X. 8. 1, f. 50. William Hakenyman of Faversham, cited on a charge of adultery, appears in the Consistory Court 15 Sept. 1398, '. . . et exhibuit litteram purgationis Officialis et absolutus est'. Cf. X. 1. 1, f. 7b, 1449. John Norton of Staplehurst, cited before the Consistory Court on a similar charge, 'exhibuit litteram correctionis sub sigillo Officialis'.
[3] *Friar's Tale*, 19 f., 'For er the bisshop caught hem with his hook, They weren in the erchedeknes book.'

parishes, neither court possessed advantages as against the other. In matters of appeal they were on the same level.[1] Appeals from both courts lay equally to the Court of Canterbury and the archbishop's Court of Audience, and not from the Court of the Archdeacon to the Consistory Court. The proctors of one court practised without discrimination in the other, so that there was no necessity for them to 'tout' for clients to resort to one particular court.[2]

In certain circumstances the courts had to co-operate in matters which concerned both jurisdictions, though the co-operation was perhaps one-sided, the archdeacon's Official always requesting, and the commissary general always granting, the favours. In matters of probate the Official frequently had to obtain the appearance of executors living in exempt parishes to administer the goods of a person who had died in a non-exempt parish. In this situation the archdeacon's Official applied to the commissary general for a citation *sub mutue vicissitudinis obtentu*, and the executor would be required to 'renounce' his own privileged jurisdiction until the matter had been settled.[3]

It must be remembered that neither the Consistory Court nor the Archdeacon's Court possessed an exclusive jurisdiction within the diocese. Although they probably dealt with the great bulk of litigation, it is apparent from a superficial survey of the surviving fourteenth-century *acta* of the archbishop's Court of Audience that many cases of a first-instance character were heard by the Auditors of this latter court during its frequent peregrination from one archiepiscopal manor to another.[4] These suits would probably be those brought by important plaintiffs, such as the heads of religious

[1] *Infra*, p. 63.
[2] *Infra*, pp. 40–45, for discussion of proctors and their practice.
[3] e.g. Maidstone, P.R.C. 3. 1, f. 133*b*. Stephen Hawker of the exempt parish of Challock cited and suspended 'sub mutue vicissitudinis obtentu'. He later appears and 'prestitit iuramentum de renunciando jurisdictionem in hac parte' as executor of Robert White, late of Chilham (28 Nov. 1500).
[4] For a discussion of the Court of Audience see Churchill, vol. i, pp. 470 et seq. As far as is known the bulk of the Acts of the Audience are lost, but there is one Act book for the primacy of Winchelsey preserved at Lambeth (MS. 244) and several fragmentary Act books preserved in the Dean and Chapter Library at Canterbury. These and extracts in Registers G and I cover a period from 1325 to 1374. Their survival is probably explained by the need of the prior and chapter to have possession of the Act books during the exercise of vacancy jurisdiction.

houses and men of noble or knightly rank who perhaps hoped for a more official or weightier consideration of their case. In matters of correction, almost all purgations of criminous clerks, and probably the more heinous cases of heresy and disobedience would be dealt with by the archbishop's higher court. This would explain the absence of such cases in the surviving *acta* of the two diocesan courts. Whether the archbishop's Court of Canterbury heard first-instance diocesan cases cannot as yet be ascertained.

### Additional Note.

THE relations between the jurisdictions in the matter of probate are illustrated by the composition made between Thomas, archbishop of Canterbury, and Richard Clifforde, archdeacon of Canterbury, with the consent of the prior and chapter of Canterbury, dated 26 March 1397. The archbishop's jurisdiction was to extend over persons having domicile in his exempt parishes, and also over persons having goods in the exempt parishes, even though they had domicile within the archdeacon's jurisdiction, in so far as those goods were concerned. Jurisdiction was divided in the case of those persons who had two domiciles, one within each jurisdiction. Jurisdiction over the goods of nobles, wherever they died ('nobles being interpreted to mean barons and their betters, and their wives'), was reserved to the archbishop; the archdeacon had jurisdiction over the goods of persons having domicile within his jurisdiction but goods within various monastic exempts, with some exceptions, notably Wingham and Maidstone; saving the prerogative of the church of Canterbury with respect to those dying possessed of goods in several dioceses.

Another dissension, 'arising out of the multitude of apparitors', was also settled by this composition (see p. 48). The archbishop was to have one mounted apparitor, and the commissary general one mounted and one on foot for his consistory, and, if he wished, one on foot in each exempt parish; the archdeacon or his official was to have one apparitor general, mounted, and an apparitor on foot in each deanery (*C.P.L.* v, pp. 483–5).

A. M. W.

# PART TWO

## PROCEDURE AND PRACTICE OF THE COURTS

### II

## TYPES OF BUSINESS AND SESSIONS OF THE COURTS

IN general, the frequency of the sessions of an ecclesiastical court depended upon the nature and quantity of the business transacted in it. The Canterbury courts transacted three main types of business:

(A) Instance: the hearing of cases between party and party.

(B) Ex Officio: the correction of faults by the judge by virtue of his 'office'.

(C) Probate: business connected with the probate and administration of wills.

Of the three, Instance business demanded regularity of session and efficient dispatch, for litigants seeking remedy in the ecclesiastical courts were not to be discouraged by confused procedure, irregular hearing, and delays in sentence. On the other hand, Ex Officio business and probate were conducted on a far more *ad hoc* basis, free from the elaborate conjunction of parties, proctors, and witnesses that Instance business involved. The sessions of the courts merely provided one of several opportunities for the dispatch of such business. Probate and the work of correction could take place on diocesan or provincial visitations, and the local ecclesiastical court might deal with only the residual stages of disciplinary actions begun by way of presentment at the visitation. The Ex Officio *acta*, therefore, may not always provide a complete description of the handling of cases of this character, and as the registrars of the courts were wont to record

Ex Officio *acta* of disparate origin in the same *Liber Correctionum*,[1] all such *acta* have to be treated with particular care and regarded as incomplete. On the whole it was not the disciplinary business which gave substance and regularity to the sessions of the two courts, but the business that arose *ad instantiam partium*. Not only was it the main occupation of the ecclesiastical lawyer and the principal source of his fees, but it has left by far the greater deposit of record material.

## (i) SESSIONS OF THE CONSISTORY COURT

The first Instance Act book of the Consistory Court dates from 1372,[2] but glimpses of the Consistory Court in session can be obtained from the 'Boniface Roll' of 1259[3] and from the Sede Vacante material of 1292–4. The court sat inside the cathedral, probably under the north-west tower of the nave, where it is found in later times. Here Richard de Clyve, the commissary general of the prior and chapter (1292–4), heard most of the cases for which documents still survive. When the Sede Vacante material has been adequately calendared it may be possible to reconstruct a time-table of the sessions of the court during those two years. The importance of these sessions of the court in the cathedral was not disputed. The prior was concerned whether his commissary could find time to attend to its business. He wrote to Richard de Clyve instructing him to conduct an inquisition at Monkton in Thanet 'Dumtamen hac occasione Consistorium vestrum apud Cantuar' non interrumperetur'.[4]

The year 1373 is the first for which a complete time-table of the Instance sessions of the Consistory Court at Canterbury can be reconstructed. The court sat for a space of three days at intervals of three weeks. Although there is no mention of law terms, no business was transacted between 26 July and 19 September, and none between 12 December and 9 January.[5] In the Act book an elaborate heading introduces the *acta* of the first day of the 'consistory' and includes the

---

[1] e.g. X. 8. 1 (1395–1410), which records *acta* under deaneries and not by sessions of the Consistory Court.
[2] Y. 1. 1 (1372–5).
[3] C. Ant. A 7b; *supra*, p. 13–14.
[4] S.V. 2, p. 107, letter dated 26 Nov.  [5] Y. 1. 1 (1372–5).

date of the first court day of the next 'consistory'. The first court day was usually a Monday, unless it fell on an important saint's day, and the second and third days follow consecutively (with the same exception). Cases introduced in one 'consistory' were usually heard again on the same court day of the next 'consistory'. In 1397 the same three-weekly sessions were maintained, but the business sometimes occupied four or five days of the week and frequently overlapped into a second week,[1] while cases were occasionally heard by the commissary general outside the regular sessions. On some days the court sat elsewhere than in the cathedral. On Saturdays, in particular, it often sat in the chapel of St. Thomas's Hospital upon the East Bridge. There is little change during the first half of the fifteenth century. In 1416 there were fourteen 'consistories' during the year. From 1454 onwards the sessions of the Consistory Court never extended over more than two days of any week; two or three more 'consistories' were being held per annum, reducing the interval between them to two weeks at certain periods of the year.[2] Generally, from 1454 until the Reformation, some eighteen or nineteen 'consistories' were held each year. Only on rare occasions did their sessions during this period last longer than two days of the week. The cathedral remained the regular 'court place' throughout this period with one notable exception; from 7 April to 6 October 1505 the court sat in the church of Adisham, five miles distant from Canterbury. The commissary general, Robert Woodward (1504–20+), was rector of Adisham at this time. Fear of plague may have provided the motive for this excursion.[3]

The Canterbury Ex Officio sessions of the court are difficult to determine. The earliest fragments of Ex Officio *acta* (other than those contained in the Sede Vacante records of the prior and chapter) date from 1364.[4] They contain corrections for moral offences imposed by the registrar, John Crane-

---

[1] Y. 1. 2 (1396–8).
[2] There is a gap in the Instance Act book series between 1425 and 1453. The increase in the frequency of the 'consistories' probably occurred during this period.
[3] Y. 2. 9 (1505–8). The Archdeacon's Court was away from Canterbury at the same time; *infra*, p. 34.
[4] Y. 1. 19, resurrected, from the mutilated covers of a book, by Mr. Maple, bookbinder to the Dean and Chapter.

bourne, who was possibly acting as deputy of the commissary general, at a session of the court in the church of St. Alphege. The Ex Officio Act book X. 8. 1 (1395–1410) contains *acta* arranged under deanery headings with no indication where the cases were heard. The next Act book in this series, X. 1. 1 (1449–57), also fails to provide indication of the place and frequency of session. The method of compilation of these books may indicate that it was easier for the registrar to treat such business as it arose, irrespective of the sessions of the court. Time and place of session, however, were recorded in the next surviving Act book, the *Liber Correctionum* of 1468–74.[1] During these years the court heard Ex Officio cases and granted probate at the priory of St. Gregory by the Northgate, on the afternoons of those days when it heard Instance cases in the cathedral during the morning.

The sessions of the Consistory Court were not confined to Canterbury. For the seventy years previous to the Reformation there is evidence of a circuit in the southern parts of the diocese. The first complete survey of this circuit can be made for the year 1464.[2] In that year the circuit was performed ten times. At Dover the court sat in the church of St. Martin; at Hythe in the church of St. Leonard, and at Romney in the church of St. Nicholas. Sometimes one or two of these places were omitted from the circuit, but generally all three were visited on three successive days. Sometimes the three-day circuit followed immediately after sessions at Canterbury. On Monday 20, and Tuesday 21 February 1463-4 the court sat at Canterbury; on Wednesday 22 at Hythe; on Thursday 23 at Romney, and on the Friday 24 February at Dover. Usually, however, the court was on circuit during the course of a different week.

Instance and Ex Officio cases were heard and probate granted at the same sessions on this circuit, and of the four surviving Act books recording the circuit[3] only one is confined to Instance business.[4] The sessions of these circuits supplemented those of the court at Canterbury. Business

[1] Y. 1. 11.  [2] X. 8. 3 (1462–8).
[3] X. 8. 3 (1462–8); Y. 1. 10 (1468–78); Y. 2. 8 (1504–9); Y. 2. 10 (1515–23). Several folios for the year 1494 are bound up in Y. 2. 2, in the Canterbury Instance series.
[4] Y. 2. 8 (1504–9).

could be transferred from one to the other.[1] It cannot be ascertained how long this circuit had been in operation before 1462. During the fourteenth century it was probably not the only one of its kind. In the Instance Act book for 1396–8 there are traces of sessions of the court at Deal, Eythorne, Folkestone, and Reculver, as well as at Hythe, Romney, and Dover.[2] It is possible that sessions began to be held in these exempt parishes as the autonomous jurisdictions of their rectors gradually lapsed.

## (ii) SESSIONS OF THE ARCHDEACON'S COURT

The pre-Reformation Instance Act books of the Archdeacon's Court survive only from 1476, but the lack of material for the earlier period is compensated by the completeness of the material surviving for the period 1476–1536. A valuable manuscript 'Account Book of the Registrar and Receiver of the Archdeacon of Canterbury'[3] contains a detailed account of the financial administration of the archdeaconry during the years 1504–17 which enables the record of sessions and circuits contained in the Act books to be checked against the items of expenditure connected with them.

There were three main fields of activity: Sessions at Canterbury, a circuit through the rural deaneries in the western part of the diocese, and sessions in the deanery of Sandwich. At Canterbury the Archdeacon's Court usually sat to transact Instance business every other Saturday, apart from the summer and Christmas vacations. Probate and Ex Officio business was transacted on the same day. The court place was not as permanent as that of the Consistory Court in the cathedral. From 11 January 1499/1500 to 12 November 1524 (a period continuously recorded in the Instance Act books) the court sat in the churches of St. George's; Holy Cross, Westgate; All Saints, and in the Hospital of the Poor Priests. In the summer of 1505 the court sat away from Canterbury at various churches in the vicinity. In the sessions

[1] e.g. Y. 2. 9, f. 139b, under date 2 Dec. 1508. Testamentary case Cheseman v. Dewer': '. . . primo introducta erat apud Romene'.
[2] Y. 1. 2. A day's session at each of these places is noted for the two years 1397 and 1398.                                     [3] Z. 3. 22.

of the court at Canterbury the Official, although dealing with business arising within the whole archdeaconry, was largely concerned with Ex Officio business and probate arising in the deaneries of Canterbury, Bridge, Westbere, and Elham.

The court went on circuit through the deaneries of Lympne, Charing, Sutton, Sittingbourne, and Ospringe fourteen times a year, usually during the week preceding the session of the court at Canterbury on the Saturday. One day was spent transacting business in the deaneries of Lympne and Charing and one day in each of the other three deaneries. The tour usually began on the Monday and finished at Canterbury on the Saturday. The route from deanery to deanery seldom varied, though the court was held at various places within the deaneries. The court usually sat at Ashford to deal with business arising in the deaneries of Lympne and Charing, though sessions were frequently held at Cranbrook, Tenterden, and Biddenden. In the deanery of Sutton sessions of the court were held at Leeds, Lenham, Harrietsham, Sutton Valence, and occasionally elsewhere. With the exception of a few isolated sessions in other parishes, Sittingbourne was the usual rendezvous for the deanery of the same name. The court visited Ospringe and Faversham alternately to deal with business arising in the deanery of Ospringe. Finally, sessions of the Archdeacon's Court were held within the deanery of Sandwich. The court sometimes sat at Northbourne or Great Mongeham, but it usually sat in one of the churches of Sandwich—St. Mary's, St. Clement's, or St. Peter's. The sessions within the deanery of Sandwich lasted one day and there were seldom more than ten during the year. They were held on any weekday and were probably appointed at the convenience of the Official.

The mobility of the ecclesiastical judges and their assistants was considerable. A survey of all the sessions of the courts in the year 1522 reveals that the courts sat 140 times in twenty-five different places. There could have been few people in the diocese who remained unacquainted with the cavalcades of ecclesiastical lawyers and their assistants. The Consistory Court perhaps had become less peripatetic than formerly, but ten circuits to Romney and the coast during the course of a year show that its personnel had no purely indoor occupation. The Official of the archdeacon, his registrar, proctors, and apparitors, following a fifty-mile circuit through Cranbrook or Ashford to Milton or Faversham in the snows of winter, or in the dust and heat of summer, had no easy task. Those proctors who worked in both courts must have been as long in the saddle as they were pleading the suits of their clients.

# III

# THE PERSONNEL AND THEIR DUTIES

As a class, the personnel of the church courts, the ecclesiastical lawyers and the apparitors, have been neglected by the historian. From the Act books of the courts much biographical detail can be gleaned, not only about the judges, but also about the registrars, proctors, and apparitors. It is apparent that there was a considerable ladder of preferment for the able lawyer and that a good living could be made by those who became registrars or practised as proctors.

## (i) THE JUDGES

The commissary general ranked as one of the higher officers in the archbishop's administration. Many of the holders of this office had already had experience as judges before they arrived at Canterbury. Many had been agents of the archbishop in other branches of his administration. A few later held positions of greater distinction.[1] Only two instances have been found of commissaries general who had served their apprenticeship as proctors in the Consistory Court: John de Raveningham and Master John Williamson. The latter first appeared as a proctor in the Consistory Court on 27 February 1485/6. Later he acted as a deputy to the commissary general and was appointed to that office himself in 1500. Among commissaries general who had been judges in other dioceses were Robert de Bourne (commissary general 1366/75+), who had been Official-Principal of Rochester 1364–5, and John Parmenter (commissary general 1462-86), who had previously been Official of the archdeacon of Ely in 1458. Robert de Malling (commissary general 1317–1323?+) is an example of an officer who had served the archbishop in other capacities. He had administered the diocese of Chichester during the vacancy of 1304–5, and the diocese of Bath and Wells during the vacancy of 1308, and had been an Auditor of Causes 1308–10. James Goldwell, commissary

---

[1] Full details and references for the following personnel will be found in Appendix No. I (i).

general during 1454, was the most distinguished holder of
the office. He became dean of Salisbury in 1463, bishop of
Norwich 1472–99, and served Edward IV in the capacity
of ambassador to the king of France.

The Officiality of the archdeaconry was not such a high
ranking post. Some Officials later became commissaries
general. Details of the early careers of many of the Officials
are lacking. Master Richard Willefords, LL.B., acted as a
proctor in the Archdeacon's Court from 1477 and was
appointed Official in 1502. Nicholas de Ystele, Official
1352–62, was a public notary who had drawn up a *Sede
Vacante* register for the prior and chapter in 1348.[1]

Neither post was a sinecure. The medieval holders of the
two offices presided over the vast majority of the sessions of
their courts, but there are brief periods when deputies acted
on their behalf. The scribe was usually very careful to note
the details of the appointment and the authority on these
occasions. Copies of the commissions of appointment of
these special commissaries are sometimes entered in the Act
books. They were usually members of the local clergy.
Walter Gerard, for example, vicar of Northgate, Canterbury,
acted as deputy at intervals to three successive commissaries
general during the years 1481–93.

## (ii) REGISTRARS AND SCRIBES[2]

If the efficiency of the courts depended on any one man,
that man was the registrar. He determined the time and order
of the hearing of cases; entered the *acta* of the court in the
various registers; supervised the dispatch of citations, letters
of suspension and excommunication, and directly controlled
the activity of the apparitors. He received the fees, examined
witnesses, and conducted inquisitions as ordered by the
judge.[3] A high standard of education and training was
required for the efficient conduct of his office. He was of
necessity a public notary. The registrar was the 'public person' and sufficient witness to the Acts of the court.[4]

[1] Now bound up in Reg. G, f. 25, 'Registrum . . . per Nicholaum de Ystele . . .
confectum.'
[2] For lists of registrars see Appendix No. I (iii).      [3] *Infra*, p. 69.
[4] For a discussion of this necessity see Phillimore, vol. ii, p. 94; cf. Fournier, p. 48.

It is not known how soon life grants of this office came to be made. A possible indication is provided by the *acta* of the Consistory Court. Adam Body, who was acting as registrar in 1397 and 1402,[1] was acting as a proctor in 1415–16, subsequent to the appointment of another registrar, John Lovelych.[2] It is possible, therefore, that life grants were not being made at this time. On the other hand, the first extant registrar's commission, that of William Bold in 1442, was an appointment for life,[3] and subsequent appointments were of a similar character. In the same year John Penwortham was appointed to hold the offices of registrar and apparitor general for the archdeaconry. These were life grants.[4] It is possible that the custom of having such appointments confirmed in the registers of the prior and chapter indicates that grants for life were becoming common during the first half of the fifteenth century; but this evidence is inconclusive and purely local in character. Even so, the Canterbury evidence shows the growing professionalism of the holders of this type of ecclesiastical office in the century previous to the Reformation settlement. The view that their office was private property to be bought and sold was perhaps a post-Reformation development, but steps had been already taken in that direction. In one instance, at least, celibacy, apparently, was no longer regarded as a necessary qualification for the holding of such an office. Despite Archbishop Chichele's decree of 1414 which included registrars and scribes in a general ban on the exercise of ecclesiastical jurisdiction by married clergy,[5] John Colman, registrar of the Consistory Court 1484–1534, was married. In 1486 he and Elizabeth his wife were granted a licence for the erection of a private oratory.[6] The earliest

---

1 Y. 1. 2, f. 58, under date 10 Sept. 1397, and Maidstone, P.R.C. 32. 1, f. 15 (7 Feb. 1402/3).

2 He first appears in Y. 1. 3, f. 1, 31 Jan. 1415/16, but was probably appointed before this.

3 Reg. S, f. 149b. Commission dated 25 May 1442; see transcript, Appendix No. II.

4 Reg. S, f. 151. Commission dated 15 Aug. 1442. Both these commissions appear in confirmations of the appointments by the prior and chapter.

5 Wilkins, vol. iii, p. 269.

6 Reg. R, f. 15. This was probably not an isolated case. John Pakyngton, chapter clerk of Lincoln and Registrar of the Acts of the Dean and Chapter, was married. See K. Major, 'The Office of Chapter Clerk at Lincoln in the Middle Ages', *Medieval Studies presented to Rose Graham*, p. 175.

recorded registrar of the Consistory Court is an Elyas of
Westgate who appears in 1259,[1] and after a long gap a fairly
complete list of his successors can be compiled from the end
of the fourteenth century onwards.[2]

The registrars appear to have employed assistants. In
the Act books the preliminary entries of cases were frequently entered in a different hand from that which recorded the events of the actual hearing. It may have been
some of these assistants who 'doodled' and drew rude
pictures of court officials in the Act books which had been
filed away.[3]

### (iii)· THE PROCTORS

It is very difficult to compile a comprehensive list of proctors who served in the courts. There is a list of proctors in
the 'Boniface Roll' of 1259,[4] and another on the dorse of
*acta* of the 'Curia Cantuariensis' for 1271,[5] but no lists of
this kind have been found for the remainder of the period.
The earlier Act books do not contain notices of the appointment or 'constitution' of proctors.[6] In the Act books of the
early fifteenth century 'constitutions' are sometimes interlarded among other *acta* of the court.[7] It is not until 1464 that
the registrar began to enter the surnames of the proctors in
the margin alongside the entry of the *acta* of the cases in
which they were concerned.[8] Such entries, however, are not
reliable indications of the appearances of proctors, for they
are frequently omitted. Until all the cases are calendared no
definitive analysis can be made of the number of proctors
employed or of the number of suits each proctor handled.
Registers of 'constitutions' do not survive from the pre-
Reformation period. Provisionally, however, some approxi-
mate indication of the numbers involved can be given. In
1374 two proctors conducted most of the business.[9] In 1397

---

[1] C.Ant. A 7b. He also appears as a witness to a charter in 1254 (Reg. A, f. 364).
[2] See Appendix No. I (iii).
[3] Particularly in Y. 1. 9 (1505–8), where the scrawl 'Johnny Draper is a Knave'
frequently occurs. John Draper was registrar in 1536 (Y. 2. 13).
[4] C.Ant. A 7b.
[5] *Supra*, p. 11.
[6] *Infra*, pp. 52–53 for the procedure of 'constitution'.
[7] Y. 1. 3 (1415–23) and Y. 1. 4 (1419–25), *passim*.
[8] Y. 1. 6 (1463–8).         [9] Y. 1. 1, John Bedel and Adam Clerk.

four regular proctors can be distinguished;[1] in 1415, three.[2] From 1464 until 1482 there were never more than four lawyers practising in the Consistory Court. In 1483 a fifth proctor appeared in the court,[3] and from 1486 to 1493 there were eight or nine proctors handling business at any one time.[4] From 1493 onwards there was a decline in numbers, but until the Reformation there were always from three to five proctors engaged at the same time. No regulations concerned with the number of proctors who could be admitted to practise in these diocesan courts have been found. The majority of the proctors of the Consistory Court practised in the Archdeacon's Court. Of thirty proctors who appeared in the Consistory Court from 1474 to 1535, eighteen appeared in one or more series of the sessions of the Archdeacon's Court; while only nine out of the twenty-seven proctors appearing in the Act books of the Archdeacon's Court fail to figure in the Act books of the Consistory Court.[5] The practising ecclesiastical lawyer made little distinction between the two jurisdictions as means of employment. There does not seem to have been any fixed principle in their division of labour. It was probably a matter of private inclination or mutual arrangement. Some confined their attentions to the Canterbury sessions of the courts, while others practised in all the sessions of both courts. The amount of business probably determined the numbers of proctors engaged in the various sessions. Generally the circuit sessions of the Archdeacon's Court in the western deaneries of the diocese and in the deanery of Sandwich did not occupy the attention of more than two proctors at any one time. Five or six proctors were employed in the Canterbury sessions of the court from 1500 to 1524.[6]

The scanty notice taken of the appearances of the proctors makes it difficult to generalize about their status or general background. It is to be doubted whether the elaborate rules

[1] Y. 1. 2, Nicholas Archer, John Wilmington, Thomas Borne, William Warrene.

[2] Y. 1. 3, Adam Body, previously registrar in 1402/3; David Mareys and John Egerden.        [3] Master John Richardson from 27 Jan. 1482/3 (Y. 1. 13).

[4] From among James Ganton, Thomas Notyngham, James Das, Thomas Ramsey, John Richardson, John Williamson, John Warde, Thomas Colman, Henry Woods, and Mercer. (Y. 1. 13, Y. 1. 14, and Y. 1. 15.)

[5] For lists of proctors see Appendix No. I.

[6] Y. 4. 3 and Y. 2. 4.

laid down for the admission, training, and conduct of proctors for the Court of Canterbury in London applied to the proctors in the inferior diocesan courts.[1] There is no distinction made between proctors and 'advocates' as in the provincial courts. It is probable that the admission of proctors rested with the commissary general and the archdeacon's Official. No notices or oaths of admission have survived. Of the thirty proctors appearing in the Consistory Court between 1474 and 1535, ten are noted as being public notaries. Eight others were beneficed, and one may have been a chantry chaplain.[2] Eight of this last group of nine do not appear in the Consistory Court before 1504. The exception is John Williamson, who appears fitfully in that court from 27 February 1485/6 onwards.[3] He seems to have specialized in handling the suits of local clergy. Two of the beneficed proctors, Dominus Stephen Galle and Dominus Richard Knepe, are found bringing suits in court for the recovery of fees,[4] the holding of benefices apparently not preventing these proctors from collecting fees. In time it may be possible to identify many of these ecclesiastical lawyers from other sources. Many of the proctors are noticed in the Act books of the courts or in the registers of the prior and chapter as holding various law degrees.[5] It seems obvious that the majority of ecclesiastical lawyers were the products of the universities and the numbers engaged in one small diocese reflect the vocational importance of contemporary university education in Canon Law. Sometimes it appears that practical experience in the ecclesiastical courts was regarded as a stepping-stone to further advancement. Some of the shorter appearances of proctors in the Act books may be cases of apprentices obtaining training

[1] Cf. Churchill, vol. i, pp. 450–2, for discussion of statutes regulating the Court of Canterbury.

[2] Thomas Cokkes, noticed as the Brencheley chantry chaplain (Y. 2. 13, f. 130, under date 6 May 1533).

[3] Y. 1. 14. He later became Official of the archdeacon in 1496 and commissary general in 1500. See Appendix No. I (i), p. 117.

[4] Y. 2. 2, f. 95, under date 17 Dec. 1504 for former; Y. 2. 6, f. 159b, under date 31 July 1520 for latter. For benefices see Appendix No. I (v), p. 122.

[5] I am greatly indebted to Mr. A. B. Emden for identifying many of the officers of the courts and the proctors as graduates of Oxford or Cambridge, as well as providing many other biographical details; see Appendix No. I for lists of officers and proctors.

in the courts. John Warde appeared in the Consistory Court in 1485/6 as the deputy substitute for Thomas Colman and Thomas Notyngham, two public notaries.[1] He acted as a proctor from 1485/6 until 11 March 1492/3,[2] and as deputy for the commissary general for two sessions on 30 and 31 January 1491/2.[3] He may be the same John Warde who appears as an English law student at Bologna in 1494.[4] In contrast to these short appearances, there are a number of proctors whose whole careers must have been spent handling suits in one or both of the Canterbury courts. James Ganton holds the long service record for the period 1474 to 1535 with probably more than forty years' service.[5] Generally the average length of service declines after 1500 and the number of lawyers who appear only for short periods increases. Of the thirty proctors practising in the Consistory Court between 1474 and 1535, nineteen appeared in 1502 and after and eleven of these practised for less than seven years. This may indicate that the position was no longer providing permanent or lucrative employment. It certainly appears as if the amount of business had begun to decline prior to 1500.

The amount of business which came the way of each individual proctor depended on a variety of elements: his reputation, the size of his clientele, opportunities provided by his clients, and his own ambition. Clients usually employed the same proctor. In 1482 a James Aylonds of Canterbury brought fifteen suits into the Consistory Court. In two of these suits he was not represented by a proctor. In the remaining thirteen he was represented by James Ganton.[6]

It is comparatively easy to estimate the total number of cases which each proctor handled during the course of a year, but it is a laborious task to assess the total number of separate appearances in court, for it involves an exhaustive analysis of the 'process' of every suit recorded in the Act books. In 1493 Master Thomas Notyngham made 567 recorded

---

[1] Y. 1. 14, under date 13 Mar. 1485/6.
[2] Y. 1. 16.
[3] Y. 1. 15. Possibly a deliberate part of his training?
[4] R. J. Mitchell, 'English Law Students at Bologna in the Fifteenth Century', *E.H.R.*, vol. li (1936), p. 282.
[5] He began to act prior to 1474 (Y. 1. 8). His last appearance was on 20 June 1513 (Y. 2. 5).        [6] Y. 1. 13.

appearances in the Consistory Court on behalf of clients.[1] There were 38 court days in that year, so that, on an average, he handled 15 suits on each court day, appearing either for plaintiffs or defendants. There were 174 cases introduced in which he appeared. On an average, therefore, he appeared from three to four times on behalf of the client in each suit. Of all the proctors, Thomas Notyngham handled the greatest amount of business in that year;[2] but it must be remembered, however, that the appearances of proctors varied in length. Sometimes the proctor would merely obtain the permission of the judge to appoint a further 'term' in the hearing of the case. At other times the appearance might involve the reading of a long 'libel'.[3]

Although the activity of each proctor varied from year to year, it is interesting to compare the maximum of suits handled by any proctor over a period of years. The following chart of cases handled in the Consistory Court shows that the maximum declined from 223 suits in 1482 to 57 suits in 1535; a further indication that the business which each individual proctor might hope to handle was declining in the fifty years before the Reformation.

| Consistory Court | 1482 | 1493 | 1511 | 1522 | 1535 |
|---|---|---|---|---|---|
| Total number of cases . . . | 636 | 568 | 198 | 223 | 93 |
| Number of cases in which proctors appear . . . . . | 265 | 360 | 143 | 150 | 77 |
| Percentage of total. . . . | 47% | 63% | 83% | 67% | 85% |
| Maximum number of suits handled by any one proctor . . . . | 223 | 174 | 83 | 69 | 57 |

The number of proctors engaged in the court obviously affected the amount of business that each could handle. The increase in the numbers of proctors after 1483 reduced the number of suits in which each appeared. While regular clients would engage the same proctor as formerly, the generality of clients who appeared for the first time had a greater field from which to choose their representative. It will be observed, however, that while the total number of suits in which proctors appeared declined, a greater propor-

[1] Excluding sessions at Hythe, Romney, and Dover.
[2] Y. 1. 16.  [3] *Infra*, pp. 50–59 for discussion of procedure.

tion of the total number of suits was being handled by proctors, so that the increase in their number may have resulted in a more efficient service for clients. Conditions did not apparently justify the retention of eight or nine proctors in the Consistory Court for long. After 1500 there were never more than five, but even these probably found that business prospects were far less bright than formerly. These conclusions are based on statistics provided by an analysis of the Act books of the Consistory Court sessions at Canterbury, but there is no evidence to suggest that the proctors who practised in that court could have hoped to augment their business in the sessions of the Archdeacon's Court. The decline in the total number of cases in this court may not be so marked, but it is sufficient to show that the decline in business was common to both courts.[1]

## (iv) THE APPARITORS

The Canterbury court records provide considerable information about that redoubtable and picturesque figure the apparitor, or summoner, the ubiquitous agent of ecclesiastical jurisdiction. The first appearance of the apparitor in the Canterbury *acta* is in 1259, when 'Ricardus preco Consistorii' witnessed the monks' publication of their appeal against Archbishop Boniface.[2] The Sede Vacante material of 1292–4 provides further glimpses of apparitors. Delinquent clergy, duly summoned *per apparitorem consistorii Cant'*, were excommunicated by the commissary Richard de Clyve for not appearing in court;[3] a certain Emma de Wyldington brought a matrimonial suit against John, the apparitor of Sutton.[4]

Notices of apparitors in the earlier Act books of the Consistory series are few, for their names were not usually entered. Citations, if not performed by a rural dean or incumbent, were noted as having been carried out *per apparitorem consistorii* or *per apparitorem decani*.[5] In 1420 Robert *apparitor Officialis*, probably one of the archdeaconry apparitors, witnessed a proctor's appointment.[6] A few names

[1] *Infra*, pp. 109–10.
[2] C.Ant. A 7b.
[3] S.V. 3, p. 45, no date.
[4] Ibid., p. 21, *acta* dated 4 June 1293.
[5] Y. 1. 1 (1372–5).
[6] Y. 1. 4, f. 33, 6 May.

can be gleaned from further Act books, but no basis for the compilation of a list exists until after 25 February 1454/5, when the registrar began to enter the names of apparitors responsible for the citation at the beginning of the *acta* relating to a suit.[1] This practice was maintained in both the remaining Consistory Act books and in all the surviving Archidiaconal Act books. This new practice may have been a clerical innovation of the registrar at that time, but it possibly reflects a stage in the establishment of a stricter control over the apparitors. In the fourteenth century and earlier, the responsibility for citation rested in the majority of cases with the rural deans and incumbents, and they are frequently noticed in the Act books as having to answer in person for failing to send a certificate on receipt of their mandates.[2] They may have employed their own apparitors to carry out the mandates of citation, but it is probable that in the majority of cases citations were addressed to them, and that they were responsible to the commissary general for carrying them out. A number of these 'omnibus' mandates or certificates of citation have survived for the 1292–4 and 1414–20 periods, and it is safe to assume in the majority of cases that the registrar dispatched mandates to the deans instructing them to cite one or a number of persons, and that the deans further instructed their own apparitors. The rights of deans and incumbents in effecting citation must have led to delay and friction between the court and the diocesan clergy, and by *c.* 1450 it may have been appreciated that the centralization of the routine of citation would speed up the hearing of suits. Thereafter the apparitors of the deaneries were made directly responsible for citing parties to court. In the Act books of the Consistory Court from 1455 onwards apparitors are noticed as certifying delivery of mandates of citation or taking oaths that they have diligently searched for the parties concerned.

The first notice of the office of apparitor general appears in 1397, when a certain Robert Otes, *Apparitor Generalis*, witnessed the appointment (or 'constitution') of proctors.[3] Confirmations of commissions of appointment to the office of

[1] Y. 1. 5.                                            [2] Y. 1. 1, e.g. ff. 9, 22, 29b, 34.
[3] Y. 1. 2, f. 35b, 28 May, and f. 50b, 25 Sept.

apparitor general appear in the Registers of the prior and chapter from 1442 onwards. The first is that of the appointment of Master John Penwortham to the office of apparitor general in the archdeaconry. He was also appointed registrar.[1] The appointment was for life. A similar life grant of the office of apparitor general for the Consistory Court was made to William à Dane in 1474. He took an oath of obedience to the prior and chapter in return for their confirmation of his appointment.[2] In 1476 John Sheffields, the archdeaconry apparitor general, did likewise.[3]

The duties of an apparitor general are indicated in detail in a commission of appointment to John Taylor as apparitor general of the city and diocese in 1500.[4] He was to summon laymen and clerks, whatever their condition or degree, to appear before the Auditors or commissaries of the prior and chapter to answer in any suit or for any crime. He was to supervise the summoning of executors and the administration of the goods of deceased persons and to see that wishes of testators were duly carried out and to sequestrate the goods of intestates. It is probable that the powers of the apparitor general were increased once the deanery apparitors had become directly responsible to the courts in matters of citation; the duties of his office may then have involved some measure of control over the subordinate apparitors within the diocese. Little, however, can be gathered from the *acta* of the courts concerning the powers or duties which the apparitor general possessed in this respect. He appears to have remained in close attendance upon the court while in session and is found performing errands in all quarters of the diocese, in contrast to the subordinate apparitors whose activities were generally confined within their particular deaneries. According to the constitutions of Archbishop Stratford, the deanery apparitors were not to use horses.[5] Whether this injunction was observed or not cannot be ascertained.

---

[1] Reg. S, f. 151. *Supra*, p. 39 and n. 4.
[2] Reg. S, f. 268b. Commission dated Lambeth 6 Oct. Oath taken 26 Oct. He began to act from 19 Dec. onwards (Y. 1. 12).     [3] Reg. S, f. 292.
[4] Reg. R, f. 41b. Commission dated Canterbury 20 Sept. For transcript see Appendix No. III. This is not a life grant, being made by the prior and chapter *sede vacante*.     [5] Lyndwood, p. 225

An analysis of the number of citations carried out by each apparitor in 1482 for the Consistory Court provides some glimpse of the division of labour. In that year the apparitor general, John Hunt, and sixteen other apparitors delivered citations in the eleven rural deaneries of the diocese. Most of the apparitors conducted most or all of their business in a particular deanery. Citations within the city and deanery of Canterbury, however, were carried out on an *ad hoc* basis by any apparitor who appears to have been available. The numbers of apparitors employed within the diocese seems to have increased in the century preceding the Reformation. Originally it would appear that the same deanery apparitor cited persons to appear in both the Consistory Court and the Archdeacon's Court, as well as perhaps the senior Courts of Canterbury and of the Audience, but in time each court developed its own corps of apparitors, probably at the same time as the system of citation ceased to be the responsibility of the rural deans.[1] In 1482 there were only three apparitors, Cary, Baker, and Smyth, who acted on behalf of both the Archdeacon's Court and the Consistory Court within their respective deaneries of Charing, Sittingbourne, and Ospringe.[2] By 1522, however, there is no record of any apparitor being employed by both courts. The two groups of apparitors were now quite distinct.[3]

The task of the apparitor was no easy one. The citation of parties in Instance cases was often dangerous, while the summoning of wrongdoers in cases of correction was permanently fraught with peril to life and limb. Apparitors frequently declared that they had been unable to cite parties to court 'propter metum mortis et membrorum suorum mutilacionis',[4] while in the Ex Officio Act books many persons are found accused of setting ambushes and assaulting agents of the courts. In 1470, a particularly bad year for assaults on apparitors, Robert Olyver of Rainham, cited originally on a charge of fornication, was accused 'quod fecit insidias Mathew Apparitori cum baculo suo et quod surri-

---

[1] *Supra*, p. 29, additional note.                    [2] Y. 1. 9, *passim*.
[3] Y. 2. 12 (Consistory); Y. 2. 4; Y. 2. 7; Y. 4. 4 (Archidiaconal).
[4] e.g. Y. 1. 16, f. 77b, under date 11 Mar. 1492/3. The apparitor Salkyn certifies to this effect in perjury suit 'William Baldock v. Roger Fower'. The phrase was common form.

puit commissionem ab eo vi ac male tractavit in eo'. He later admitted that he had abducted the same apparitor *vi et armis* to a house outside Rainham.[1]

The apparitors may have contributed to their own unpopularity by abuse of their powers. The opportunity for victimization and blackmail of the simple was always present. Prosecutions might be suspended in exchange for money payments. Many people were cited before the courts for saying that the apparitors were thieves and blackmailers,[2] but few indications of irregularity have been found in the Act books. One man who had been citing persons in the past came before the Consistory Court accused of acting as an apparitor without authority;[3] another was suspended from office by the archdeacon's Official, but no reasons are given.[4] The normal work of the apparitors was sufficient, however, to generate hostility, quite apart from the irregularities of individuals. The great bulk of Ex Officio business coming before the courts originated in the inquisitions of apparitors.[5] They collected the reports of ill fame and acted as a kind of ecclesiastical gestapo. To the subjects of the archbishop they were the ubiquitous symbols of ecclesiastical jurisdiction, and their conduct and behaviour were no doubt largely responsible for the ill favour with which that jurisdiction came to be so frequently regarded.

Such were the men who staffed the ecclesiastical courts. Before dealing with the problems of their remuneration and the profits and expenses of ecclesiastical jurisdiction, it is necessary to survey the work they performed.

---

[1] Y. 1. 11, f. 105*b*.

[2] e.g. Y. 1. 11, f. 305, under date 15 Sept. 1473. 'Ricardus Herford de Chylham notatur quod publice dixit in foro publico apud Godmersham: omnes officiarii Consistorii Cant' fuerunt latrones et bribors'; cf. Y. 1. 11, f. 178.

[3] Y. 1. 11, f. 59, under date 18 Dec. 1469. 'Henry Graf notatur quod occupat officium apparitoris sine aliqua auctoritate.' He failed to appear and was suspended.

[4] Maidstone, P.R.C. 3. 4, f. 123, under date 2 Apr. 1519. William Allen suspended from office under pain of excommunication.

[5] *Infra*, p. 69.

# IV

# PRACTICE OF THE COURTS. INSTANCE

IN the following survey of the activities and procedure of
the courts attention is directed to what occurred rather
than to what ought to have occurred. No attempt has
been made to correlate practice with Canon Law, Provincial
Constitutions, or Lyndwood's gloss. The survey is intended
to illustrate two main points:

(*a*) How a person began and prosecuted a suit.

(*b*) How the personnel of the courts conducted the hearing of a suit.

## (i) CITATION

A party wishing to introduce a suit notified the registrar
and requested the citation of the defendant. Unless the latter
voluntarily appeared in court *apud acta*, a mandate of citation
was drawn up and dispatched to the apparitor concerned
requiring him to summon the defendant to appear on the
day assigned for the hearing. Sometimes a letter of citation
was dispatched for delivery to the defendant. The registrars
noted the delivery of such letters in the Act books.[1] Whether
these letters were in Latin or English cannot be ascertained.
Comparatively few defendants received them. The plaintiff
would probably only incur the expense of a letter if he knew
the defendant to be literate. The apparitor (or rural dean in
the thirteenth and fourteenth centuries) returned his mandate
of citation to the registrar, certifying that the citation had
been carried out. The 'certificate' consisted of the signature
of the apparitor written on the dorse of the original mandate.
Only one certificated mandate of citation survives for the
pre-Reformation period. This is not a primary citation, but
a mandate of citation for a party to appear to hear sentence,
but there is no reason to suppose that the procedure differed.[2]

---

[1] The usual notice is *citatus litteratorie*.
[2] Citation dated 28 Jan. 1528/9, inserted in binding of Y. 2. 7.

In many cases a primary citation was sufficient to bring the defendant into court. If he failed to appear he was in contempt of court, and if he persisted in absenting himself he might incur the penalty of excommunication.[1] There are large numbers of cases, however, where the record proceeds no farther than the notice of citation, with or without some mark of dismissal, and no entry of penalties for non-appearance. These still-born suits probably indicate that the plaintiff had achieved his purpose. The threat of court action embodied in the appearance of an apparitor may well have prompted the defendant to satisfy the plaintiff's claims and have rendered the prosecution of the suit unnecessary.

In many cases the party to be summoned could not be found. It was possible that the person was elsewhere on his lawful occasions, out of reach of the apparitor. The latter would certify to that effect.[2] If, however, the person deliberately avoided the apparitor, or prevented him from performing his duty by threat of violence, then a citation *viis et modis* could be prepared and dispatched.[3] No such mandates have survived for this period, but it is probable that they were addressed to the local incumbent, instructing him to make proclamation in church or elsewhere, as was the case in later times. Citation *viis et modis* was not employed very often. There are only three cases in the Consistory Court *acta* for 1486, three in 1490, none in 1511, one in 1522, and only two in 1535. When the first court day arrived the defendant might still fail to appear because of some genuine disability. In this event he could proffer an 'exception'. There are frequent notices of such exceptions being made. Among the loose papers still contained in the Archidiaconal Act book Y. 2. 7 is a letter of excuse from one 'Bery' of Sutton pleading infirmity.[4] Absence on the king's business was another frequent excuse for non-appearance.

---

[1] *Infra*, p. 93.

[2] e.g. Y. 1. 3, f. 59 (probably 5 Nov. 1417). Testamentary suit 'Thomas Frost *v.* John Gylys of Rinwould' . . . 'rea . . . non comparente vide certificatorium in dorso mandati quod dicit quod est in mare ad piscandum igitur non citatur'.

[3] e.g. Y. 1. 3, f. 4*b*, under date 19 Mar. 1416/7. *Viis et modis* decreed against John Egerden of Elham. The parish chaplain was afraid to cite on the original mandate.

[4] Y. 2. 7 (1520–5). No date.

(ii) CONSTITUTION OF PROCTORS

Before or during the case, one or both of the parties, if they so desired, appointed proctors to represent them. The proctors could act on their behalf in most of the stages of the case, but the personal presence of the 'principal party' was required for answering the libel, to hear sentence, and, on rare occasions, for interrogation. The plaintiff usually appointed his proctor as part of the preliminary measures taken to begin the suit. The defendant, on the other hand, usually waited until after his own first appearance in court. If the proctor was appointed *apud acta*, during the public session of the court, no witness to the 'constitution' was necessary, but if a proctor was 'constituted' out of court, then the presence of two witnesses was required. Taverns were favourite rendezvous for appointing proctors,[1] but sometimes less hospitable surroundings appeared adequate.[2]

When the proctors appeared in court to represent their 'lords' they provided material evidence of their appointment, or took an oath that they had been appointed by the particular person they claimed to represent.[3] Proctors were required by Canon Law to take an oath to their clients.[4] The formula employed by the registrar when recording 'constitutions' of proctors remained the same throughout the period: 'A constituit B procuratorem suum in omnibus causis suis cum quibuscunque clausulis necessariis una cum clausula substituendi et cautione de rato.' Substitutions of one proctor by one or two others were frequent. The *cautio de rato* was the guarantee that the 'lord' of the suit would ratify the actions of his proctor.[5] Proctors were not bound to prosecute a suit if they thought it hopeless or irregular. If a proctor

---

[1] Cf. Y. 1. 3, f. 39, under date 18 Jan. 1416/7, for the substitution of one proctor by another: 'Adam Body, procurator originalis Alicie Smyth . . . in hospicio de Flor de Lis in parochia omnium Sanctorum Cant' situato substituit Johannem Chapman . . . presentibus Hans de Colonia Ricardo Frogynhale de Cantuar'.' The 'Fleur de Lis' still exists.

[2] e.g. Y. 1. 3, f. 28, under date 14 Sept. 1416. . . . 'in alto vico coram ostio Rogeri Dyer in parochia omnium sanctorum Cant' situato comparuit Willelmus Sone de parochia de Recolver' et constituit magistrum David Mareys. . . .'

[3] Several 'constitutions' of proctors survive in the Sede Vacante Scrapbooks. Clergy appointing proctors usually employed the seal of their rural dean.

[4] Gibson, vol. ii, p. 991, from Constitutions of Otho, 1237.

[5] For the *cautio de rato* cf. Fournier, p. 40.

declared a case *desperata*, the principal party was summoned to appear in person to carry on the suit if he so desired.[1] Only one instance has been found of a proctor not fulfilling his duty.[2]

## (iii) CONTESTATION OF THE SUIT

After the initial appearance of the parties or their proctors the judge either heard the case summarily or assigned a court day for the production of the libel. Many cases, particularly testamentary and perjury suits, were handled summarily.[3] The production of a libel and the elaborate contestation of the suit through the stages of full procedure were not usually required where the plaintiff was petitioning that the defendant fulfil some previously recognized obligation. On the other hand, if the points at issue were uncertain and complex, the judge decided that the case was to be contested stage by stage according to the rules of plenary procedure. The libel was produced, 'articulated' if necessary, the defendant called to 'answer', and three 'terms probatory' assigned for the admission of witnesses and proofs. A term was later assigned for the parties or proctors to 'propound all acts', and finally the judge decreed that the parties be summoned to hear sentence. Each of these stages took at least one court day of any one session of the court. As the courts rarely sat more frequently than at intervals of two or three weeks, it follows that a case could not be terminated within less than three months of its introduction. Superficially it would appear that the mills of the ecclesiastical courts, when geared to full procedure, ground exceeding slow. The Act books, however, indicate that the plenary hearing of a case was not always as inflexible or as relentless as it might appear.

The judges retained considerable powers of discretion.

---

[1] e.g. Y. 1. 3, f. 148, under date 2 July 1420. Testamentary suit 'Executors of John Wylmot of Stone *v.* Simon Odyerne of Wittersham'. Thomas Fen, the defendant's proctor, 'dimisit causam desperatam'.

[2] Y. 1. 3, f. 28*b*, under date 15 Sept. 1416, 'Churchwardens of Ham *v.* John Cely of Eastry': '. . . in termino ad proponendum omnia actore non comparente rea per David in penam actoris non comparentis dominus Commissarius decrevit procuratorem eorum puniri et dictos parochianos citandos erga proximum.'

[3] *Infra*, pp. 82–92 for discussion of types of case.

They could penalize those who would interrupt or purposely delay a process, intervene to prevent the rules from injuring the parties' proper presentation of their cases, or shorten the process if both the parties so desired. They were not well disposed to plaintiffs who failed to prosecute their suit at the time assigned. Plaintiffs who failed to produce a libel on the day allotted were summoned on an ex officio charge of *temeraria fatigatio* or condemned in the costs which the defendant and the court had sustained.[1] Parties failing to produce witnesses lost automatically the benefit of the particular *productio* or 'term probatory'. On the other hand, these *productiones* could be extended to cover more than one court day if the judge saw fit. If the business was unfinished, the case was continued at the stage already reached.[2] If both parties wanted a speedy termination, then the judge could satisfy their petition by curtailing the 'terms'.[3]

Both sides kept a close scrutiny upon the defaults of the other and formally petitioned for the intervention of the judge when they occurred. An efficient judge would see that no unfair advantage was taken in this way of genuine disabilities. The term assigned for answering the libel was a critical stage in the case. If the defendant failed to appear, the plaintiff could claim that the non-appearance of the party was tantamount to a confession of the truth of the accusation. In one case, when the defendant's proctor put forward the excuse that the defendant was unable to enter Canterbury for fear of arrest, the judge appointed a special term for hearing his 'answers' in the church of St. Dunstan's, outside the walls.[4]

---

[1] e.g. Y. 1. 3, f. 162b, under date 21 Feb. 1421. Perjury suit 'Crispina Stevenys of Birchington *v*. John Copyn of Whitstable': '. . . in termino ad libellandum nullo libello porrecto dimissa est pars rea in pena actoris non libellantis et commissarius decrevit partem actricem citandum super temeraria fatigatione.' Condemnation in costs was the more frequent penalty after 1454. It could be reinforced by excommunication.

[2] A very frequent entry: 'continetur causa in statu quo tunc usque proximum'.

[3] e.g. Y. 1. 3, f. 34. Matrimonial suit 'Joan Olyver of Faversham *v*. Thomas Bert of Lyminge'. On the day assigned for second *productio*, '. . . ex consensu partium renunciatis ulterioribus productionibus . . . publicatum est in causa et datur ad concludendum in proximo consistorio'.

[4] Y. 1. 3, f. 59b, under date 22 Nov. 1417. Testamentary suit 'Agnes Lucas of Biddenden *v*. John Brynchele': '. . . commissarius assignavit ecclesiam Sancti Dunstani pro loco tuto ad personaliter respondendum in proximo secunda hora post prandium.'

Once the defendant had answered the libel negatively, it was usual for the judge to elicit the *de calumpnia* oath from the plaintiff or his proctor.[1] It is to be doubted whether this had any influence upon the conduct of any case. It must have been regarded as purely formal, remaining merely an ideal guarantee that the plaintiff's motives were good and that his conduct of the case would be honest.

## (iv) PROOFS

In those cases which were seriously contested the most frequent form of proof was by witnesses, but documentary proof was common, and compurgation was frequently employed in summary hearings.

Parties usually managed to produce their witnesses on the days assigned for the *productio testium*, but sometimes they petitioned for a 'compulsory' order to effect the appearance of witnesses in court. Witnesses compulsorily ordered to attend were presumably subject to penalties for contempt if they did not appear, but no examples of the suspension or excommunication of witnesses have been found. This is not surprising, for the numbers of *mandata compulsoria* were small. Only one instance has been found in the Consistory Court *acta* for 1511, and none at all in 1522.[2] It was probably only rarely that a party required the presence of an unwilling witness and requested official assistance of this kind, but whether witnesses were willing or unwilling, it was probably a difficult task to get them to attend court at the right time. Their expenses had to be paid and various hazards attended their journey. They might be threatened by the supporters of the opposite party[3] or be arrested on their way.[4] In medieval

---

[1] Gibson, vol. ii, p. 1052 n. for terms of this oath: 'Quod credit se bonam causam habere; interrogatus non negabit quod verum esse credit; nec utetur scienter falsa probatione; Et quod dilationem non petat in fraudem; Nec dedit nec dabit, nec promisit, nec promittet, aliquid pro hac causa, nisi illis personis quibus leges dare permittunt'.  [2] Y. 2. 5 and Y. 2. 12 respectively.

[3] e.g. Y. 4. 3, f. 207, under date 26 Jan. 1509/10. Defamation suit 'John Kempe of Stodmarsh *v.* Robert Cokke'. On 24 Mar. the plaintiff's proctor nominated William Saukyn and Ralph Swan as necessary witnesses: '... allegans eos non audere accedere metu arrestationis a parte rei sicut actor fuit antea arrestatus modis partis rei'. The judge summoned Cokke to answer Ex Officio articles 'perturbationis et impedimenti iuris ecclesiastici'.

[4] e.g. Y. 1. 12, f. 262, under date 15 Sept. 1477. Defamation suit 'John Gavelonde

conditions the three 'probatory terms' were not too generous an allowance for the production of witnesses.

In general, witnesses had to appear publicly in court to be admitted and sworn, but infirm or important personages were allowed special privileges. Commissions were appointed to visit such persons in their own homes.[1] When the witnesses had been admitted and sworn, and if no immediate 'exceptions' had been brought against them, a place and occasion was assigned for their examination. This usually took place on the same day after the public session of the court. Witnesses were examined in private without the presence of the parties or their proctors. In the period 1412–20 the Consistory Court examinations were usually conducted by the commissary general, but the registrar sometimes deputized for him. During the year 1412 Assheton, the commissary general, conducted thirty-nine distinct examinations, mostly in his own house in All Saints' parish, but he employed the Chapter House of the Dominicans on two occasions and the house of the registrar once. John Lovelych, the registrar, conducted only two examinations that year. If special commissions were dispatched to examine witnesses outside Canterbury or away from places where the court sat, the registrar usually presided.[2]

The examiners questioned the witnesses from set 'interrogatories' which the parties or their proctors had prepared. The answers were probably written down roughly by the scribe and later incorporated into a fair copy. It was this final deposition that was published on the next court day appointed for the continued hearing of the suit. The depositions were entered in special books or quires to remain among the archives of the court. If the parties so requested, copies

*v.* Juliana Whyte'. Both the plaintiff and the witness he was fetching from London were arrested while on their way to Canterbury.

[1] e.g. Y. 2. 13, f. 148, under date 14 Apr. 1534. Defamation suit 'Agnes Bolney of St. Andrew's *v.* M. John Cokke, rector of St. Andrew's, Canterbury'. On 20 Oct. the prior of Christchurch, Sir William Hawte, and four others were required as witnesses: '. . . Iudex decrevit predictos Reverendissimum Priorem et Willelmum Hawte quia egregie persone domi examinandos fore atque alios testes predictos compellandos fore'; cf. Y. 1. 3, f. 21*b*, under date 17 June 1416. Matrimonial suit 'Thomas Bergrove *v.* Joan Dyne of Reculver'. Commission to John Lovelych, registrar, to examine John Bukwell at Westbere, the witness being infirm.

[2] e.g. X. 10. 1, f. 12*d*, 16 May 1412. The registrar examined witnesses at St. Mary's, Faversham.

would be written out and handed to them. The routine of examination and the formulae of the 'interrogatories' of the fifteenth century differ little from those of the thirteenth. The depositions of the earlier period are perhaps more succinct. The 'interrogatories' were employed to elicit the 'common fame' as well as the personal knowledge of the individual witness. Although the 'interrogatories' themselves were constructed to elicit direct and unequivocal replies, there was no system of cross-examination. In Canon Law the concordance of two witnesses was sufficient 'proof'. The opposite party attempted to refute the attestations of his opponent's witnesses by producing witnesses of his own, and it remained the task of the judge to evaluate the worth of the statements that the witnesses of both sides had deposed.

Notices of 'instruments' exhibited in court are frequently found among the court *acta*. Ecclesiastics in particular could draw upon documents from among their own archives,[1] while the exhibition of wills or copies of wills frequently occurred in testamentary suits. The registrar would turn up official copies of wills from the archives.[2] Sometimes suits were brought against parties for illegally detaining muniments, and the judge would order them to be exhibited.[3]

Compurgation, although primarily employed in Ex Officio procedure, is often found among the Instance *acta* of those Act books dating from an earlier period than 1425. It was employed in defamation suits in particular. Defamation contained a disciplinary element, for it often involved the plaintiff in suspicion of having committed acts open to correction. Some plaintiffs, therefore, purged themselves of the 'ill fame' before beginning a suit.[4] The defendant, on the other hand,

[1] e.g. Y. 2. 1, f. 64*b*, 20 May 1504, two Bulls were exhibited in a tithe suit on behalf of the abbot of Faversham; Y. 4. 3, f. 188, under date 5 Oct. 1509. 'Causa subtractionis quorumdam cereorum'; 'abbot of St. Radegund's *v.* parishioners of Capel le Ferne.' On 17 Nov. Richardson, the abbot's proctor, 'introduxit quendam librum ex archive sive armario monasterii sancte Radegundis'.

[2] e.g. Y. 1. 3, f. 24, under date 9 July 1416. Testamentary suit 'Joan Clerke, Robert Nethersole, and Alice his wife *v.* Thomas Ovynden'. The registrar produced a copy of the latter's deceased wife's will.

[3] e.g. Y. 1. 16, f. 192*b*, under date 8 July 1494. 'Robert Ames, John Poole *v.* William Baldwyn of Sturry.'

[4] e.g. Y. 1. 3, f. 40, under date 26 Jan. 1416/17. Richard Ravenisdale of Lenham 'purgatus est cum vi^ta manu vicinorum suorum quod non vendidit ii vaccas suas et

sometimes employed compurgators to swear that he had
never spoken the words in question.[1] The number of compurgators employed varied from two to twelve. The number
probably depended on the nature of the offence and the worth
of the compurgators concerned.[2] After 1454, when the series
of Instance Act books recommence, there is no trace of the
employment of compurgation in Instance suits. Possibly it
came to be regarded as redundant. If the plaintiff won his
suit for defamation he was cleared of the suspicion, and
regained his 'good fame', while the defendant was awarded
penance.[3] If he lost the suit, then he himself was liable to
correction.

## (v) CONCLUSION AND SENTENCE

Once the parties had enjoyed the 'probatory terms' and
produced their witnesses and instruments, the judge called
upon the proctors to 'propound all acts'. After this summing
up of the positions of both sides the judge 'concluded' the
case and assigned a day for the principal parties to appear to
hear sentence. The sentence determining the suit was known
as the 'definitive sentence' to distinguish it from the 'interlocutory sentences' whereby the judge terminated points at
issue incidental to the hearing of the suit. During the vacancy
of 1292–4 it was the custom to inscribe the sentence upon
the dorse of the depositions of witnesses. During the fourteenth century the sentences published by the judges of the
Consistory Court were interlarded among the *acta* of the
suits in the Act books.[4] Later, they were not written out in

imbursavit pecuniam pro eis receptam et postmodo imposuit vicinis suis quod ipsi
easdem subtraxerunt seu abduxerunt'. He later brings suit for defamation against
William atte Downe (f. 41*b*).
    [1] e.g. Y. 1. 3, f. 7, under date 24 Mar. 1415/16. Defamation suit 'Robert Marshall
*v.* Thomas Bertram': '. . . datur parti rei ad purgandum se in proximo die Jovis
cum vi*ta* manu quod non est causa diffamationis vicinorum et precipue Roberti
Marchall'.
    [2] Cf. Y. 1. 3, f. 11*b*, under date 9 Apr. 1416. A vicar and a chaplain were enough
to clear William Verich of St. Laurence, Thanet, from a charge of theft. (A suit was
later brought against his defamer Richard Cokelyn.) Eight compurgators were
required to clear William Tropham of Chartham (ibid., f. 16, 18 May).
    [3] *Infra*, pp. 87–89 for discussion of defamation suits.
    [4] Y. 1. 1 (1372–5) and Y. 1. 2 (1398–2). In Y. 1. 1 each sentence is followed by
the signature of the registrar: 'Lata fuit sententia predicta per commissarium predictum in foro predicto—J. Cranebourne subscripsi.'

the Act books, probably being filed elsewhere, but no independent book or file of Sentences survives. The registrars were careful to name two witnesses against the entries that sentence had been given.

## (vi) ARBITRATION

In a few cases the parties to a suit agreed to compromise and accept the judgement of arbitrators rather than proceed with the suit in court. One or two arbitrators would be appointed by each side, and the parties undertook in court to accept their verdict on pain of certain penalties. These took the form of money fines. The money was to be contributed towards the upkeep or repair of churches.[1] During 1416 there were four cases introduced into the Consistory Court in which the parties agreed to compromise, and only one case in 1417. Later, arbitration is very rare. Analyses of cases heard in the Consistory Court for the years 1475, 1482, 1486, 1499, 1511, and 1522 provide no examples. There was one case in 1535. In the Archdeacon's Court in 1517 a woman was required to answer why she should not be excommunicated for not obeying the decisions of arbitrators in a testamentary case.[2]

## (vii) DISPOSAL OF INSTANCE SUITS

Only a minority of cases was given a plenary hearing. If the assignment of a court day for the presentation of a written libel is accepted as the criterion of a plenary hearing, then it can be estimated that approximately a third of the total number of cases introduced into the Consistory Court between 1416 and 1535 were contested according to the rules of full procedure. The number of suits which involved the production of witnesses was smaller still, approximately a tenth of the number of plenary suits.[3] Unfortunately the

---

[1] e.g. Y. 1. 3, f. 37, under date 15 Dec. 1416. Testamentary suit 'John Bocher of Westwell and Thomas Bocher of Parva Chart *v.* William Hurst, butcher of Westwell': '. . . Compromiserunt dicte partes in Johannem Darell et Johannem Hawte.' The penalty for disobeying their verdict was the payment of 25s. to Christchurch and 25s. to the church of Parva Chart.

[2] Y. 2. 7, f. 181*b*, under date 19 Mar., Dionisia Gore of Sheldwich. The arbitrators were John Colman and Thomas Laurence. [3] See Appendix No. IV.

number of suits in which definitive sentence was given cannot be ascertained, for the Act books did not serve as clearance registers in this respect. Although the record of a particular suit may end with the entry of assignment to hear sentence, there is no guarantee, in the absence of files or books of Sentences, that a definitive sentence was actually given; even so, the number of cases where a day was assigned *ad audiendam sententiam* is very small.

The mere numbers of plenary suits cannot indicate the relative amount of time that the courts spent upon them. Each case may have engaged the court ten or twenty times as long as a summary case which could be heard in one or two days. It is probable that the comparatively few plenary suits which were contested to a finish occupied the courts longer than all the rest of the cases together.

The very large number of uncompleted cases must not be taken as a measure of efficiency. The courts had no concern in seeing that sentence was given in suits where the responsibility for their prosecution rested with private persons. The judges only took the initiative where matters of correction were involved.[1] Nor must it be assumed that the plaintiff had been frustrated in his purpose. He may have come to some agreement with the defendant to drop the case, or the defendant may have conceded the issue in dispute. Many cases are recorded as adjourned (*continuatur sub spe concordie*), indicating that some private agreement was being reached in this way. On the other hand, the plaintiff's initial determination might have been outweighed by the expenses of litigation. It is also probable that a large number of cases foundered upon the rock of the defendant's refusal to come into court at all.[2] Except for this last, there is little indication of the reasons for dropping a case. Often there is no indication of dismissal. Another group of cases were removed from the jurisdiction of the courts by appeal or by prohibition.[3]

## (viii) COSTS

Whether cases were finished or not, the expenses of the courts had to be met. In unfinished cases it was the plaintiff

[1] *Infra*, p. 83.
[2] *Infra*, p. 100.
[3] *Infra*, pp. 107-8 for discussion of prohibitions.

who had to defray the common expenses of the court; but where definitive sentence had been given, the party who had lost the suit was generally condemned in the costs incurred by the successful party. No bills of costs survive for the thirteenth century, and there is insufficient data in the Act books to furnish information respecting the rate of costs until the half-century previous to the Reformation. It is fortunate that three bills of costs remained inserted among the leaves of two Act books for this period. Two of these can be checked against the *acta* of the cases concerned.[1] From these three bills of costs can be established the fixed and the variable items of some of the expenses incurred in the prosecution of a suit. Significantly, the fixed costs are common to both courts and it is probable that there was a customary, if not stipulated, scale of charges.

The introduction and dismissal of a suit each cost 3*d*. Letters of citation, whether of the defendant or the principal party, cost 4*d*. The writing of the libel cost 2*s*. 1*d*. Examination of the principal party cost 1*s*. Unfortunately no indication is given of the charge for examining witnesses, but it is probable that copies of witnesses' depositions were priced according to their length. The drawing up of the definitive sentences cost no less than 7*s*. 8*d*., an expensive item which may help to explain why so few suits reached the stage at which sentence was given. It cost 8*d*. to purchase the letter of execution, while the drawing up of the bill of costs itself cost 4*d*. Proctors were paid at the rate of 6*d*. for each appearance. The 'constitution' of a proctor cost 2*d*. The charge for the certification of the various citations varied. This served as the apparitor's fee and varied in relation to the distance the apparitor had to travel. It was probably rated at 1*d*. a mile. It cannot be ascertained how the personnel of the courts

[1] A. Consistory Court: bill of costs, testamentary suit, 'Executors of Richard Forde *v*. Roger Bounsse of Molash'. The case *acta* under date 15 May 1497 (Y. 1. 17, f. 118*b*). For transcript of both Bill and *acta* see Appendix No. V.

B. Archdeacon's Court: bill of costs, suit for adultery. 'Margaret Marley of Chilham *v*. James Prowde.' Case *acta* under date of 27 Oct. 1515 (Y. 2. 4, f. 76).

C. The third bill of costs inscribed 'Halke contra Torner expense', found inserted in Y. 2. 4 (f. 33), probably related to a suit prosecuted in the Archdeacon's Court.

shared out these fees, but it is doubtful whether the apparitors received more than their 1*d.* a mile rate, or the proctors more than their 6*d.* a day rate. The judge and the registrar probably divided the remaining fees between them.[1]

The payment of costs was enforced by disciplinary action and threat of excommunication.[2] A time limit was imposed, and occasionally payment by instalments was allowed. It was not often that the judge assigned an indefinite time limit as in the case of John Castlyn of Frittenden, who was allowed by the archdeacon's Official to pay *cum ad pinguiorem fortunam pervenerit.*[3]

Theoretically the Church allowed poor suitors to plead *in forma pauperis,* but cases in which plaintiffs or defendants were allowed to conduct their suits free of charge were infrequent. There was only one case from a total of 198 suits introduced into the Consistory Court during 1511.[4] In many years there were none at all. Either the very poor were not involved in Instance litigation or else the courts were not eager to subsidize their suits.

---

[1] *Infra,* pp. 75–78 for discussion of income of personnel and expenses of the courts.

[2] Cf. Y. 1. 3, f. 22*b*, under date 20 June 1416. Perjury suit 'John Sparows *v.* Thomas Mattie'. Costs taxed at 20*s.* to be paid in three instalments of 6*s.* 8*d.* Thomas to appear to say why he should not be excommunicated if he failed to pay.

[3] Y. 1. 9, f. 56, under date 24 Sept. 1482, at Tenterden. Perjury suit 'Ralph Blechynden of Headcom *v.* John Castlyn of Frittenden'.

[4] Y. 2. 5, f. 92*b*, under date 24 Nov. Matrimonial suit 'Alice Kynge of Ulcombe *v.* William Cressefelds of Lenham'. Alice was allowed to plead *in forma pauperis.*

# V

## PRACTICE OF THE COURTS. APPEALS IN INSTANCE CASES

IN the question of appellate jurisdiction both the Consistory Court and the Archdeacon's Court were on an equal footing. No appeal lay from the Archdeacon's Court to the Consistory Court. There is no evidence to suggest that the latter ever possessed, or even claimed, an appellate jurisdiction over the former. This was probably due to the comparatively late development of the Consistory Court as a purely diocesan court.[1] Appeals lay equally from both courts to the provincial Court of Canterbury and to the archbishop's Court of Audience.

The first surviving document in an appeal from the Consistory Court to the Court of Canterbury is a 'remission' in a matrimonial suit of 1294,[2] but the vacancy of 1292–4 does not provide a representative picture of appeal business, however, for the jurisdictional disputes between the prior and chapter and the archdeacon gave rise to an inordinate number of appeals to the Court of Canterbury at that time. The Consistory *acta* of 1372 onwards, on the other hand, provide information for a period free from any serious disputes of this kind. Cases in which parties attempted to prosecute appeals were few. In the Consistory Court there was only one appeal from a total of 195 cases introduced during 1416. From 1474 to 1483 there were no appeals at all from the 6,580 cases introduced during these years. From 1484 to 1500 there were 5 cases of appeal. From 1500 to 1536 there were 33; an increase relative to the total number of cases handled, but still very few. The *acta* of the Archdeacon's Court do not allow such complete statistics to be compiled, but 20 appeals have been noted in the *acta* of the Canterbury sessions of the Archdeacon's Court between the years 1501 and 1524.

---

[1] *Supra,* p. 12. The clause relating to the hearing of appeals, in some commissions of the Commissary General (Churchill, vol. i, p. 59), probably related to appeals from exempt parishes.

[2] 'Muriel of Dunham *v.* John Burnoth of Chartham', dated 22 July 1294.

As yet no comparison can be made between the numbers of appeals originating in the Canterbury diocesan courts and those originating in the other diocesan courts of the province, but it is possible that the Canterbury figures will be found to be comparatively small. The archbishop's Court of Audience also served as a court of first instance for his own diocesan subjects, and in attracting many of the more weighty cases to it direct, it perhaps lessened the incidence of appeals from the inferior courts.

Appeals were of two types, direct and tuitorial. They were heard in both the Court of Canterbury and the Court of Audience. There do not appear to have been any restrictions on the types of case which qualified for tuitorial appeal. Despite Archbishop Pecham's ruling that tuitorial appeals could not be made in matrimonial cases,[1] an appeal of this type was made in a matrimonial case in 1416.[2]

Another distinction can be made between appeals which followed a definitive sentence and appeals which arose from some 'gravamen' or grievance incurred at the time of the hearing of the case. Most of the recorded cases of appeal followed a definitive sentence. The *acta* of cases where the appeal followed from a *gravamen* do not usually indicate the reason. In 1524, however, a party is found appealing on the grounds of the non-competence of the judge.[3] If an appeal followed from a definitive sentence, the party, or his proctor, demanded in set form that *apostolos* should be granted him: 'apostolos petiit primo secundo tertio instanter instantius et instantissime'. The *apostolos* were letters dimissory granted to appellants by the judge if he recognized the validity of the appeal. These were dispatched to the provincial court together with the written appeal of the appellant.[4]

---

[1] Churchill, vol. i, p. 462. For an account of proceedings in the Court of Canterbury, ibid., pp. 460–9.

[2] Y. 1. 3, f. 18*b*, under date 28 Mar. 'Thomas Hokerygge of Cranbrook *v.* Godeleva Lucas of Benenden.' Miss Churchill may have overlooked the fact that, later, the restriction applied only to appeals from *gravamina* in matrimonial suits; cf. Wilkins, vol. ii, p. 683, for Archbishop Stratford's ruling on this point.

[3] Y. 2. 12, f. 92*b*, under date 5 Apr. Matrimonial suit, 'John Barber of Dover *v.* Joan Stylman of Dover.' The protest against the judge was made on 14 May, and inhibition was announced on 6 June.

[4] No letters dimissory or written appeals survive for the period 1372 to 1536.

The local judge could refuse to grant *apostolos*,[1] but this did not prevent the appeal from going forward. The fact that an appeal had been made was sufficient reason for it to be considered at the provincial court, provided that the appellant prosecuted his appeal within thirty days.[2] This was probably the rule in appeals *a gravamine* where *apostolos* were hardly likely to have been granted by the judge. In both cases the appellant probably notified the provincial court by way of a notarial instrument to avoid the trouble of appearing in person with witnesses to attest the mere fact of appeal. Once the provincial judge had received notification of appeal, an 'inhibition' was dispatched to the local judge. This recited the reasons for the appeal contained in what was now termed the *suggestio* of the appellant; ordered the parties to be summoned to appear before the provincial court and enjoined that the local judge was to act no further in the matter.[3] If the appellant failed in his appeal, a *remissio* would be dispatched to the local judge ordering him to proceed.[4]

With tuitorial appeals the procedure was similar, in so far as it related to the appeal for tuition. An inhibition was dispatched to the local court ordering the parties to be cited to the provincial court to establish whether tuition was to be granted or not, for this was the initial matter for consideration in appeals of this kind. Once tuition had been granted it theoretically lasted for a year and a day, to enable the appellant to appeal to Rome. Presumably the local judge would have been within his rights if he had resumed the case after the period had elapsed, but it is probable that in the event of the case being heard at Rome an inhibition would have arrived from the Curia, and in the event of the case being heard in the Court of Canterbury, or the Audience, it is unlikely that the inferior judge would have reopened the case without the

[1] e.g. Y. 2. 11, f. 13*b*, under date 30 Apr. 1521. Testamentary suit 'Elinor Groverst of Doddington *v.* Margaret Ferrar'. On 26 Feb. 1522 the defendant's proctor '. . . peciit apostolos et judex recusavit sibi tradere . . .', but inhibition announced 1 July; cf. Y. 2. 13, f. 171, under date 16 Sept. 1534. Matrimonial suit 'Robert Danyell *v.* Thomasina Orgar', 2 Mar. 1534/5. Appeal declared *frivola et inepta* in that no good reason had been given.
[2] Reg. L, f. 102*b*, where instructions are given for prosecuting appeals. Date *c.* 1337.
[3] For transcript of an inhibition in a tuitorial appeal see Appendix No. VI.
[4] For transcript of a *remissio* in the same case see Appendix No. VI.

usual 'remission'. No inhibitions in tuitorial appeals have survived for the period 1372–1536, but an inhibition of 1293 rehearses the reasons for appeal and forbids the commissary general to attempt anything to the prejudice of the appellant.[1]

For information concerning the standing of an appellant after making an appeal, the *acta* of the courts must be deserted in favour of surviving Provincial Statutes[2] and tracts on procedure. There survives at Canterbury a valuable treatise on the practice of the Court of Canterbury at the beginning of the fourteenth century (MS. D. 8). This cannot be analysed in any detail here, but some provisional generalizations can be made from its contents upon the standing of appellants.[3]

In cases of direct appeal to the Court of Canterbury the definitive sentence of the inferior court stood until it had been confirmed or cancelled by the superior court, and there was no immediate remedy against acts performed to the prejudice of the appellant. A cleric who had lost his benefice would remain deprived until the sentence of the inferior court had been cancelled, but if the appellant had been excommunicated, however, the superior judge could temporarily absolve him *ad cautelam* (subject to some pledge or security being given) upon the appellant's petition, which, as it preceded the hearing of the case, was known as the *articulus ante omnia*. If the direct appeal had arisen from a *gravamen*, the appellant remained in the same state as at the time of making the appeal.

The effects of tuitorial appeal were far more complex, and varied according to the timing of the *provocatio*. This was the call for the protection of the archbishop (*pro tuitione*) which could be made upon the mere anticipation of an adverse sentence or of acts to the appellant's prejudice, and could be followed by the formal appeal to Rome, once the sentence had been given or the acts performed. The advantages of

---

[1] S.V. 1, p. 103. Inhibition in divorce suit 'Roger le Corveysor and Alice Finchelot *v.* William de Rywode', dated 5 May 1293.

[2] e.g. Archbishop Greenfield's Statutes of 1311 for the province of York, see Wilkins, vol. ii, p. 412; cf. ibid., p. 681, for Stratford's Statutes for Court of Canterbury.

[3] MS. D. 8 has been transcribed by the late W. P. Blore. Professor N. Adams is working on this MS. in connexion with her forthcoming study on 'Thirteenth Century Ecclesiastical Suits' for the Selden Society.

having made a *provocatio* were considerable. If the judge of the provincial court upheld the *provocatio*, tuition was granted to the appellant; the sentence of the inferior court was revoked, not merely suspended, and all acts done to the prejudice of the appellant since the making of the *provocatio* were revoked also. Theoretically a clerk who had lost his benefice after making a *provocatio* would be restored to it. Sentences of excommunication would be rendered null and void.

The making of a *provocatio* had its drawbacks. It ensured the revocation of anticipated injuries only; not those already committed. The writer of MS. D. 8 urges his readers to see to it that they are in a 'good state' when they make it, and not excommunicated. The *provocatio* need not particularize the injuries that were anticipated. General precautionary *provocationes* could be made to ensure subsequent confirmation of jurisdictional rights. From 1278 to 1327, one of the first steps which the prior and chapter took at the beginning of a vacancy was the publication of a *provocatio* against would-be usurpers of their rights. It was a curious legal weapon. The prior and chapter called for the protection of the Court of Canterbury, which they themselves controlled, in the exercise of jurisdiction of the same court and that of the Consistory Court.[1]

The mechanics of this double-barrelled procedure of *provocatio* and appeal still have to be worked out in detail. It would appear that the *provocatio* as a separate instrument—a mere call for protection—without a simultaneous appeal, was a rather primitive institution belonging to a period when appeal jurisdiction was still ill defined.[2] Later it would appear that the *provocatio* and the appeal were made simultaneously as a matter of form. The terminology is confused by the employment of the word *provocatio* to cover both the initial call for protection and the whole procedure including the appeal.

---

[1] For transcript see Appendix No. VII.

[2] The suffragans complained about the misuse of the *provocatio* in 1282. Cf. Articles of Complaint against Archbishop Pechham, printed *Reg. Epp. Jo. Peckham*, vol. i, pp. 334–7, Article XI, where they complain that excommunicates are being absolved 'quando frivola provocatio proponitur praecessisse'. They petition that the publication of the revocation be delayed until the appellant has himself instructed the Court of Canterbury of the grounds of his *provocatio*.

# VI
## PRACTICE OF THE COURTS.
## EX OFFICIO

### (i) EX OFFICIO PROMOTO

THIS was a very rare type of action whereby an ecclesiastical judge undertook the prosecution of a person or persons at the 'promotion' of a third party. The registrars generally recorded them in the Instance Act books. The procedure was similar to Instance procedure. In 1416 a proctor, David Mareys, brought a testamentary suit *ex promotione officii* against Henry Austin of Herne. The latter produced witnesses who were examined in the usual way.[1] A more characteristic case of this type was the action brought by the parishioners of Westwell against William Edynton and John Rusyll whom they had elected churchwardens. The parishioners petitioned that they be compelled to fulfil their duties.[2] This form of action apparently suited parishioners who were attempting to remedy the faults and misdemeanours of their churchwardens. Costs of prosecution were no doubt borne by them and not by the court.

### (ii) EX OFFICIO MERO

One of the more interesting features of late medieval enforcement of canonical discipline disclosed by the Canterbury *acta* is the comparative insignificance of the regular visitations in the process of checking and punishing crimes and misdemeanours which were answerable *in foro ecclesiastico*. The visitations of the archdeacon's Official seem to have been little more than formal annual tours, the chief object of which was the collection of procurations. He spent little more than one day in each deanery. The paucity of the information contained in the surviving Archdeaconry Visitation

---

[1] Y. 1. 3, f. 28b, under date 15 Sept.
[2] Y. 1. 5, f. 20, under date 21 May 1454.

books reflects the cursory nature of the Official's tour.[1] The criminal business entered in them is quite negligible when compared with the amount of business originating at other times. The great bulk of Ex officio business arose not upon presentment after detection but as the result of a continuous process of 'inquisition'. The registrars distinguished the few cases arising out of visitations by employing the phrases *ut in billa detectionis* or *detectus in visitatione* after the description of the charge and the name of the defendant.[2]

The usual formula employed by the registrar to record Ex Officio cases is 'A. notatur de crimine B, citatus per C' (the apparitor). It cannot be ascertained how individual delinquents were brought to the notice of the courts. Incumbents may have requested the assistance of the judges to deal with refractory parishioners;[3] churchwardens may have unofficially 'presented' suspect persons; but it is probable that the majority of cases arose from the general 'ill fame' connected with suspected delinquency and that the whole was sifted and sorted by the inquisitorial activity of the apparitors. The judges probably acted upon their intelligence or perhaps even at their instigation. Archdeacon Hale found that this was the case in the diocese of London from his survey of the early Act books of the London diocesan courts.[4] From a review of post-Reformation Act books it can be seen that one of the great permanent changes in the application of ecclesiastical jurisdiction during the later sixteenth century was the substitution of a regular visitation and presentment system for the hitherto haphazard process of hauling people into court upon the instigation of the apparitors. It appears that in Elizabethan times there were very few Ex Officio cases which had not resulted from presentment by churchwardens at visitations, which were more frequent and thorough than they had been in immediate pre-Reformation times.

Citation of offenders in matters of correction was

[1] Visitation books survive from 1498 onwards. *Infra*, p. 142.

[2] e.g. Maidstone, P.R.C. 3. 1, f. 20, under date 18 Sept. 1490. 'William Marshall de Westgate detectus in visitatione quod non abfuerat propriam ecclesiam in audiendo divina' [*sic*].

[3] Scrapbook A, No. 60. No date, but early sixteenth century. Letter from incumbent requesting judge to send his apparitor to cite certain *generosi*. Largely illegible.

[4] W. H. Hale, *Precedents in Criminal Causes* (London, 1847), p. lxiii.

'peremptory'. No elaborate citation mandates were drawn up. There was no one to pay for them. The apparitors cited offenders by word of mouth, their commission of appointment being sufficient authority. That this was the usual practice is made quite clear by the prosecution of people who asserted that it was irregular. In 1469/70 William, the parish clerk of Ewell, was summoned for saying that apparitors could not cite offenders without a written mandate.[1] An instruction for citation still remaining between the leaves of the Archdeaconry Act book for 1505–12[2] illustrates the informal manner in which persons were summoned. It is to be noted that the apparitor was to cite persons whose names were not yet known. It is probable that the apparitor already had full details of the delinquencies for which the persons were to be cited.

If the person was accused of a heinous offence, or several offences, it was usual for the court to draw up articles which were read out to him in court,[3] but in most cases the defendant was dealt with summarily, by word of mouth, probably with nobody else present but the judge and the registrar. The latter noted the brief details of the case in the Act book. If the defendant denied the charge, he was required to purge himself. The numbers of compurgators are not usually given, so it cannot be ascertained whether Archbishop Stratford's injunctions of 1342, that a maximum of six compurgators should be called in fornication cases and a maximum of twelve in cases of adultery, were observed.[4] If the defendant failed to find the necessary compurgators, or had confessed, he was admonished or awarded penance.[5]

The expenses of Ex Officio business were small, not amounting to more than the citation fees of the apparitor, and the cost of letters of suspension or excommunication, if such had been dispatched. Persons cited to answer Ex Officio

[1] Y. 1. 11, f. 77b, under date 29 Jan. 1469/70. 'Willelmus . . . clericus parochie de Ewell notatur quod predicat et publice dixit quod nullus apparitor debet citare aliquem ex officio sine citatione in scriptis. . . .'
[2] Maidstone, P.R.C. 3. 3, at f. 58. For transcript see Appendix No. VIII.
[3] e.g. Y. 1. 5, f. 81b, under date 31 Mar. 1455. Articles of accusation against James Mocock of Wittersham for rude and irreverent criticism of a sermon.
[4] Wilkins, vol. ii, p. 700.
[5] For discussion of ecclesiastical censures see *infra*, pp. 94–102.

charges might be called upon to pay such costs if they were found guilty or if they had been suspended or excommunicated.

There is no evidence in the Canterbury *acta* of any appeals being made by defendants in these types of case. This appears to have been the rule in the enforcement of canonical discipline by ecclesiastical judges acting by virtue of their office.

# VII

## PRACTICE OF THE COURTS. PROBATE

PROBATE *acta*, containing the details of the process of proving testaments and granting letters of administration, were entered in the Ex Officio Act books.[1] Most of the surviving Ex Officio Act books of the Archdeacon's Court have found their way to the Kent County Record Office at Maidstone, but the two surviving Sandwich Act books of the Archdeacon's Court and the few Consistory Ex Officio books remain at Canterbury. Surviving Registers of Wills and boxes of Wills proved in both courts are preserved at Maidstone.[2]

None of these Probate Registers can be regarded as comprehensive for the period they cover, for probate was often granted on visitations as well as during sessions of the courts; while the inhibition of inferior jurisdictions during the course of archiepiscopal visitations temporarily interrupted probate unless instructions were given for it to be carried on.[3]

The *acta* of probate usually contain the name of the deceased, the names of the executors or administrators, the notice of the grant of execution upon the exhibition of the inventory, the value of the goods, and the fee charged. Numbers of inventories still remain among the leaves of the Archidiaconal Act books. Some are stitched to the page against the details of the case to which they refer. The books also contain various claims upon goods of the deceased, letters to the court requesting payments of debts or wages, and many other miscellaneous papers which still require to be sorted. The goods of intestates were collected by the appari-

---

[1] For an account of procedure see E. F. Jacob, Introduction, *Chichele* (C.Y. Soc.), vol. ii.

[2] For details of Act books and Registers see *infra*, pp. 140–2. A few copies of wills from the *sede vacante* period 1292–4 survive in S.V. 2, pp. 188–91.

[3] Chichele reserved probate during his visitation of the diocese in 1414–15 (Churchill, vol. ii, p. 146). Warham granted the exercise of probate jurisdiction to the archdeacon during his visitation of 1511 (Lambeth, Reg. Warham, f. lxxxvii).

tors, and proclamation was made three times to allow persons to claim any debts owing to them by the deceased.[1]

Regular fees were charged for probate. The archdeacon's Official, in the ten years previous to the meeting of the Reformation Parliament, was charging the same fees as had been customary in Lyndwood's day.[2] The fees entered in the Act book of the Sandwich session of the Archdeacon's Court for the years 1520–30 have been compared with the total of the inventories as entered in the *acta*.[3] No deviation from the Lyndwood scale has been found. No fees were charged if the total value of the goods was less than 30s.; 1s. was charged for totals ranging from 30s. to 100s.; 3s. for totals between 100s. and £20; 5s. for totals between £20 and £40; 10s. for totals between £40 and £100; 20s. for totals between £100 and £150, and thence an additional 10s. for every increase of £50. From a cursory examination of the other Archidiaconal Act books at Maidstone it would appear that these rates were charged uniformly throughout the archdeaconry. If the recorded figures represent the fees actually charged, then there were no grounds for complaints of irregular extortion. It is perhaps significant that the framers of the Act of 1529 which established a new scale of probate fees could only rehearse complaints made in Statutes enacted more than a century earlier.[4] It cannot be ascertained whether probate charges in other dioceses were as regular as those of the archdeaconry of Canterbury, but the local evidence suggests that the 1529 Act was directed at the existing scale rather than at any irregularities or arbitrary extortions.

The most important aspect of probate jurisdiction which the Probate Registers reveal is the exercise of the 'prerogative' by the commissary general. The prerogative jurisdiction of the archbishop over the probate of testaments drawn up by

---

[1] Maidstone, P.R.C. 3. 3, f. 98*b*, under date 8 May 1506, for person cited before archdeacon's Official for impeding an apparitor: 'Johannes Skell de Apuldore impedit apparitorem nostrum facere inventorium de bonis. . . .'

[2] Cf. *Chichele* (C.Y. Soc.), vol. ii, introduction, p. xxxiv.

[3] Y. 4. 4.

[4] 21 Hen. VIII, c. 5. The new rates were to take effect on 1 Apr. 1530. They appear in the Sandwich Act book Y. 4. 4 from Oct. 1530 onwards. Nothing was to be charged for testaments where the goods did not exceed £5 in value, with the exception of 6*d*. for registration. The other rates were £5–£40, 3s. 6*d*. (inclusive of 1s. for scribe); over £40, 5s. (inclusive of 2s. 6*d*., or fee by length for scribe).

persons possessing *bona notabilia* in more than one diocese was delegated to the commissary general in so far as the person concerned left goods within the diocese of Canterbury. The Consistory Court was yet another channel through which prerogative jurisdiction operated.[1] This is made abundantly clear by the number of 'prerogative' wills contained in the Consistory Registers. From them it can be seen that the commissary general had exercised this jurisdiction from at least 1400.[2] The exercise of it was never specifically granted in any of the commissions of commissaries general until 1500. In that year the prior and chapter granted John Williamson the right of confirming and proving the testaments and wills of all persons within the city and diocese and those of others who had goods in several dioceses of the province of Canterbury, provided the diocese of Canterbury was one.[3] The archdeacon did not exercise the prerogative jurisdiction.

[1] For a discussion of the archbishop's prerogative jurisdiction see Churchill, vol. i, pp. 380–423.

[2] Maidstone, P.R.C. 32. 1 (1396–1455), the earliest register of the series. The 'prerogative' wills to be found *passim*.

[3] Reg. R, f. 41, dated 2 Sept. 1500; for transcript see Appendix No. IX; cf. Reg. T, f. 430 for further grant dated 1 Mar. 1502/3; cf. Churchill, vol. i, pp. 609–10. The commission of Christopher Nevinson of 1547 has been the earliest case of the exercise of this jurisdiction hitherto.

# VIII

## FINANCIAL ADMINISTRATION

SUBSTANTIAL information can be gathered regarding the financial aspect of court administration. A valuable manuscript 'Account book of the Archdeacon's Receiver and Registrar' survives for the years 1504 to 1517.[1] Nothing as comprehensive as this has been found among the Consistory Court records, but fragments of accounts kept by the prior and chapter during the vacancies of 1443 and 1452 indicate that the items of income and expenditure were similar for both courts.

One of the more significant features revealed by this account book is that the archdeacon's income was in no way dependent on fees paid by the clients resorting to his court, except on the fees received for probate of wills. The income of the archdeacon was derived from probate fees, procurations, Peter's Pence, pensions, induction fees, vacant benefices, and commutations of penance. In the year 1505–6 probate fees amounted to £27. 13s. 4d. out of a total income of £129. 11s. 4d. No other items of income derived from the business of the court figure in these accounts except small amounts received from commutations of penance.[2]

Apart from the Official's annual stipend of £10, and a small sum for dress allowance, no items of remuneration of personnel appear under the heading of expenditure.[3] It is clear that the remaining personnel maintained themselves directly from the fees arising from the business they transacted in the courts. While the personnel were self-supporting in this way, the archdeacon was relieved of charges for their maintenance. On the other hand, he had no financial interest in the business of the court, apart from the fees charged for probate and small sums derived from the commutations of

---

[1] Z. 3. 22, compiled by Thomas Laurence.

[2] These were 3s. 4d. for 1505–6 and 16s. 8d. for 1506–7.

[3] Z. 3. 22, f. 42 (1515–16), 'pro togis Officialis et computatione xxvi s. viii d.' The *computatio* may have been a counting-board or possibly a calendar.

penance. Instance business could dwindle to zero without affecting his income.

The only items of expenditure relating to the court which the archdeacon or his receiver had to meet were the Official's travelling expenses. These expenses are detailed under the heading 'Expense domini Officialis et aliorum secum equitantium in esculentis et poculentis ac pabulo equorum'. The sums expended at the various places where the court was held were totalled for each financial year. They amounted to £7. 3s. 10d. in the year 1506–7 and to £10. 0s. 2d. in the year 1516–17. This probably covered only the expenses of the Official and his servants. The expenses of the registrar and proctors were probably not included. In 1443 the prior of Christchurch drew up similar accounts for the conduct of the Consistory Court during the vacancy following the death of Archbishop Chichele, but he divided the expenses 'Commissariorum tam in progressis curie quam etiam in visitationibus diversorum locorum per eosdem' from the payment 'pro regardo servientium commissarii Cantuar' on the same trips. The first amounted to £4. 9s. 10d., the second to £1. 3s. 4d.

The judges had little need either of stipends or fees, for they were well beneficed. The rectories of parishes in the archbishop's collation were usually occupied by his officers. The provostship or the prebends of the college of Wingham were frequently occupied by the commissaries general. The Officials of the archdeacon were likewise provided for from churches in the archdeacon's collation.[1] Nevertheless, the judges probably supplemented their private income from fees. Unfortunately, no information can be gained about the division of fees between the judges and the registrars.

Although the registrars could augment their income from private practice as public notaries, they were dependent on the fees they received from the courts. Even if it is assumed that half of the fees not specifically appropriated by proctors or apparitors did not finally enter the registrars' pockets, their income must still have been considerable. From the one case 'Executors of Richard a Forde v. Roger Bounsse', where

[1] For benefices held by commissaries general and Officials see lists, Appendix No. I.

the costs were taxed at 20s., the registrar would have collected some 7s. on that basis.[1] He probably collected more. In the year in which that case was heard (1497), 409 suits were introduced in the Consistory Court. Many of them were of an ephemeral character, but even if the registrar collected only 6d. from each suit, he would have earned £10 during the year. The registrars' actual income from court fees may have been as much as £30 per annum.

The income which proctors derived from their fees can be estimated with some accuracy, for the number of appearances they made on behalf of clients can be checked from the *acta* of each individual case. During 1493 Master Thomas Notyngham appeared 567 times on behalf of clients in the Canterbury sessions of the Consistory Court. If he obtained his fees, he would have earned, at the rate of 6d. per diem, a total of £14. 3s. 6d.[2] He probably earned more than any other proctor during that year. From an analysis of the numbers of suits in which proctors appeared it may be estimated that a busy proctor could earn an average of £10 per annum from his practice in one court. At the end of the fifteenth century he might have earned £20 if he practised in both courts.

The incomes of apparitors cannot be accurately estimated. It cannot be ascertained how much any individual apparitor made from his citation fees, but assuming that an average sum of 4d. was collected upon each citation (at the 1d. per mile rate), then Byrchet, an apparitor who cited 115 persons in Instance cases to the Canterbury sessions of the Consistory Court during 1482, would have earned 38s. 4d. for so doing. With the addition of fees collected for other citations effected during the course of a case, and fees accruing from probate duties, he might have earned £5 during that year. The average yearly income of an artisan at the end of the fifteenth century was £7. 10s.[3] It is impossible, however, to compare standards of living where details of additional income from possession of property are lacking.

While judges drew private incomes from their benefices,

---

[1] Y. 1. 17, f. 118b. *Supra*, p. 61 and Appendix No. V.
[2] *Supra*, p. 44 for numbers of suits in which proctors appear.
[3] Cf. J. E. Thorold Rogers, *Six Centuries of Work and Wages*, p. 388.

and registrars and proctors augmented their incomes from the possession of property or practice as public notaries, it yet remains true that the personnel of the courts as a whole were directly interested in the amount of business transacted in them. Their personal incomes depended in a large degree upon the numbers of cases they handled. This was in direct contrast to the lack of financial interest on the part of the ecclesiastics whose authority they exercised.

# IX

# NUMBERS AND TYPES OF CASE

## (i) EX OFFICIO

THE surviving Ex Officio Act books do not cover a sufficiently long period of time for comparisons in the amount of Ex Officio business to be made, but it would appear that the amount depended upon the energy of the courts in enforcing canonical discipline. The personnel, except, perhaps, unscrupulous apparitors, benefited little by the transaction of such business. They probably regarded it as a duty rather than as a source of profit. It is possible that with the decrease in Instance business after 1500[1] the courts, and particularly the apparitors, had more time to spare for ferreting out delinquencies. The number of cases of correction dealt with in the Canterbury sessions of the Archdeacon's Court tends to rise after that date, and the impression is obtained that people are being summoned on less important and even frivolous charges.

An analysis of the Ex Officio cases of the Consistory Court during the year 1474 provides some indication of the types of offence. A total of 158 charges were brought against persons appearing in the Court. No less than 110 of these were sexual in character. Charges of a more social character included: 11 for not attending church, 11 for illicit Sunday trading, 3 for obstructing ecclesiastical jurisdiction, 2 for perjury, and single charges of defamation and of temerarious administration of a deceased person's goods. Charges brought against clerics included 9 of occupying cures without showing letters of ordination, 3 of apostasy from monastic rule, 1 of celebrating more than three masses in one day, and 1 of non-residence.

The Canterbury *acta* provide no evidence on the types of cases reserved for the archbishop. Major heresy would be beyond the scope of the local judges and it is probable that it was reserved for a more competent tribunal, such as the

---

[1] *Infra,* p. 84.

archbishop's Court of Audience. The Kentish heretics who
figure in Archbishop Warham's Register have left no trace in
the records of the local courts.[1] The offences of a heretical
character which are noted in the Act books are rather those of
momentary disgruntlement than constructive principle. In
1472 John Sprat, senior, of Willesborough came before the
Consistory Court for declaring he would rather confess to a
tree than to a priest,[2] and in the following year Thomas Whyte
of Ringwold was in trouble for saying it would profit him as
much to be buried in a marsh as in a churchyard.[3] The archdeacon's registrar thought a certain Thomas Widerley's
opinions, however, to be sufficiently heinous to write them in
large letters across two pages.[4] The latter's criticism of the
nature of priestly orders was certainly more serious than the
usual type of petty disaffection. The pursuit of occupations
on the Sabbath was a frequent cause of prosecution. In 1488
Thomas Samson of St. Peter's in Thanet was before the
archdeacon's Official for looting a shipwreck in preference to
attending divine service.[5] In 1505 William Brygge and his
wife continued to ply their trade of making beehives on feast
days.[6]

The judges of both courts repeatedly organized 'drives'
against butchers who sold meat on the Sabbath. In 1474
eleven butchers from Canterbury and the neighbouring
villages appeared in the Consistory Court charged with
Sunday trading. All were awarded penance except a man
from Littlebourne who was dismissed *sub spe melioris vitae.*[7]
In 1519 fifteen butchers appeared before the archdeacon's
Official for the same offence. In 1526 the registrar recorded
injunctions directed against this selling of meat. This time

---

[1] Lambeth Reg. Warham, ff. clxiiii et seq.

[2] Y. 1. 11, f. 199*b*, under date 16 Nov. '. . . ipse mallet citius confiteri arbori
quam sacerdoti'.

[3] Ibid., f. 302, under date 12 July 1473: '. . . dicit quod tantum prodest anima
sive corpus suum in stagnus [*sic*] vel paludem sicut in aliquo cimiterio sepeliri. . . .'

[4] Maidstone, P.R.C. 3. 1, f. 148*b*, under date 24 Oct. 1501. Thomas Widerley
of Bridge 'opinatur quod sacerdos non est sacerdos nisi tempore celebrationis
misse'.

[5] Y. 4. 2, f. 104, under date 7 Nov. 'notatur quod in die omnium sanctorum
abfuit a divinis navigando in mari ratione acquirendi bonos de naufragio'.

[6] Maidstone, P.R.C. 3. 3, f. 9, under date 19 Oct. 1505. 'notantur quod non
coluit [*sic*] sabbatum quia in die martis in septimana penticostis excercuerunt opus
eorum viz makyng of Beehevys.'      [7] Y. 1. 11, f. 350, under date 28 Nov.

any two of the butchers within Canterbury were allowed to sell meat on Sundays and festivals, and these two were only allowed to have one shop window open.[1] Barbers, too, are cited for neglecting the Sabbath. John Ravyn of Monkton in Thanet shaved customers at time of divine service.[2] Unlucky was Lucas Pancake of Otterden, who shaved his own beard. He refused to perform the first penance awarded, but on his second appearance in court promised to perform another.[3] Charges such as these raise a suspicion that apparitors victimized individuals against whom they bore a grudge. The unfortunate Lucas Pancake was cited eighteen months later, accused 'de crimine blasphemie et quod fovet lenocinium'. On this occasion he was admonished to reform.[4] It would be interesting to discover who informed the court of the gluttony, or fast breaking, of a certain Robertson of Thanet who was accused of eating too much bread and butter.[5]

Brawling, attacks on clerics,[6] ill treatment of wives and children were perennial offences before the notice of the courts. Women were cited for fortune telling and sorcery. Joan Mores of East Langdon was cited for divining the future from the croaking of frogs.[7] Persons were prosecuted for asking alms under false pretences.[8] A priest was cited for unsuccessful practice as a surgeon.[9] There was the usual

---

[1] Maidstone, P.R.C. 3. 6, ff. 51–52b. '. . . quod ipsi duo solomodo habeant unam fenestram apertam'.

[2] Y. 1. 11, f. 16, under date 10 Oct. 1468 'notatur quod solet radere barbas diebus dominicis precipue in tempore divinorum. . . .'

[3] Maidstone, P.R.C. 3. 5, f. 139, under date 15 Nov. 1520. 'notatur quod non servat sabbatum quia rasit sibi barbam die dominica. . . .'

[4] Ibid., f. 149b, under date 10 Apr. 1522.

[5] Maidstone, P.R.C. 3. 6, f. 81b, under date 23 May 1528. '. . . notatur quod commedit panem et buteriam in veneris iiii temporum et quod rarfacit se commediturum imposterum [sic] . . . fatetur se commedisse non tamen animo delinquendi Nichilominus Iudex injunxit eidem quod debet contribuere ad usum dicte ecclesie i libram cere et quod abstineat se abhinc in futurum. . . .'

[6] e.g. Maidstone, P.R.C. 3. 5, f. 46, under date 26 July 1524. 'William Cristiane de Ebony notatur de violentia iniectionis manuum in dominum Ricardum Harvy curatum proiiciendo eum in aquas profundas violenter in periculum vite eiusdem domini Ricardi. . . .'

[7] Y. 4. 4, f. 77, under date 17 Jan. 1524/5 '. . . utendo sufflationibus ranarum. . . .'

[8] e.g. Y. 4. 4, f. 109b, under date 13 June 1531. 'Robertus Thomson heremita notatur quod dolose exiget elemosinas xpi fidelibus sub colore non vero. . . .'

[9] X. 8. 1, f. 9b (1399). 'Dominus Thomas Forster notatur quod pretendit se

assortment of bibulous clerics.[1] The list of offences could be extended. The Ex Officio Act books provide many vivid cameos of the Kentish scene in late medieval and early Tudor times, but it is important to remember that the courts spent only a small part of their time in correcting offences of brawling, non-attendance at church, and the like. It is difficult not to allow the more piquant quality of some of these offences to detract from the great weight of cases of immorality which burdened the courts from year to year.

## (ii) INSTANCE

Numbers of suits introduced into the Canterbury sessions of the Consistory Court can be accurately assessed for most of the years between 1454 and 1535 and for many years between 1372 and 1425.[2] For the purposes of classification, types of case which were sometimes more specifically described by the scribe are included under the general headings.

### Matrimonial

Under this heading are included other cases which were described by the scribes as *divortii*, *reclamationis bannorum*, and *restitutionis conjugalium*. Lanfranc had reserved matrimonial cases for the cognizance of the archbishop.[3] Jurisdiction in such cases was later delegated to exempt rectors[4] and to the commissary general. It is doubtful whether the archdeacons ever exercised jurisdiction in matrimonial cases other than those arising during certain vacancies of the see. By the composition drawn up between Simon Langton and the prior and chapter in 1241 the archdeacon obtained such jurisdiction for the duration of the vacancy following upon the death of Edmund Rich.[5] It is possible that Simon's

medicum ad sanandum equos a gallidis etc cum non est et destruxit oculum unius mulieris cuius curam accepit et posuit in eius oculo pulverem de arsnekis et sandwert ita quod mulier est monocula. . . .' He appeared 19 Nov. 1399 and successfully purged himself.

[1] e.g. X. 1. 1, f. 2 (1449). 'Dominus Robertus [Vicar of St. Mary Bredman, Canterbury] notatur quod he tippled apud Cardynals Hat.' Possibly he merely served behind the bar. 'Tipple' may mean to retail ale.

[2] See chart, p. 84.

[3] Churchill, vol. i, p. 43. *Supra*, p. 19.

[4] Ibid., pp. 84–94, for discussion of commissions of exempt rectors.

[5] Churchill, vol. i, p. 551.

successors attempted to employ that grant as a precedent in subsequent vacancies, but it is doubtful whether the Archdeacon's Court ever exercised this jurisdiction after the victory of the prior and chapter in the matter of *sede vacante* rights in 1292–4.[1] The Act books of the Archdeaconry Court which survive from 1476 onwards contain no trace of matrimonial litigation.

The *acta* of matrimonial cases form the great bulk of the Consistory Court material which survives for the vacancy of 1292–4. Sixty-two matrimonial suits of that period can be listed from the various Sede Vacante collections. Probably a few of these had originated in the autonomous exempt parishes. One had been heard originally by Anselm, the rector of the exempt parish of Eastry.[2]

The judges retained a greater disciplinary interest in matrimonial suits than in most other Instance suits. They could not allow them to remain undecided, for the relationships between the parties to such suits had to be clarified. The judge, in publishing definitive sentence, often decided whether the parties were really man and wife or whether a solemnization of marriage was of no effect. In many cases the judge declared that he was going to proceed to definitive sentence whether the parties attended the court or not.[3] Precautions were taken to keep the various parties apart while the case was being heard. The woman was often warned not to cohabit with the opposite party or to enter into matrimony with another.[4] Sometimes this warning was reinforced by the penalties of excommunication or a fine.[5] At the end of the fifteenth and the beginning of the sixteenth century the women were often 'sequestrated' until judgement had been

[1] *Supra*, p. 16.

[2] S.V. 3, p. 66. Inhibition in a suit 'John de Stokbury *v*. Katherine de Newenham', dated 16 Oct. 1294, addressed from the Official of the Court of Canterbury to the commissary, Richard de Clyve. *Supra*, p. 24.

[3] e.g. Y. 1. 3, f. 29*b*, under date 17 Sept. 1416, 'John Curdy of Hythe and John Skynner of Harrietsham, competitors, *v*. Margaret Smallwode'. John Curdy is warned 'quod sive venerit sive non Commissarius in dicta causa procedere intendit usque ad sententie diffinitive prolationem in eadem'.

[4] e.g. Y. 1. 3, f. 33*b*, under date 27 Oct. 1416, 'John Wythot *v*. Alice Tur'. The latter so ordered.

[5] e.g. Y. 1. 3, f. 18, under date 23 May 1416, 'John Spender *v*. Matilda Rodyng'. The fine was 40*s*.

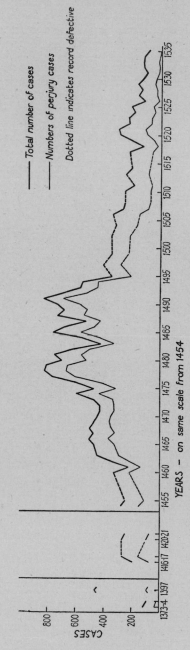

CHART ILLUSTRATING AMOUNT OF 'INSTANCE' BUSINESS HANDLED BY THE CONSISTORY COURT, 1373–1535

given. A prioress of a nunnery, or a responsible citizen, was usually placed in charge of them.[1]

During the years 1373 and 1374, thirty-nine and thirty-one matrimonial suits respectively were introduced into the Consistory Court at Canterbury, constituting approximately a third of the total number of suits heard in those years. Forty-seven suits were introduced during 1397, but between 1415 and 1507 the number of matrimonial suits introduced during years for which a complete record survives never exceeded twenty, and was frequently less than ten. The number tended to increase after 1500. It remains obscure whether the fifteenth century was a period when matrimonial complications were fewer, or, perhaps, a period when the material incentives behind matrimonial litigation were less.

## Testamentary

Under this heading are grouped not only those cases generally designated *testamentaria*, but also those cases more specifically described as *impedimenti ultime voluntatis* and *temerarie administrationis bonorum defuncti*. The majority of cases labelled *testamentaria* are cases of debt. The executors of the deceased may be claiming debts still owing to him or other parties may be claiming debts owing to them by the testator. Many of these cases developed subsequent to the grant of probate by the courts. A comparative study could be made of the probate *acta*, the testamentary cases, and the actual wills, and the difficulties confronting executors and tradesmen trying to recover debts could be gauged thereby. The numbers of testamentary suits obviously depended upon a host of circumstances and cannot be related with any accuracy to mortality rates or to economic indices. There was a very large number of testamentary cases introduced into the Consistory Court during 1397: 187 cases from a total of 461. From 1454 to 1500 the average number of suits

---

[1] e.g. Y. 2. 11, f. 36b, under date 1 Oct. 1521, 'Francis Plott *v*. Elizabeth Eston', the latter placed in the custody of the prioress of St. Sepulchre's, Canterbury. Cf. Y. 2. 5, f. 92b, under date 25 Nov. 1511, 'Richard Piers *v*. Joan Bowman': '. . . Dominus monuit mulierem quod non contrahat cum aliquo alio nec quod promittat matrimonium solempnizare lite pendente sub pena excommunicationis et . . . sequestravit mulierem et commisit custodiam Johanni Hale seniori civitatis Cant'.'

introduced each year was between thirty and forty. After
1500 the decline in the number of testamentary suits is not
as great as in other types of case.

## Tithe ('Subtractionis Decimarum')

Tithe cases included actions between rectors and
parishioners as well as those between rival ecclesiastical
authorities for revenues of certain lands or churches. The
number of tithe suits introduced into the Consistory Court
in any one year varied between thirty-nine during 1397 and
four during 1531; but there is no well-defined fluctuation in
the numbers of tithe cases from which phases of tithe litigation might be determined.[1]

## Ecclesiastical Dues

This heading covers a miscellaneous series of suits which
were usually described by the scribes as *subtractionis iuris
ecclesiastici*, and included actions brought against parties for
non-payment of customary offerings, rent paid to local
churches from houses or shops, rent for cattle hired from the
churchwardens, and for almost any kind of return which
figures in contemporary Churchwardens' Accounts. In the
majority of these suits the plaintiffs were churchwardens. No
marked fluctuations in the numbers of these suits can be
distinguished. There was a slight decline in the numbers,
however, after 1517.

## Other Miscellaneous 'Church' Suits

It is difficult to distinguish cases which were sometimes
described as *subtractionis iuris ecclesiastici* from those cases
which were described as *subtractionis pensionis* and *subtractionis
mortuarii*. Without an analysis of each case it is impossible to
decide whether the scribes were consistent in distinguishing
cases which concerned the parishioners from cases which
concerned rectors or incumbents. However, the number of
cases for the recovery of pensions or mortuary fees were

---

[1] The Canterbury Act books can provide much new information on problems
of tithability and the *modus decimandi*, particularly with regard to the customs of
Kent and the Weald. For a discussion of tithability in Kent, particularly on the
matter of *silva cedua*, see N. Neilson, *Cartulary and Terrier of Bilsington*, pp. 29–33;
cf. N. Adams, 'The Judicial Conflict over Tithes', *E.H.R.*, vol. lii (1937), pp. 19–21.

very few; usually one or two, and never more than six, in any one year. Likewise the number of suits brought by the clergy for assaults (*iniectionis violentarum manuum*), for brawling (*perturbationis divinorum*), and sacrilege (*sacrilegii*) were very few. Actions to determine responsibility for repair of churches, or to compel persons or monastic houses to undertake such repair, were very infrequent. Actions in disputes over pews are first noticed in the year 1462.[1]

## Salary

Suits described as *subtractionis salarii* or *suffragii* cover actions brought by proctors against their clients and those brought by parish clerks or *aquebaiuli* for the payment of wages. There were generally less than six such cases in any one year, but the number rises to nineteen in 1499 and fifteen in 1504 and 1506.

## Vexatious Litigation

This was a type of case arising directly from the conduct of a suit. Defendants occasionally brought actions *temerarie fatigationis* against plaintiffs who failed to prosecute their suits. Sometimes the judge brought an Ex Officio action of this kind.[2]

## Usury

The Act books of both courts contain only a very small number of *causa usurie pravitatis*. There were three introduced into the Consistory Court in 1373, and three in 1374; one in 1415 and none recorded thereafter until 1513, when a single case is recorded in an Archdeaconry Act book. Very few persons are found being cited upon an Ex Officio charge. From the evidence of the Act books it would appear that Kentish people were either not tainted by this particular sin, or, as is more probable, not concerned at its prevalence.

## Defamation

Cases of defamation were frequent throughout the period from 1372 onwards. From an analysis of the *acta* it can be seen that the number of cases introduced into the Consistory

[1] Y. 1. 7, f. 153b. Four cases between various parishioners of Smarden.
[2] *Supra*, p. 54.

Court increased after the middle of the fifteenth century. From 1454 onwards there were usually more than fifty cases each year. In 1485 there were 105, and although this figure in not reached thereafter, defamation suits become an increasing proportion of the total number, and after 1522 they are the most numerous type of case. Many of these cases were heard summarily, and the scribes obviously relished noting the offensive words that were the subject of the action, for they are usually written out at length. In some cases it is not really clear why the plaintiff should have taken exception to such a degree as to bring a suit into the ecclesiastical court, but the majority of plaintiffs were trying to clear themselves of charges which might lead to actions being brought against them. Great numbers concern imputations of crimes of a sexual character and so rendered the plaintiff liable to answer for them *in foro ecclesiastico*, but many of the crimes were answerable in a secular court;[1] evidence that there was no move as yet to make any distinction between the two types.[2] It had, however, been enunciated in the fourteenth century that prohibitions should lie in defamation cases where the plaintiff was attempting to vindicate himself of a crime of which he had been found guilty in a secular court.[3] This principle was ignored in at least two suits recorded in the Canterbury *acta*. In 1416 Thomas Austyn of Canterbury brought a defamation suit into the Consistory Court against an Isabella Laybrooke who had previously accused him of theft of fruit for which the borough court had fined him 10 marks.[4] In 1517 John Bull of Newington brought a suit in the Archdeacon's Court against William Flawne who had sued him successfully in a secular court for theft. The undersheriff, who had saved John Bull from the extreme penalty on that occasion, wrote to the Official on John's behalf supporting his suit for defamation.[5] The chance survival of

[1] e.g. Y. 2. 1, f. 116, under date 27 May 1505, 'Robert Cudworth, chaplain of Faversham *v.* Richard Vyan'. The latter confessed that 'dixit quod dominus Robertus occultavit quendam Willelmum Knokke homicidum in camera sua'.

[2] Cf. Holdsworth, vol. viii, p. 348.

[3] Ibid., vol. iii, p. 410, discussion of 1 Edw. III, st. 1, c. 11.

[4] *Acta*, X. 1. 3, f. 1, under date 17 Feb. 1415/16. Depositions of witnesses, X. 10. 1, f. 9b, et seq.

[5] Y. 2. 7, f. 115, under date 18 June. For transcripts of *acta* and letter see Appendix No. X.

the under-sheriff's letter is the only indication of the con-
nexions of this suit with previous secular litigation. It is not
unlikely that many defamation suits were brought into the
Canterbury courts as counter-measures to secular actions. No
prohibitions interrupted either of these two cases, and the
numbers of prohibitions recorded in the Act books are so
infinitesimal that it is probable that many defamation suits of
this kind were heard unchallenged.[1]

## Perjury ('Fidei lesionis')

The most important feature of Instance business disclosed
by an analysis of the numbers of cases is the very large
number of cases entered under the heading *fidei lesionis et
periurii*. Numbers of perjury cases increased as the fifteenth
century advanced. In the Consistory Court for the years 1373
and 1374 perjury suits were somewhat less than a quarter of
the total number of suits introduced. In 1417 they provided
about half the total: 148 cases out of 265. There were 150
cases during 1454 and there was an increase thereafter until
1482. Five or six hundred cases were handled in some years
and a maximum of 684 cases was reached in 1491. After that
date, there was a steady decline until the second decade of
the sixteenth century. After a brief revival in the period 1519
to 1523 the number of perjury cases dwindled rapidly until
there were only four introduced during 1535. They had
ceased to be the most numerous single class in 1521. Figures
from the other sessions of the two courts indicate that this
development was common to both.

Most perjury cases were heard summarily and it is therefore possible to discover the details of the issues involved in
many of them. Such suits were brought against parties for
breach of contract or breaking of their word in non-payment
of money, non-provision of supplies, or even for non-fulfilment of a building contract.[2] If the defendant confessed to

---

[1] Cf. Holdsworth, vol. iii, p. 410, for cases in which prohibition was granted
temp. Edward IV.

[2] These cases are to be found *passim* throughout the Instance Act books. For
non-fulfilment of a building contract cf. Y. 4. 3, f. 32, under date 20 Feb. 1500/1,
'Master James Ganton (a proctor) *v.* William Stoks'. The defendant 'fatetur
violationem fidei in non edificando quandam domum et datur ei ad perimplendum
fidem suam citra festum Nativitatis sancti Johannis Baptiste'. Later he was suspended. Cf. Y. 1. 9, f. 118, under date 18 Dec. 1482, 'Robert Cheyne of Milstead

the obligation, or if the existence of the obligation had been proved, the judge usually warned him to pay the debt or fulfil the obligation within a specified time under pain of excommunication. The majority of perjury cases for which details were recorded were nothing more than actions for recovery of debt. Often the amount involved was noted by the scribe. Usually it was less than 40*s*., but greater sums are sometimes found. The greatest amount found hitherto is the £19. 5*s*. which the rector of Burmarsh sought from Stephen White of Burmarsh in the Archdeacon's Court at Ashford in 1482. The defendant was ordered to pay it in instalments of 40*s*.[1] Sometimes the exact amount involved had not been calculated and a further court day was assigned for the parties *ad computandum*. These debt cases provided the bulk of the Instance business of the Consistory Court during the fifteenth century, long after the Common lawyers had staked their claims over litigation for recovery of debt. Without investigation of contemporary ecclesiastical court records from other dioceses it is impossible to decide whether the Canterbury evidence of the amount of perjury business in matters of debt is of more than local significance, but it will probably be found that ecclesiastical courts throughout the kingdom were similarly employed. The complaint of the judges in the Exchequer Chamber in 1459 against the hearing of these cases by the Spiritual Courts was probably not without foundation.[2]

There is evidence that some ecclesiastical lawyers, on their part, were not very satisfied with the handling of perjury cases for debt by the Canterbury Consistory Court. Until 1495 parties were baldly ordered to pay their debts *sub pena sententie excommunicationis*. After that date a distinction was increasingly being drawn between the act of breaking faith and the particular subject of the contract. From 1500 to 1511 parties are awarded penance for their perjury but are not ordered to pay the money they owe. The penance was awarded immediately.[3] In 1511, however, the old formula

---

*v*. William a Park of Rodmersham'. Robert 'petit unum par de thollys pro le cart et unum par rotarum pro aratro'. William failed to provide them and was excommunicated.    [1] Y. 1. 9, f. 26, under date 4 Nov.

[2] Holdsworth, vol. ii, p. 305. Cf. ibid., vol. iii, pp. 413–16, for earlier complaints of Common lawyers on the handling of debt cases by ecclesiastical courts.

[3] e.g. Y. 2. 2, f. 67*b*, under date 5 Apr. 1502. 'Henry Scott *v*. William

'monitus est ad solvendum . . . sub pena sententie excommunicationis' reappears in the Consistory Act books. The number of perjury cases introduced into the Consistory Court had declined from 230 in 1499 to 71 in 1511, and the judges may have felt that the mere award of penance to the defaulting debtor hardly satisfied a plaintiff who wanted his money back. This brief experiment in a more scrupulous handling of perjury for debt was confined to the Consistory Court. There is no evidence to suggest that the archdeacon's Officials of this period imitated their colleagues' example.

Reasons for the fifteenth-century increase in the number of perjury cases can only be conjectured. Perhaps the secular courts were unable to cope with the amount of petty debt litigation. They were slow in improving upon their ancient procedures.[1] The statute 17 Edw. IV, c. 2, limited the jurisdiction of Piepowder Courts to actions arising from transactions taking place during the period of fairs. An appeal had been taken to the King's Bench from the Canterbury Piepowder Court some years previously (36 Hen. VI) and the judges had asserted that the latter court had been exceeding its jurisdiction.[2] It is possible that people were seeking an alternative forum for the settlement of debt disputes. Unfortunately no records of the operation of the Statute Merchant and Statute Staple jurisdiction at Canterbury survive for the fifteenth century, and it is therefore impossible to discover the extent and efficiency of that jurisdiction.[3]

It is possible that actions were commenced in the ecclesiastical courts to enforce the observance of obligations taken in a secular court. In 1415/16 a perjury suit was undertaken by John Byrcholt in the matter of a debt owed to him by John Cophurst. From the depositions of the witnesses in this case it appears that the original obligation had been undertaken in the Guildhall (the 'speche hows') at Canterbury. No details of the nature of the *conventio* are given, so it cannot be

Bachelor'. The latter was ordered 'ad recipiendum penitentiam in prox'.'. Cf. Y. 2. 2, f. 59, under date 28 Feb. 1501/2, 'Prior of Christchurch *v.* Thomas Estwell'. The latter 'submisit se ad recipiendum penitentiam'.

[1] H. Hall, *Select Cases on the Law Merchant*, vol. ii (Selden Soc.), p. xxxix.

[2] Ibid., vol. i, pp. xxi and xxiv.

[3] A Merchant Seal was granted to Canterbury in 1337 (ibid., vol. ii, p. lix). Cf. H.M.C. 9th Report, pp. 129–77, for description of these records.

ascertained whether it was a purely private arrangement or whether recognizances were recorded under Statute Merchant regulations; but the official nature of the place in which the obligation was incurred may indicate that it was not a purely private agreement.

Reasons for the decline in the number of perjury suits are equally obscure. It is hardly likely that it was entirely due to the drying up of debt litigation. It is possible that the early Tudor stimulation of efficiency in secular courts of all kinds had begun to take effect in the period after 1500. In 1490, 130 perjury suits had been introduced into the Sandwich sessions of the Archdeacon's Court. In 1522 only twenty-seven such suits were introduced. It may be that the drawing up of revised and uniform statutes for the Cinque Ports in 1505/6 reflected a general overhaul of the methods of local secular courts.[1] The city of London may not have been the only corporation to establish a 'Court of Conscience' for the enforcement of the payment of petty debts.[2] The improved efficiency of secular courts may have begun to outweigh the disadvantages of the ecclesiastical courts as institutions for enforcing payment of debts. The lack of effective sanctions and the disregard of sentences of suspension and excommunication had always been handicaps to the ecclesiastical jurisdiction. It is remarkable that clients had resorted to ecclesiastical courts with suits so secular in character for so long.

Whatever the reasons for the decline in the number of perjury cases, overt action on the part of the secular courts did not count among them. Hardly any prohibitions were brought into the Canterbury courts.[3] In any case they were virtually useless instruments to prevent the handling of summary cases which were dispatched on one court day. There may have been indirect pressure to drop this type of case, but this cannot be estimated.

[1] M. Bateson, *Borough Customs*, vol. i (Selden Soc.), pp. xxi–xxii. Sandwich customs in debt litigation had been very primitive (ibid., pp. 131–2).

[2] Established in 1518. It sat in the Guildhall and its jurisdiction extended to debts of 40s. and under among the citizens of London (J. R. Tanner, *Tudor Constitutional Documents, 1485–1603*, p. 302). Was this perhaps a deliberate attempt to attract debt litigation away from the Consistory Court of the bishop of London?

[3] *Infra*, p. 108.

# X

## THE ENFORCEMENT OF DISCIPLINE

THE three sanctions employed by the courts to enforce obedience were suspension, excommunication, and 'aggravated' excommunication *cum communicantibus*.[1] If suspension *ab ingressu ecclesiae*, excommunication, and an *aggravatio* of the latter sentence had failed to bring an offender to obedience, the archbishop, as a last resort, could be requested to send a signification (or 'letter of caption') to Chancery invoking the aid of the secular arm to effect the imprisonment of the excommunicate.

### (i) SUSPENSION

Suspension *ab ingressu ecclesiae* was generally employed as the first sanction. If defendants did not appear on the court day allotted, and the apparitor had publicly called them in vain, they were usually suspended for their contumacy in not appearing. A letter of suspension was drawn up and dispatched to the incumbent of the defendant's parish church. He publicly announced the suspension of the culprit to the congregation and returned a certificate to the court.[2]

### (ii) EXCOMMUNICATION

The sentence of excommunication was sometimes decreed without a previous order of suspension, but usually only in those cases where the culprit's offence was 'manifest', i.e. in his refusing to obey the court outright or hindering the

---

[1] The terms 'minor' and 'major' are nowhere used to describe the grades of excommunication. Lyndwood does not mention the 'aggravated' sentence *cum communicantibus*. It would appear that the boycott of the excommunicate was the main contemporary differentiation between the two grades.

[2] No letters or certificates of suspension survive. Letters of suspension and excommunication were prepared by the Registrar at the end of the day or session. In Y. 1. 13, at f. 188*b*, there survives a memorandum slip still attached to the top of the page: 'fiat littera S. pro Sampsone Gryme de Petham ad instantiam fratris Lyndsay iiii Junii'. Sampson had failed to appear to defend a perjury suit that same day. The case is recorded on the same page.

apparitor in his duty.[1] Generally, however, it was retained
as the reserve penalty for continued obstinacy or followed a
previous monition which had stipulated it as a penalty. A
letter of excommunication was dispatched to the local incumbent, who 'denounced' the sentence in the presence of the
congregation.[2] It is probable that the full cursing in the
vernacular and the spectacular ceremonial were reserved for
cases of 'aggravated' excommunication. The theoretical effects
of excommunication were serious. The excommunicate was
cut off from the sacraments of the Church and could not be
given a Christian burial.[3] When the greater sentence had been
issued, the excommunicate was cut off from the society of the
faithful and subjected to an economic boycott. Persons con-
sorting with these excommunicates were themselves liable
to be excommunicated.[4]

Even if the religious horror of excommunication affected
few, the opportunities for vexation at law which it gave to
one's enemies must have rendered it extremely irksome. The
Common lawyers recognized the secular disabilities of the
excommunicate.[5] At the end of the thirteenth century it was
still being used as a powerful weapon to counter secular
accusations. Sir William de Brokhele[6] attempted to bring
the rector of Saltwood before the justices in eyre on a charge

[1] e.g. Y. 1. 3, f. 31b, under date 7 Oct. 1416. Defamation suit 'Richard Peraune
v. John Studle'. The apparitor certified that the latter 'noluit comparere nec curavit
de commissario aut aliquo de curia'. The judge decreed him excommunicate *propter
manifestum contemptum*.

[2] No letters or certificates of excommunication survive for this period.

[3] Cf. Reg. Q, f. 19b, for *provocatio* against those who would bury the excommunicate vicar of Chilham c. 1297; cf. MS. D. 8, f. 16, for 'Articulus ex officio ad
exhumandum defunctum in excommunicatione'. Post-mortem absolutions could
be granted to allow burial; cf. *Winchelsey* (C.Y. Soc.), p. 402.

[4] Cf. Lyndwood, p. 266. The court *acta* throw little light on distinctions between
excommunications decreed by the judge (*ab homine*) and excommunications *ipso
facto* (*sententiae a jure*). For practical purposes persons incurring the latter penalty
would still be declared excommunicate by name. The knowledge by defendants of
general sentences against persons committing crimes meriting *ipso facto* excommunication is frequently emphasized in interrogatories. These general sentences were
usually pronounced four times a year. Cf. Myrc's *Instructions to a Parish Priest*,
E.E.T.S., Original Series, No. 30, pp. 60–67.

[5] Cf. Bracton, f. 426b. 'Excommunicato enim interdicitur omnis actus legitimus.'
Cf. Lyndwood, p. 266.

[6] Possibly a member of the De Broc family, ancient enemies of Becket. He was
probably constable of Saltwood Castle. Cf. *Winchelsey* (C.Y. Soc.), p. 327, for con-
cession of privilege of private services in the chapel, dated 24 Apr. 1299.

of homicide. The rector, William le Archier, denounced him excommunicate for defaming a cleric. The knight appealed to the commissary general, Richard de Clyve, who was probably glad to find an excuse to interfere in the conduct of an exempt jurisdiction. The commissary summoned a number of persons 'learned in the law' to inquire into the circumstances of the excommunication, and in default of the rector's personal appearance temporarily relaxed the sentence. The rector, however, appealed to the Court of Canterbury. The subsequent developments are lost, but the existing documents in the case illustrate how even a minor ecclesiastic could vex a local potentate with the anathemas of the Church.[1]

## (iii) SIGNIFICATION

In England the Church possessed the right of applying to the secular arm for the arrest of excommunicates after they had persisted in their disobedience for forty days or longer. The exercise of the right of applying to Chancery for a writ *de excommunicato capiendo* was restricted to bishops and a few other ecclesiastics.[2] There is no evidence that the archdeacons of Canterbury ever exercised this right *sede plena*, but Simon Langton was granted vacancy rights of signification in 1241,[3] and Hugh de Mortimer 'signified' an excommunicate to Chancery during the vacancy of 1270–2.[4] After that date it is only the archbishop, the Official of the Court of Canterbury, and the prior and chapter of Christchurch (as *custodes spiritualitatis* during vacancies) who are found addressing significations to Chancery. If the commissary general or the archdeacon's Official wanted to have excommunicates captured by the secular authorities, they had to apply to the

[1] The documents are E.S. Roll No. 134, containing 'process' of the suit; MS. Z 20 and complaint of rector in S.V. 3, p. 76; cf. *Rot. Parl.*, vol. ii, p. 76a, for complaint of sheriffs and other officers against bishops who excommunicate those who attach clerks to appear before secular courts (1334).

[2] For analysis of persons exercising signification rights see R. C. Fowler, 'Secular Aid for Excommunication', *T.R.Hist.S.*, 3rd Series, vol. viii, pp. 113–17.

[3] Churchill, vol. i, p. 551.

[4] P.R.O. Significations File 1, No. 56, dated Orpington, 11 Nov. 1271. He styles himself 'Custos Spiritualitatis'. He had been signifying excommunicates as Official of the Court of Canterbury 1246-69 (ibid., File 1, *passim*).

archbishop. In one instance a letter from the archdeacon's Official to the archbishop requesting signification was sent straight on to Chancery.[1]

Signification was an extreme weapon for the judges of the inferior courts. Far more than forty days had usually elapsed before signification was decreed. The culprit had usually been suspended, excommunicated, and excommunicated *cum communicantibus* at intervals of two or three weeks before the judge decreed that he would write to the king for the 'capture of his body'.[2] In the only instance where the *acta* of the Consistory Court can be checked against a surviving signification writ[3] the archbishop moved comparatively quickly in applying to Chancery. Nicholas Chelmyngton had been found guilty in the Consistory Court of assaulting a cleric, one John Benyngton. He had appealed to the Court of Canterbury, but had lost the appeal and had been condemned in costs. He refused to appear to hear taxation of costs, either for the original suit or for the appeal, and after a citation *viis et modis* had proved vain, the commissary general applied for signification on 22 May 1416.[4] The signification dispatched to Chancery by the archbishop's scribe is dated London, 2 June.[5]

While the ecclesiastical authorities might work rapidly in this matter, the ultimate capture of the excommunicate depended on the speed and co-operation of the secular

---

[1] P.R.O. Significations File 23, No. 4, from Simon Hogges requesting signification of Robert Marten of St. Margaret's, Canterbury, dated 14 Feb. 1487/8. Cf. Y. 4. 3, f. 33, under date 20 Feb. 1500/1. Tithe suit 'Rector of St. Mary de Castro *v.* Joan London'. On 9 Mar. 1502/3 'iudex decrevit rescribendum fore ad Archiepiscopum ad scribendum regie majestati pro litteris Significationis'. There is no trace of this signification in the P.R.O. files.

[2] e.g. Y. 1. 3, f. 13*b*, under date 28 Apr. 1416. Perjury suit 'John Dawndelyon of Thanet *v.* Hamo Tody': '. . . dictam partem ream prius ab ingressu ecclesie suspensam et excommunicatam Commissarius decrevit sententiam excommunicationis contra eandem fore aggravandum et decrevit partem citandam citra proximum ad dicendum causam quare pro ipsius corporis captione scribi non debet regie maiestati etc.'. The decree was issued on 20 May. There is no trace of this signification in the P.R.O. files.

[3] It is possible that a more exhaustive analysis of the Act books will reveal persons who are named in signification writs, but none of the notices of signification in the Act books can be correlated with surviving writs, except the case in question.

[4] Y. 1. 3, f. 18.

[5] P.R.O. Significations File 14, No. 6. The writ was copied into the Archbishop's Register. For text see *Chichele* (C.Y. Soc.), vol. iv, pp. 152–3.

authorities. The speed of the issue of a writ *de excommunicato capiendo* and the energy and success of the sheriffs in executing it remain to be investigated. It may be found that the expenses incurred in Chancery, and the lack of efficiency or co-operation of the local authorities, partially accounted for the extremely infrequent use of the sanction of signification by the Canterbury courts.[1]

## (iv) ABSOLUTION

Absolution was granted to suspended and excommunicated persons after they had appeared in court or pleaded legitimate excuse and had paid the fees of their contumacy. These fees covered the costs of letters of suspension and excommunication and the certification fees of the apparitor. Letters of suspension cost 4*d.*, and it is probable that letters of excommunication cost the same amount. In Instance litigation the costs were awarded to the plaintiff who had petitioned for suspension or excommunication and defrayed the expenses of their execution. Absolution was usually granted in open court or in the house of the judge or registrar.[2] Occasionally commissions of absolution were dispatched to local incumbents.[3] Once the defendant had been absolved, the case proceeded at the point at which it was interrupted. So many processes of suits end without record of absolution or dismissal that it is probable that many scores of persons remained suspended or excommunicated without taking steps to obtain absolution.

## (v) PENANCE

Penances were awarded as penalties for committing specific actions open to correction by the Church. They tended to become less severe in character as the centuries passed. At

---

[1] Cf. Fitzherbert's *Natura Brevium* (London, 1677), pp. 140 et seq., for writs *de excommunicato capiendo* and *de admittenda cautione*. The commentary indicates some of the technical difficulties which might provide excuses for hindering the signification process.

[2] *Infra*, p. 112 and n. 2.

[3] e.g. Y. 1. 14, f. 163*b*, under date 20 June 1486. Perjury suit 'Margaret Clyffords *v.* Thomas Quynt of Milton'. Commission dispatched to the curate of Milton. No details of the reason for this commission are given. An excuse may have been sent to court, or the case may have been settled privately.

the end of the thirteenth century the commissary, Richard de Clyve, frequently ordered the delinquent parties in matrimonial suits to be whipped.[1] Penances of this character are seldom found in the Act books of the fifteenth and early sixteenth centuries. During this latter period it was usual for the judges to enjoin the carrying of candles in the Sunday procession and the making of offerings at altars. Sometimes the penitent was ordered to bear a placard proclaiming the nature of his sin.[2] In 1502 Geoffrey Bocher of Horton, one of the butchers found selling meat on Sundays, was ordered to walk before the cross in his parish church in the Sunday procession with a candle in one hand and a shoulder of lamb in the other.[3] The person awarded penance took an oath in court to fulfil it, and the local incumbent probably returned a certificate to state that it had been duly performed. In the absence of Certificates of Penance, it cannot be ascertained whether penances were performed or not. Persons were summoned to court for not performing penance, but it is unsafe to assume they represent all those who did not do so.

Many penances were commuted into money payments. Sometimes the amount is recorded by the scribe,[4] but usually the entry *composuit* is the only notice to show that a commutation has been made. Moneys received from commutation of penances were theoretically devoted to charitable uses and were therefore separately entered in accounts. The receiver of the archdeacon accounted for 3s. 4d. from this source during the year 1505–6 and 18s. 8d. during the year 1506–7.[5] It is possible that the sums accruing from commutations arranged by the commissary general were paid to the archbishop's almoner. In 1471 an Ex Officio action was brought

[1] e.g. S.V. 3, p. 145. Sentence in matrimonial suit 'Angelina de Lustyntone and Ivona *v.* Walter de Lustynstone'. Walter was found guilty of marrying Angelina while under contract to Ivona. Walter was to be whipped 'septies circa forum Cant' et toties circa ecclesiam ubi est parochianus'.

[2] e.g. Y. 2. 12, f. 214b, under date 29 Oct. 1527. Perjury suit 'Stephen Wykham *v.* Thomas Derbye.' The latter was ordered to wear a placard on his chest inscribed 'I doo this for my perjury'.

[3] Maidstone, P.R.C., 3. 1, f. 159, under date 29 Jan. 1501/2: '. . . cum cereo in una manu valoris duorum denariorum et scapula mutilis in alia manu sua.'

[4] e.g. Y. 1. 11, f. 220, under date 27 Apr. 1473. Thomas Harry of Maidstone commuted penances for himself and his wife for the sum of 10s., to be paid in two instalments.                                                    [5] Z. 3. 22, f. 14b and f. 18b.

against Thomas Swetman of Northgate, Canterbury, for saying that all commutations of public penances were extortions,
that the Church had no power to grant them, and that the
almoner of the archbishop was immoral.[1] During 1474 one
person was suspended for not paying a commutation of
6s. 8d.,[2] and a chaplain was summoned before the Consistory
Court for retaining commutation money.[3] It cannot be ascertained how scrupulous the courts were in arranging commutations. It is quite possible that many commutations of penance
went unrecorded, the court officials or the local incumbents
collecting the proceeds; but no examples of this kind of
irregularity have been detected. They certainly would not
have been recorded in the Act books.

It is impossible to construct reliable tables of the number
of suspended and excommunicated persons from the limited
evidence of the Act books. In the absence of certificates it is
impossible to discover whether the sentences of suspension
and excommunication were actually 'denounced'. The registrars sometimes noted that the letters had been issued (by
writing *emanavit* after the notice of the decree), but there are
many cases where absolutions are recorded without the issue
of the letters being so noted. Again, decrees of suspension
and excommunication could be made more than once during
the course of a case without information being provided as to
whether the previous sentences had been rescinded or not,
making it impossible to compute how many persons stood
suspended or excommunicated at any one time.

Care must be taken in making any comparison between the
employment of ecclesiastical censures in Instance and Ex
Officio business. In the former the plaintiff was responsible
for petitioning for the decree of these censures, and he paid
the expenses of their execution. In the latter the censures were
decreed on the initiative of the judge. Judges would be more

---

[1] Y. 1. 11, f. 123b, under date 1 Apr.: '. . . notatur quod affirmat et dicit quod
omnes commutationes publicarum penitentiarum sunt extortiones anglice brybus
et quod ecclesia non habet potestatem condendi tales leges. . . .' He failed to purge
himself with four laymen and four clerics as stipulated, failed to perform penance,
and spoke rudely of the archbishop's almoner.

[2] Y. 1. 11, f. 332b, under date 18 Apr. Richard Barton of Barfreston.

[3] Y. 1. 11, f. 342, under date 27 July 1474: 'Dominus Nicholaus Wylkys capellanus de Cranebroke notatur quod tenet in manu sua vis viiid de correctione
Ricardi Fayrewey.' He paid it.

likely to be consistent in the enforcement of discipline than plaintiffs in petitioning for the application of sanctions. Censures decreed in Ex Officio business are more likely, therefore, to indicate the extent of the disobedience of the defendants.

The number of cases in which defendants were suspended for not appearing after initial citation in Instance suits amounted to approximately a quarter of the total during the second half of the fifteenth century, but amounted to a much smaller proportion in the years preceding the Reformation. The great majority of suspensions of this kind decreed in the Consistory Court between 1454 and 1511 were of persons failing to appear as defendants in perjury suits. From 154 Ex Officio cases recorded in the Consistory Court Act book for 1474, there were 60 in which the defendant failed to appear, approximately 40 per cent. of the total. In the Canterbury sessions of the Archdeacon's Court in 1513, 16 out of 50 defendants were suspended for not appearing; in the sessions of the same court in the western deaneries during 1522, 21 out of 88. The proportion was less than 25 per cent. in both instances.

The majority of excommunications decreed in Instance suits introduced into the Consistory Court between 1454 and 1500 were of persons failing to obey the judge's monition to pay their debts. During 1486 only 22 defendants out of a total of 144 were excommunicated for reasons other than non-payment of debt. After 1500 the number and proportion of cases in which excommunications were decreed falls considerably. The number of excommunications decreed in Ex Officio cases was much smaller, in proportion, than those decreed in Instance cases. Out of 154 defendants cited Ex Officio to the Consistory Court during 1474, only 3 were excommunicated. None of the 50 defendants cited to the Canterbury sessions of the Archdeacon's Court in 1513 were excommunicated. During 1522 only 2 out of a total of 88 defendants cited to sessions of the same court on its circuit through the western deaneries incurred that penalty.

The number of significations recorded in the Act books is very small. None are found in the Ex Officio Act books. Two are recorded in the Instance *acta* of the Consistory

Court in 1416, and one for the year 1420. Only one case has been found in the *acta* of either court for the period 1454–1535.[1]

In Instance business it is quite impossible to gauge the efficacy of the sanctions of the courts with any certainty. While the record of many cases continues after defendants were noted as suspended or excommunicated, it cannot be ascertained whether those defendants, apparently left by the scribe suspended or excommunicated, had in fact satisfied the plaintiff out of court. The impression remains, however, that the majority of these persons either did not satisfy the plaintiff or bother to seek absolution. In Ex Officio business it is easier to assess the extent of disobedience. The majority of persons cited appeared in court, and very few of these were subsequently recalcitrant. As for those who were suspended for not appearing, the judges could well cite again if their crime was sufficiently heinous. Nevertheless, there were large numbers of people who refused to obey the injunctions of the Church.

People were frequently cited to appear before the courts for disregarding the sentences of suspension[2] and excommunication[3] by entering a church or receiving communion, and incumbents came before the courts for allowing such persons to enter churches.[4] There were probably many who regarded such sentences with the same contempt as John Gray, who was presented at archbishop Warham's visitation in 1511 for saying 'that he settith not a straw by the suspension of the commissary or officiall'.[5] Such cases, however, must not detract from the high percentage of people who did obey the citations and mandates of the Church. It is doubtful whether the percentage of the 'contemners' of ecclesiastical jurisdiction exceeded that of those outlawed for contempt of the kings' courts.

1 *Supra*, p. 96, n. 1.

2 e.g. Y. 1. 3, f. 30*b*, under date 5 Oct. 1416. Perjury suit 'William Sone *v.* Edmund Lacey': the latter 'ex confessione propria iudicialiter emissa dicit quod intravit ecclesiam non obstante publicatione littere'.

3 e.g. Y. 1. 11, f. 43, under date 21 Mar. 1469/70. John Ashert cited for receiving communion while excommunicated.

4 e.g. X. 8. 1, f. 9*b*. Dominus William Kibbeworth appears before the Consistory Court on 25 June 1399 for allowing excommunicates to receive communion.

5 Lambeth, Reg. Warham, f. xlix*b*.

The decline in the employment of the weapon of excommunication in the first thirty years of the sixteenth century admits of no one explanation. In Ex Officio business it had been sparingly used for the last fifty years of the fifteenth century. In Instance business the decrease in the number of perjury suits removed one of the more frequent causes of its being used, but this did not altogether account for the general decline. From 1495 onwards the commissaries general increasingly awarded penance to persons found guilty of perjury in not paying their debts, and excommunication was less employed as a sanction to enforce payment of debt.[1] In both courts the penalty of excommunication began to be 'reserved'. Reservation of the issue of letters of excommunication was increasingly frequent. The time limit was usually noted by the scribes.[2] This development was probably due to a combination of niggardliness on the part of plaintiffs and court personnel and of a greater scrupulousness on the part of the judges. The plaintiffs were probably unwilling to incur the expenses of obtaining the excommunication of defendants who might not appear to pay the costs. The registrar and apparitors of the court may have become increasingly reluctant to issue or carry letters of excommunication without being paid cash down. This may well explain the reservation of the issue of an excommunication for more than two months in a case where the plaintiff resided in the diocese of Norwich.[3] The judges, perturbed by the weakening of the sanction by frequent and ineffective use to enforce payment of debts in perjury cases, may have been reluctant to grant it, preferring to award penance for the perjury. It is possible that the courts expected these penances to be commuted, but the *acta* do not indicate that their expectation was fulfilled.

[1] *Supra*, p. 100.
[2] e.g. Y. 2. 7, f. 217b, under date 20 Mar. 1521/2. Testamentary suit 'Margaret Chapleyne *v.* Richard Turner.' '. . . pena reservata ad octem dies'.
[3] Y. 2. 12, f. 24, under date 17 June 1522. Testamentary suit (subtraction of legacy) 'William Nobyll *v.* John Hokbourn'.

# XI

# THE COURTS AND SOCIETY

Having examined the operation of the courts and the duties of their personnel, it is possible to obtain a more general perspective of their evolution and their wider social relationships.

At the beginning of the thirteenth century the administration of the diocese of Canterbury was largely in the hands of the archdeacon and the rural deans. The archbishop and his Official exercised a general but probably vague and ill-defined supervision over the whole, reserving only matrimonial litigation exclusively in their own hands. By the end of the century the jurisdiction of the archdeacon was overlaid at a number of points by the activities of the commissary general, representing perhaps a more general contemporary tendency on the part of bishops to exercise their authority more effectively through the agency of commissaries directly subordinate to themselves. In the diocese of Canterbury this process was given particular stimulus by the removal of the Court of Canterbury to London (and the subsequent need for definition of the diocesan jurisdiction) and by the activity of the prior and chapter of Christchurch in upholding their *sede vacante* rights within the diocese against the rival claims of the archdeacon. Archbishops Pecham and Winchelsey were both eager to consolidate their authority over the *congeries* of parishes exempt from the archdeacon's jurisdiction which were ruled by independent minded and frequently recalcitrant rectors. The autonomous jurisdictions of the exempt rectors were gradually reduced and finally submerged within the jurisdiction of the Consistory Court during the course of the fourteenth century.

The delimitation of jurisdictions was accompanied and followed by a continuous but slow process of centralization and by the increasing professionalism of the personnel who operated the jurisdictions. Both courts, which had originally shared the older agencies of the rural deans and the deanery apparitors for the purpose of citation and execution of sentences, gradually built up a more dependable corps of apparitors of their own, and in so doing obtained a more direct contact with the subjects of their jurisdictions. They not only sat at Canterbury but went on circuit, exercising a continuous pressure against delinquents which greatly exceeded that of the now largely nominal visitations. As the years pass, a general strengthening of the business routine can be detected not only from the activities recorded in the Act books but from the very appearance and form of the Act books themselves, the contents of which were set out in a more orderly and stereotyped fashion. There was a more exact distinction between different types of business. In the years 1470 to 1500 the Act books give the impression that business was being handled with precision and that the registrars and judges were operating well-oiled machinery. This was, in part, no doubt due to the increasing professionalism of the ecclesiastical lawyer.

At the end of the thirteenth century the judges and registrars were local clergy. By 1500 the judges, registrars, and proctors are obviously engaged in an occupation which occupied the major part, if not the whole, of their attention. During the fifteenth century the registrars were beginning to receive life grants of their offices and the proctors were almost all public notaries, professional men, not perhaps in their capacities as proctors, but trained in professional habits. Generally the second half of the fifteenth century appears to have been the apogee of the medieval ecclesiastical court, both as regards efficiency and volume of business. Instance business, largely owing to the increase in the handling of petty debt, increased to such an extent that extra proctors were brought in to handle it. The reasons for this volume of litigation are obscure at the moment, but civil disorder and the expensive or inefficient character of secular courts may have contributed towards it. There can be no doubt that the ecclesiastical courts, in so far as Instance business was concerned, were very popular with many different elements of the population.

An index of the plaintiffs introducing suits into the courts would include all the important persons of east Kent, all the religious houses within the diocese, and many of the wealthy citizens and mayors of Canterbury and the Cinque Ports. The Church was well represented by the heads of houses and colleges; monks and nuns licensed to appear by their superiors; rectors, vicars, chantry chaplains, curates, and churchwardens. The personnel of the courts brought their own suits into them. The judges brought suits in their own and in each others courts. In one case a proctor sued an apparitor of the same court.[1] An analysis of the suits brought by clerics into the Consistory Court during 1482 gives some indication of the numbers and types of suits brought by the different ranks of ecclesiastics. Heads of religious houses brought 8 suits for perjury and 1 testamentary suit. Rectors and vicars brought 13 suits for perjury, 14 tithe suits, 1 testamentary suit, and 2 other suits for the recovery of 'dues'. Churchwardens brought 10 suits for the recovery of 'dues'. Out of 636 cases introduced into the Consistory Court in 1482, 77 were brought by ecclesiastics, clerics, and churchwardens. The great bulk of the remaining cases were those of 'middling' people who resorted to the courts to recover debts, bring suits for defamation and for recovery of legacies.

The amount of Instance business depended in some degree upon the frequency with which individual clients brought suits into the courts. In 1482 James Aylonds of Canterbury brought fifteen suits into the Consistory Court, all of them suits for perjury. This was the maximum number brought by any one party. Thomas Ramsey, public notary and proctor, was the second most litigious client, introducing eight suits for perjury.[2] The Roper family, in particular, of St. Dunstan's, brought much litigation to the Consistory Court throughout the period.[3]

While it is impossible to compile a comprehensive social index of the clients of the courts, it is probable, to judge from the expense of litigation and the very few admissions *in forma pauperis*,[4] that the majority of plaintiffs belonged to the wealthier sections of society. Most of the cases were concerned with the recovery of material wealth, unlikely to be

---

[1] Y. 1. 16, f. 251, under date 7 July 1495. Perjury suit 'James Ganton *v.* James Bellynger, apparitor'. The latter failed to appear and was suspended.

[2] Y. 1. 13.

[3] The family into which Margaret More married.  [4] *Supra,* p. 62.

brought by the poor. It is probable that it was only in matrimonial or defamation cases where poor plaintiffs appeared in any great strength, to avoid ill fame and to rebut criminal charges.

Until *c.* 1490 it is apparent that many hundreds of clients resorted to the courts, to persist in their suits despite the travail and expenses of litigation, apparently hoping that these latter would be ultimately outweighed by the rewards of success. During the century preceding the Reformation official costs, at least, were not at all excessive, but official costs were not the whole story. They were, no doubt, only part of the total expenses of litigation. As with all medieval justice, the client often had to be prepared to meet a considerable expenditure in tips and *douceurs* to help accelerate the working of the court machinery. Costs, as has been seen,[1] were based on a regular or customary scale of charges. There is no evidence that this scale was altered or departed from in the years previous to the Reformation, and if prices were rising generally, the official expenses of an ecclesiastical suit cannot have been considered excessive. The plaintiff who had his case heard summarily would not have had to pay for more than its introduction, the citation of the defendant, the dismissal of the suit, and possibly one or two days' salary for a proctor. If he won his suit, the defendant would have had to defray those expenses. A plaintiff, however, had to be prepared to have his suit plenarily contested with the likelihood of having to pay 20*s.* or more, not including unofficial *douceurs*.

Fortunately it is possible to obtain a glimpse of the travails and expenses of litigation from the point of view of a plaintiff. Items of expenses in suits occasionally figure in Churchwardens' Accounts. An account survives of the expenses of two suits brought by the churchwardens of St. Dunstan's next to Canterbury, into the Consistory Court in 1490.[2] Useful comparisons can be made with the *acta* of the suits recorded in the Act book[3] and with the items of surviving bills of costs. The first suit was brought for the recovery of

---

[1] *Supra,* p. 61.
[2] J. M. Cowper, 'Accounts of the Churchwardens of St. Dunstan's Canterbury', *Arch. Cant.,* vol. xvi, pp. 299–303.
[3] For transcript of *acta* and accounts see Appendix No. XI.

six years' arrears of a yearly rent of half a pound of wax. After 2s. had been spent, the defendant gave in and promised to pay. The second suit, however, had had a long history dating from before 1486. Three cows owned by the church had been let out to farm to one William Belser. He had died and the previous churchwardens had endeavoured to recover £3 worth of cows and stock from his executors. In 1486 action was taken in the Consistory Court. The suit was 'stentyd and put to arbytrement', but unhappily both the arbitrators, John Roper and Roger Brent, and the 'umpire', Commissary Master Parmantory, had died, leaving matters where they were before. In 1490 Churchwardens Richard Denyse and John Long with the support of their vicar, Mr. Roper, and the parishioners, made a fresh attempt to recover the £3. They went into action in great style. A bottle of wine was bought for one of the proctors, Master Ramsey, at the cost of 6d., while the vicar entertained the commissary, the proctors, and the registrar to dinner, the churchwardens defraying 2s. 4d. towards the expenses of this entertainment, the vicar standing the remainder. In the end, 30s. were recovered from Belser's executors, and costs were awarded to the extent of 15s. 8d., hardly a handsome compensation for the 33s. 2d. which they had expended on the whole suit.[1] This case gives some indication of the trouble and expense in bringing a suit into an ecclesiastical court, and the earnestness with which it could be prosecuted.

It is interesting to find that the ecclesiastical court was regarded by some clients as only one possible channel for obtaining redress. If medieval man failed to obtain what he wanted in one court he resorted to another. In 1490 the churchwardens of St. Andrew's, Canterbury, brought one suit into two courts. They were attempting to recover revenues for a chantry; 10s. 4d. was spent on a suit in the Court of the Archdeacon, and 8s. 8d. on the preparation and prosecution of a plea in a Common Law court.[2] It is perhaps remarkable to find that the Instance business

[1] This sum was equivalent to a quarter of the churchwardens' annual receipts. In 1490 these amounted to £6. 8s. 6d. (Arch. Cant., vol. xvi, p. 303.)
[2] C. Cotton, 'Churchwardens' Accounts of the Parish of St. Andrew, Canterbury, 1485–1625', Arch. Cant., vol. xxxii, pp. 214–15. Details of the suits are not entered.

of the two courts was conducted without any interference from secular jurisdictions. The Canterbury *acta* provide little information on writs of prohibition.[1] Two actual writs survive for the period of the 1292–4 vacancy, addressed to the custodians of the spiritualities, and no doubt filed away by the registrar of the commissary Richard de Clyve.[2] The details of the cases to which they refer are lacking. In the later series of Act books the interruption of a case by the production of a writ of prohibition was merely noted by the words *prohibita est*, which were sometimes written in large letters in the margin against the case to which they referred. The number of cases interrupted by prohibitions were few. There were two in the Consistory Court during 1398 and single cases in 1374, 1417, and 1420. Only one of these five was a perjury suit. No notices of prohibition have been found for the years 1373, 1416, and 1421, while none have been found in the Act books of either court for the whole period 1454 to 1535, except one doubtful example in the Archdeacon's Court in 1503. In that year a testamentary suit was interrupted by one of the Canterbury sergeants *ad clavem*.[3] This may have been a purely local and possibly irregular interference. In none of the few cases where prohibition was recorded did the suit continue. There are no traces of 'consultations'. Although more thorough search might reveal a few more examples of prohibition, the general picture of almost complete absence of secular interference would remain. The reasons for this absence of writs of prohibition must be sought elsewhere. It was certainly not due to lack of provocation. That a great weight of litigation for recovery of debt was conducted without overt interference is possibly the greatest proof of the vigour and independence of the Courts Christian of the diocese of Canterbury during the fifteenth century.

[1] The most important work on writs of prohibition has been done by G. B. Flahiff in *Medieval Studies of the Pontifical Institute of Toronto*, vol. iii, pp. 101–16, 'Use of Prohibitions by Clerics against Ecclesiastical Courts in England', and ibid., vol. vi, pp. 261–313, 'The Writ of Prohibition to the Court Christian in the 13th Century'.

[2] Ch.Ch. Letters, vol. ii, Nos. 350, 351. The form is identical.

[3] Y. 4. 3, f. 59, under date 16 July 1502. 'Richard Grey *v.* William Kelsam'. On 24 Jan. 1502/3, 'Christopher Breche unus servientium ad clavem Cant' inhibuit M. Ricardum Willefords' (then Official).

Another feature of the operation of the courts is the lack of any evidence to suggest that they suffered any disturbance from political disorders. Unfortunately the Act books do not cover the periods of the Peasants' Revolt or the Cade rebellion, so it is impossible to tell whether these movements affected the operation of the courts. The insurgents of 1381 may have been responsible for the loss of most of the records of the courts for the period before that date, as the historian Somner suggests,[1] but the Wars of the Roses seem to have disturbed the courts little. The Consistory Court continued to sit at the usual times with the same regularity. Only one serious disturbance is recorded. On 28 January 1469/70 a 'dominus' Christopher Alcham invaded the Consistory Court (then in session at St. Gregory's) with a band of ruffians, threatened the commissary general, John Parmenter, and interrupted the proceedings. The registrar dipped deep into his vocabulary in his recording of this untoward affray.[2] The Fauconbridge rising of 1471 and the Buckingham rebellion of 1483 have left no trace in the Consistory Act books, though it is possible that the disturbances of the latter year were responsible for the comparatively small amount of Instance litigation that year.[3] The disturbed state of the country in the years 1469–74, however, may account for the general picture of unrest which emerges from the Ex Officio Act book for these years.[4] More people are summoned into the Consistory Court for abusing the Church and manhandling its officers than at any other period for which record survives.

The courts survived the political disturbances of the fifteenth century to be weakened by new conditions prevailing during the reigns of the first two Tudors. By the year 1500 there is every evidence of a serious decline in Instance business,[5] the loss of much of the litigation for the recovery of

---

[1] Somner, p. 174.

[2] Y. 1. 11, f. 114. Unfortunately the Act book employed by the registrar of the Consistory Court at the time of the fracas caused by the pursuit of Bernard the Goldsmith does not survive. Cf. E. F. Jacob, 'Chichele and Canterbury', *Essays Presented to F. M. Powicke*, p. 389.

[3] A total of 423 cases, as against 636 for 1482, and 551 for 1484 and 764 for 1485.

[4] Y. 1. 11.       [5] See chart, p. 84.

petty debt, and the corrosion of the efficiency which had reached such a high peak so recently. The reasons for this decline can only be hinted at. The greater efficiency of secular courts, particularly urban courts, and the development of new 'courts of conscience' may possibly be the principal reason for the desertion of the ecclesiastical courts. The decline in the litigiousness of plaintiffs within the borough of Canterbury was greater than that of the plaintiffs living in the country-side. In 1482 parties resident in Canterbury brought 195 suits into the Consistory Court out of a total of 636. One hundred and sixty-three of these were suits for perjury. In 1522 plaintiffs from Canterbury introduced only 24 suits in a total of 223, and of those only 6 were suits for perjury. The proportion of suits introduced by Canterbury residents had fallen from approximately a third in 1482 to approximately a tenth in 1522, while the proportion of perjury suits had fallen to a still greater extent. It would certainly appear that the inhabitants of Canterbury were turning elsewhere to settle their disputes, possibly to a more efficient borough court.

The decline in the amount of Instance business was immediately reflected by the lowering of the income of the personnel who operated the machinery of the courts, for their livelihood largely depended upon the fees they could collect. Their morale and professional standards probably suffered as a result. It appears that the proctors no longer practised in the courts for prolonged periods and that people who were not trained as public notaries were beginning to be employed to represent clients. Local clergymen appear to take a hand once more.[1] It can be assumed that the personnel would now be more prone to exploit the procedure of the courts to delay the hearing of cases in order to augment their fees as well as to succumb to the temptation of corrupt practices, but it is difficult to discover whether the decline in business after 1500 did, in fact, have these effects. The proportion of suits in which proctors are engaged rises,[2] and the number of summary suits decreases,[3] but the variable factors are so

[1] *Supra*, p. 42.                        [2] *Supra*, p. 45.
[3] The decline in the number of perjury suits largely accounts for these developments.

imponderable that it is impossible to discover from comparisons of lengths of hearings whether cases were being deliberately delayed or obstructed. The 'trade union' interest of
the proctors in fees, however, is illustrated by an entry in an
Archdeaconry Act book for 1516. The proctors apparently
insisted that in future parties should pay them their fees for
one court day before being granted a day for the presentation
of the libel. The archdeacon's Official ordered that this should
be done.[1] This payment of 6d. would serve as a deposit and
some guarantee that plaintiffs would proceed with the case.
Such joint action on the part of the proctors is symptomatic
of a period of restriction and incorporation of professional
bodies. In 1511 Richard Bodewell had begun to associate
the doctors and advocates of the provincial courts in London
and other civil lawyers in a society from which the later
Doctors' Commons was to develop.[2]

The court records are not the place to find general evidence of malpractice and corruption, but it can certainly be
assumed that the decline in business served to enhance rather
than diminish the defects and disadvantages of ecclesiastical
justice. Such evidence as is provided by the Act books is
limited. 'Ye be a parciall judge', declared John Skome to the
archdeacon's Official at his court at Lenham in 1506,[3] and
a certain 'Juliana at Nash' had scandalized the whole Consistory Court in 1472 by saying that all of them there were
dishonest and fit for hanging;[4] but the expressions of dis-
appointed parties should not be taken at their face value.
While the evidence of corruption, on even a small scale, is
lacking, opportunities were certainly not lacking. Whether
the personnel of the courts took advantage of them cannot be
ascertained.

The opportunities for corrupt practice on the part of
apparitors were notorious. Their ill favour no doubt rose

[1] Y. 2. 4, f. 86, under date 15 Mar. 1516. 'Facta conventione inter procuratores
super illo termino (de precepto libello etc in proximo) Iudex de consensu procuratorum
decrevit non imposterum ille terminus obtineatur nisi refuse sint expense unius diei.'

[2] Holdsworth, vol. iv, p. 235.

[3] Cited Ex Officio he refused to appear and was suspended but later submitted to
correction.

[4] Y. 1. 11. f. 168b, 1472. 'Juliana at Nash de parochia Sce. Mildrede. Notatur
quod scandalisat totam curiam dicendo quod omnes ibidem sunt falsi et digni . . .
suspendi.'

with their increase in number. Approximately thirty apparitors were at work within the diocese in the years preceding
the Reformation, and possibly there were unofficial preten-
ders to the office as well. The other agents of ecclesiastical
jurisdiction also had opportunities. The judges and registrars
had several opportunities for accepting payments 'out of
court' and manipulating the official record. Fees need not be
paid in court.[1] Absolutions from sentences of excommunication and suspension could be granted in private.[2] Gifts were
certainly received to augment the official fees.[3] The opportunities were perhaps less in Instance business than in Ex
Officio business. Proctors of the party affected adversely by
underhand transactions would hardly be slow to protest; Ex
Officio cases, however, could be quietly dropped. But while
evidence of corruption on a scale large enough to shock the
medieval conscience is lacking, we must remain silent and
assume that the judges and registrars accepted the enter-
tainments given to them by interested clients, but did not
deliberately pervert the course of justice for personal gain.
On the whole, the impression gathered, even from the Act
books of the period immediately preceding the Reformation,
is that these higher officials of the courts regarded their
occupations as a duty and not as an opportunity for plunder.
Thomas Laurence, the registrar of the archdeacor at the
time of the Reformation, who in his old age was unfortunate
enough to become entangled in the Elizabeth Barton affair,[4]
frequently scribbled in the covers and end-papers of his
registers the Augustinian dictum, 'militia est vita hominis
super terram'. He was no doubt contemplating the day-to-day
spectacle of human frailty and the tedious nature of his office.

[1] Cf. Y. 2. 5, f. 7b, under date 2 June 1511. Perjury suit 'John Beke v. Richard
Goodhewe'. The latter was suspended, and on 16 June 'allegavit quod soluit feodos
contumacie domino commissario . . .'.
[2] Cf. Y. 1. 1, f. 151, under date 21 June 1482. 'Collectors of Goods of Richard
Frognal Kt. v. John Wode of Tong'. The latter suspended but absolved by Official
in the latter's house.
[3] Supra, p. 106.
[4] Cf. L.P. Henry VIII, vol. vi, 1460 n. He was appointed registrar 30 June 1494
(Reg. S, f. 389b) and died before 18 Nov. 1536, when probate of his testament was
granted (Maidstone, P.R.C. 3. 8, f. 82b).

# APPENDIX

## I. LISTS OF OFFICERS OF THE COURTS

THE following abbreviations are used:

| | | | |
|---|---|---|---|
| adm. | admitted. | lic. | licensed. |
| app. | appointed. | ord. | ordained. |
| bp. | bishop. | pr. | priest. |
| coll. | collated. | prof. | professed. |
| d. | died. | r. | rector. |
| dcn. | deacon. | re-app. | reappointed. |
| dioc. | diocese. | subdcn. | subdeacon. |
| exch. | exchanged. | S.V. | 'sede vacante'. |
| fr. | frater. | v. | vicar. |
| ind. | inducted. | vac. | vacated or resigned (benefice). |
| inst. | instituted. | | |

If officers have been specifically designated 'magister', 'M' is placed before the name. The term 'Churchill' indicates that reference is to lists of commissaries general and Officials of the archdeacon in Churchill, vol. ii, pp. 229–30. Benefices are in Kent unless otherwise stated. Cross references are made between the lists.

### (i) COMMISSARIES GENERAL

WALTER DE ACRISE. Acting as deputy of the Official of the Court of Canterbury (1259) in the 'Consistory Court'.[1]

ROBERT DE SELESEYA. A monk of Ch.Ch., acting during the vacancy of 1278–9.[2]

M. JOHN DE RAVENINGHAM. Acting c. 1279[3] and in 1280.[4] Had been a proctor in 1271/2.[5]

M. MARTIN DE HAMPTON. App. 5 May 1282,[6] still acting 1305.[7] R. of Wittersham in 1282.[8]

RICHARD DE CLYVE. A monk of Ch.Ch. (prof. 1286, d. 1326).[9] Commissary S.V. 1292–4; app. 14 Dec. 1292,[10] and again with M. Hugh de Forsham S.V. 1313.[11] Acting as provisional Official of the Court of Canterbury at beginning of latter vacancy.[12]

M. HUGH DE FORSHAM. Acting in 1307[13] and 1310;[14] app. S.V. 27 May 1313,[15] and again S.V. 23 Nov. 1327 with Hugh de St. Margaret, a monk of Ch.Ch.[16] Had been dean of Shoreham in 1301.[17]

[1] C. Ant. A 7b.  [2] S.V. Scrapbooks, passim.  [3] S.V. 3, p. 7.
[4] Churchill.  [5] E.S. Roll, No. 21.  [6] Churchill.
[7] Reg. I, f. 261.  [8] Churchill, vol. ii, p. 13.  [9] Ibid.
[10] Ibid.  [11] Churchill.  [12] Reg. Q, f. 93.
[13] Reg. I, f. 280b.  [14] Churchill.  [15] Reg. Q, f. 93.
[16] Ibid., f. 138b.  [17] Churchill, vol. i, p. 118.

THOMAS DE CHARTHAM. Acting 1314–17 and 1325–6.[1] Had been Official of the archdeacon in 1309 (q.v.). R. of Chartham in 1314.[2] D. by Oct. 1327.[3]

ROBERT DE MALLING. App. 30 May 1317,[4] still acting 1323.[5] Had administered dioc. Chichester S.V. 1304–5[6] and dioc. Bath and Wells S.V. 1308.[7] Auditor of Causes 1308–10.[8] Official of the archdeacon in 1315 (q.v.). R. of Eastry in 1317.[9]

M. THOMAS OF CANTERBURY. Probably acting in 1328 (citation from 'T de C');[10] S.V. commission with Fr. James de Oxene for vacancy 1333–4.[11] S.V. dean of Croydon 20 Oct. 1333 and of Shoreham 25 Oct. 1333.[12] Probably continued to act as commissary general until vacancies of 1348–9, when again app. S.V.[13] Still acting 2 June 1349.[14] R. of Dymchurch in 1325.[15] R. of Brookland in 1333.[16]

M. JOHN DE WYMBOURNE. Acting 1350–61.[17] Had been Official of the archdeacon in 1348 (q.v.). Commissioned to exercise exempt jurisdiction of Reculver, 21 Oct. 1333, as R. of Denton,[18] and as R. of Wittersham to exercise exempt jurisdictions of Reculver, 10 Sept. 1348,[19] and of Wittersham, 4 Oct. 1348.[20] R. of Aldington, exch. 1360; R. of Westwell, adm. 1360.[21]

M. RICHARD DE WARMINGTON, B.C.L. S.V. commission 30 Apr. 1366[22] (probably acting as commissary general for vacancy of 1366). Auditor of Causes, app. 13 April 1359,[23] still acting as such S.V. in 1374, commission S.V. 9 June 1374.[24] 'Chancellor' in 1369.[25] R. of Godmersham, coll. 1360, exch. 1361.[26] R. of Aldington, adm. 1361, vac. 1369.[27] R. of Adisham, adm. 1369, till death.[28] Canon of Wingham, adm. 1369, till death.[29] Will proved 7 Mar. 1379.[30]

ROBERT DE BOURNE. App. 8 Nov. 1366;[31] S.V. commission 2 Dec. 1368;[32] re-app. 16 Jan. 1368/9;[33] probably acting from 1366–76.[34] Had been Official Principal, dioc. Rochester, during vacancies of 1364,[35] 1368,[36] and 1373.[35] Auditor of Causes S.V. 1366,[37] commission as such S.V. 9 Dec. 1368.[38] Commission S.V. as Official of the archdeacon 26 May 1374.[39]

[1] Churchill.
[2] Churchill, vol. ii, p. 13.
[3] Churchill.
[4] Churchill.
[5] Reg. I, f. 387b.
[6] Churchill, vol. i, p. 210.
[7] Ibid., vol. ii, p. 154.
[8] Ibid., p. 242.
[9] Reg. Reynolds, f. 20.
[10] Reg. I, f. 426.
[11] Churchill.
[12] Reg. Q, f. 174.
[13] Churchill.
[14] Reg. G, f. 50.
[15] Reg. Reynolds, f. 291b.
[16] Reg. G, f. xxvib.
[17] Churchill.
[18] Reg. G, f. xxix.
[19] Ibid., f. 27b.
[20] Ibid., f. 28b.
[21] Reg. Islip, f. 285b.
[22] Reg. G, f. 120b.
[23] Churchill, vol. ii, p. 243.
[24] Reg. G, f. 196b.
[25] Churchill, vol. i, p. 17 n.
[26] Reg. Islip, ff. 285b, 286.
[27] Reg. Whittlesey, f. 73.
[28] Ibid., f. 72b; Reg. Sudbury, f. 128.
[29] Reg. Whittlesey, f. 24b.
[30] Ibid., f. 100b.
[31] Churchill.
[32] Reg. G, f. 164.
[33] Churchill.
[34] Y. i. 1 and Churchill.
[35] Churchill, vol. ii, p. 263.
[36] Reg. Trillek, Roch. i, f. 333.
[37] Reg. G, f. 155.
[38] Ibid., f. 162b.
[39] Churchill, vol. i, p. 49.

R. of 'Woldham' in 1350, when ord. priest.[1] R. of Freckenham, Norfolk, in 1366,[2] exch. 1368. R. of Southfleet, adm. 1368.[3]

M. ROBERT BRADEGARE, B.C.L. App. 18 Oct. 1376;[4] acting in 1381[5] and 1386;[6] commission S.V. 3 Aug. 1396.[7] 'Chancellor' in 1378.[8] Vicar General, dioc. Rochester, deputing powers, in 1389.[9] R. of Biddenden in 1375.[10] Canon of St. Paul's, app. 20 Jan. 1373/4, till death.[11] R. of Hollingbourne, with exempt jurisdiction in 1378[12] and 1382,[13] till death. Canon of Wingham till death. D. by Sept. 1409.[14] Founded college at Bredgar 19 July 1392.[15]

M. ROBERT DE MALBERTHORP. App. 10 Sept. 1378.[16] R. of Magna Chart in 1381[17] till death. D. by May 1401.[18]

M. WALTER CHELTENHAM. App. 5 Jan. 1381/2.[19] R. of 'Wythyndon' till death. Will proved 15 Sept. 1385.[20]

M. THOMAS CHILLENDEN. App. S.V. 13 Jan. 1396/7.[21] Prior of Christchurch 1391–1411.[22]

M. WILLIAM HUNDEN, B.C. and CAN.L. App. 12 Feb. 1396/7,[23] acting until 1400?[24] Notary 1390. Archdeacon of Rochester 1401, resigned 1408. Archdeacon of Totnes 1408. Chancellor of Exeter. Canon of Lincoln 1415. R. of Ruxley 1397, exch. 1399. R. of Hadstock, Essex, resigns 1400. R. of N. Crawley, Bucks. Will dated 27 Jan.; probate 10 Mar. 1415/6; *Summa bonorum* at £362. 14s. 10d.[25]

M. ROGER BASSET, D.C. and CAN.L. (Cambr.). Acting 1402–5?[26] R. of St. Dunstan by the Tower, London, adm. 1401, exch. 1402.[27] R. of E. Tarring, Sussex, adm. 1402.[28] Ord. subdcn. and dcn. 1402, pr. 1403.[29]

M. JOHN LYNTON. Commissary general S.V.? acting June 1414.[30]

M. MATTHEW ASSHETON, D.C. and CAN.L. (Oxon.). First appears as commissary general 18 Nov. 1403;[31] acting 1405–9;[32] re-app. 2 Mar. 1416/7,[33] first reappearing 8 Mar. 1416/17[34] and acting until July 1420.[35] Official,

[1] Reg. Islip, f. 308b; place not identified.
[2] Reg. G, f. 120b.
[3] Reg. Trillek, Roch. i, f. 334b.
[4] Churchill.
[5] Reg. G, f. 222.
[6] Churchill.
[7] Reg. G, f. 242.
[8] Churchill, vol. i, p. 486.
[9] Ibid., p. 219.
[10] Reg. Sudbury, f. 6.
[11] Le Neve, vol. ii, p. 433.
[12] Churchill, vol. i, p. 92.
[13] Reg. Courtenay, f. 18.
[14] Reg. Arundel, ii, f. 54b.
[15] Reg. Morton, i, f. 124.     [16] Churchill.
[17] Reg. G, f. 226b.
[18] Reg. Arundel, i, f. 276b.
[19] Churchill.
[20] Reg. Courtenay, ff. 211b–12, place not identified.
[21] Churchill.
[22] Smith, p. 233.
[23] Churchill.
[24] Ibid. and Y. 1. 2.
[25] A. H. Lloyd, 'Notes on Cambridge Clerks petitioning for Benefices 1370–1399', B.I.H.R., vol. xx, pp. 191–2.
[26] Churchill.        [27] Reg. Arundel, i, f. 278.
[28] Ibid. i, f. 282.
[29] Ibid. i, ff. 329b, 330, 330b.
[30] X. 10. 1, f. 70.
[31] Maidstone, P.R.C. 3. 1, f. 15.
[32] Churchill.
[33] Ibid.
[34] Y. 1. 3, f. 41.
[35] Y. 1. 3 and Y. 1. 4. No trace has been found of him acting after this date. Cf. *Chichele* (C.Y. Soc.), vol. i, p. lxxv, where he is stated to have acted from 1417 to 1422.

dioc.Norwich S.V. with archdeacon of Norwich.[1] R. of Slapton in 1400.
R. of Ivychurch, vac. 1413. Provost of Wingham, app. 1413.[2] D. 1435.[3]

M. ROBERT RAULYN, B.CAN.L. App. 14 June 1414, acting until death Feb.
1416/17.[4] Clerk in household of Bp. of St. David's. Prebend in Collegiate
Church of Abergwilly 20 Dec. 1401. R. of Wallingford, Berks., by 24 Aug.
1401. Canon of St. David's 29 Oct. 1403 (prebend of Clyde). V. General
of St. David's, 1405. R. of Rossely 22 Oct. 1406. Prebend of Llandysilio
in Abergwilly 30 Jan. 1507/8. R. of Frittenden 26 Nov. 1415, exch. for
St. Mary's, Romney Marsh, 14 April 1416. Buried in All Saints, Canterbury. He left the R. of All Saints a Bible and Book of Decretals; John
Lovelych, his registrar, 'Johannes in addicionibus'; John Chapman, 'Unum
corpus iuris civilis', and 6s. 8d. for the proctor David Mareys.[5]

RICHARD GODMERSHAM, D.CAN.L. Monk of Ch.Ch. S.V. commission Feb.
1414.[6] Joint commission with Thomas Moonie 28 July 1420,[7] acting until
9 Jan. 1420/21 while Archbishop Chichele *in remotis agendis.*[8]

M. THOMAS MOONIE, B.CAN.L. First appears 28 July 1420,[9] acts alone from
3 Feb. 1420/1,[10] continues to act 1421–25[11] and probably until re-app.
8 Aug. 1443,[12] and until last appearance 12 Aug. 1451.[13] V. of Hackington,
adm. 1417. Successively R. of Deal 1421 and Acrise 1429. 'Commendarius',
Bishopsbourne 1430. R. of Ruckinge 1432. Provost of Wingham 1435.[14]

M. RICHARD RAYNHILL, B.C. and CAN.L. Acting Jan. 1451/2.[15] Official of the
archdeacon 1453/4 (q.v.).

JOHN WODNYSBURGHE, D.CAN.L. Monk of Ch.Ch. Commissary general S.V.
acting 2 Apr. 1454, colleague to James Goldwell.[16]

M. JAMES GOLDWELL (Oxon. All Souls), B.C.L. (1449), B.CAN.L. (by 1450),
D.C.L. (1452). App. 2 Nov. 1452;[17] acting until last appearance 29 Oct.
1454.[18] Salient details of subsequent career:[19] Canon of St. Paul's 1457.
Dean of Salisbury 1458. Registrar, Order of the Garter 1460. Archdeacon
of Essex, 1461. Bp. of Norwich 1472 until death 1499. Benefices not noted
in *D.N.B.*: R. of St. Mary Bredman, Canterbury, adm. 1450,[20] vac. before
1 Apr. 1452.[21] R. of Cheriton, adm. 1450,[22] vac. 1453.[23] R. of Harrietsham, adm. 1453,[24] vac. before 26 Feb. 1471/2.[25]

M. DAVID BLODWELL, B.CAN.L. (Cambr.). App. 1454;[26] first appearance
29 Oct. 1454.[27] Dean of St. Asaph in 1455, dispensation to hold second
benefice.[28] R. of Adisham, coll. 4 May 1456.[29] D. 1462.[30]

[1] *Chichele* (C.Y. Soc.), vol. i, p. xcvii.
[2] Reg. Arundel, ii, f. 66; Slapton, county not identified.
[3] *Chichele* (C.Y. Soc.), vol. i, p. lxxv.
[4] Y. 1. 3, f. 41. Note of death in margin.
[5] *Chichele* (C.Y. Soc.), vol. ii, pp. 110–12 and p. 672.  [6] Reg. G, f. 277.
[7] Y. 1. 4, f. 28.    [8] Ibid.    [9] Y. 1. 4, f. 28.    [10] Y. 1. 4.
[11] Y. 1. 3 and Y. 1. 4.    [12] Churchill.    [13] X. 1. 1, f. 43.
[14] *Chichele* (C.Y. Soc.), vol. iv (Index), p. 576.
[15] Maidstone, P.R.C. 32. 1, f. 56, and X. 1. 1, f. 51.
[16] Y. 1. 5.    [17] Churchill.    [18] Y. 1. 5.
[19] *D.N.B.*    [20] Reg. Jo. Stafford, f. 105b.    [21] Reg. S, f. 194.
[22] Reg. Jo. Stafford, f. 105b.    [23] Reg. Jo. Kemp, f. 325b.    [24] Ibid.
[25] Reg. Bourchier, f. 107b.    [26] Churchill.    [27] Y. 1. 5.
[28] *C.P.L.* xi. 22.    [29] Reg. Bourchier, f. 63b.    [30] Le Neve, vol. i, p. 529.

M. John Parmenter, leg. lic. (Cambr.). First appearance 29 Mar. 1462,[1] acting until 7 Mar. 1485/6.[2] Had been dean of Bocking in 1454.[3] Official of archdeacon of Ely in 1458.[4] R. of Newchurch, vac. before 18 Mar. 1472/3. R. of Adisham, adm. 1473.[5] Canon of Wingham in 1475.[6] D. before 3 Dec. 1487, when executors noticed.[7]

M. Edward Payne, b.can.l. (Cambr.). App. S.V. 2 Apr. 1486;[8] acting until Nov. 1489.[9] V. of St. Clement's, Sandwich, adm. 1479,[10] vac. 1490.[11] R. of St. George's, Canterbury, pres. 1480.[12] V. of Herne Hill, adm. 1490.[13] V. of Monkton, till death. D. 1497.[14]

M. Henry Cooper, ll.b. (Oxon.). First appearance 1 Dec. 1489;[15] acting until June 1500.[16] R. of Great Mongeham, vac. by 6 Apr. 1492.[17] R. of Adisham in 1491 till death.[18] Canon of Wingham, coll. 1491,[19] vac. 1493.[20] D. 1500.[21]

M. Robert Woodward, d.can.l. (Oxon.). First appearance 23 June 1500;[22] ceases to act 16 Sept. 1500 upon vacancy following death of Archbishop Morton;[23] reappears 29 Jan. 1503/4;[24] re-app. 5 Feb. 1503/4;[25] acting until Oct. 1520.[26] Commissary of Calais with Adam Redeshefe, app. 3 Feb. 1503/4.[27] R. of Adisham, coll. 1500.[28] R. of St. Mary Magdalen, Canterbury, adm. 1504, vac. 1505.[29] R. of Little Mongeham, ind. 1513/14.[30] Canon of Wingham, adm. 1505, and still, 1511.[31]

M. John Williamson, b.can.l. (Cambr.). App. S.V. 2 Sept. 1500[32] and again 1 Mar. 1501/2;[33] acting from 5 Oct. 1500[34] until 9 Jan. 1504.[35] Practised as proctor, Consistory Court, since 1486/7.[36] Official of the archdeacon 1495–6 (q.v.). Commissary for Calais, app. 1 March 1501/2.[37] V. of Willesborough, adm. 25 May 1479,[38] vac. before 28 Apr. 1481. R. of Swalecliff, adm. 1481.[39] V. of Minster in Thanet in 1492[40] till death.[41] R. of St. George's, Canterbury, till death.[42] Prebendary of Wingham, vac. 1516.[43]

M. Peter Ligham, d.can.l. (Oxon.). First appearance 6 Nov. 1520;[44] acting until Jan. 1523[45]. Commissary general S.V. 30 Sept. 1532.[46] Official of Court of Canterbury in 1530.[47] V. of Minster in Thanet, ind. 29 Mar.

[1] Y. 1. 7, f. 116b.
[2] Y. 1. 14.
[3] Churchill, vol. ii, p. 233.
[4] Lib. Arch. El., p. 288.
[5] Reg. Bourchier, f. 107b.
[6] Ibid., f. 112.
[7] Y. 1. 14.
[8] Reg. R, f. 3b.
[9] Y. 1. 15.
[10] Reg. Bourchier, f. 123.
[11] Reg. Morton, ii, f. 148.
[12] Reg. S, f. 305.
[13] Reg. Morton, ii, f. 147b.
[14] Ibid. ii, f. 164.
[15] Y. 1. 15.
[16] Y. 1. 18.
[17] Reg. Morton, ii, f. 151b.
[18] Ibid., f. 151.
[19] Ibid., f. 149b.
[20] Ibid., f. 154b.
[21] Ibid., f. 168b.
[22] Y. 1. 18.
[23] Ibid.
[24] Y. 2. 1.
[25] Churchill.
[26] Y. 2. 10.
[27] Churchill, vol. i, p. 518 n.
[28] Reg. Morton, ii, f. 168b.
[29] Reg. Warham, ff. 321b and 325.
[30] Z. 3. 22, f. 37.
[31] Reg. Warham, ff. 37b and 324.
[32] Reg. R, f. 41.
[33] Reg. T, f. 430.
[34] Y. 1. 18.
[35] Y. 2. 1.
[36] Y. 1. 14.
[37] Reg. T, f. 430.
[38] Reg. Bourchier, f. 121.
[39] Ibid., f. 127b.
[40] Reg. Morton, ii, f. 151b.
[41] Reg. Warham, f. 374.
[42] Ibid., f. 37b.
[43] Ibid., f. 360.
[44] Y. 2. 10.
[45] Y. 2. 12.
[46] Y. 2. 13.
[47] Churchill, vol. ii, p. 238.

1522.[1] R. of Saltwood, adm. 1526.[2] Master, Hospital of St. Thomas on Eastbridge, Canterbury, in 1524/5.[3]

M. RICHARD BENGER, D.CAN.L. (Oxon.). First appearance 26 Jan. 1523;[4] acting until 1532.[5]

## (ii) OFFICIALS OF THE ARCHDEACON OF CANTERBURY

ROBERT, vice-archdeacon, in 1168.[6]

RALPH, 'quondam vice archidiaconus', before 1195.[7]

M. EVERARD, vice-archdeacon, 1195 × 1200.[6]

JOHN DE LONDINIIS, Official, acting 1239.[8]

M. OMER. Acting in 1257 and 1259.[9] Official of the Court of Canterbury in 1279.[10]

ROBERT DE HORLANSTON. Acting 1270/1.[11]

M. WILLIAM DE SWANTON. Acting 1292–4.[12] Examiner of the Court of Canterbury, 1304.[13]

THOMAS DE CHARTHAM. Acting 1309.[14] Commissary general 1314–17 and 1325–6 (q.v.).

ROBERT DE MALLING. Acting 1315.[15] Commissary general 1317–1325 (q.v.).

M. JOHN DE WYMBOURNE. Took oath of obedience to prior and chapter, S.V. 1 Oct. 1348.[16] Commissary general acting 1350–61 (q.v.).

NICHOLAS DE YSTELEY. Acting 1352–62.[17]

M. JOHN DWYT. Took oath of obedience to prior and chapter S.V. 20 July 1366.[18]

M. RICHARD SELLYNG, LL.B. (Oxon.). Took oath of obedience 21 July 1368.[19] Public notary. R. of Charlton, vac. 1361.[20] V. of Minster, adm. 1361.[21]

M. WILLIAM MENNESSE, B.C.L. Took oath of obedience 2 July 1372.[22] R. of 'Kingswode' in 1375, exch. 1376.[23] R. of Biddenden, adm. 1376.[24]

M. ROBERT DE BOURNE. The commissary general (q.v.) app. Official during vacancy of archdeaconry 1374–5.[25]

M. JOHN DE PETHAM. Took oath of obedience Feb. 1375/6; still acting 1383.[26] R. of St. Mildred's, Canterbury, in 1368, 1376.[27] Lic. to study for two years 1368.[28]

[1] Z. 3. 4, f. 56b.    [2] Y. 2. 12.    [3] Reg. Warham, f. 391.
[4] Y. 2. 12.    [5] Y. 2. 13.
[6] C. R. Cheney, *English Bishops' Chanceries 1100–1250*, pp. 132 and 143; cf. ibid., pp. 143–6, for discussion of vice-archdeacons.
[7] Lit. MS. B. 7, f. 7b.    [8] Gervase, *Opera* (R.S.), vol. ii, p. 167.
[9] *Arch. Cant.*, vol. xiii, p. 121; C. Ant. A 7b.
[10] M. Morgan, 'Early Canterbury Jurisdiction', *E.H.R.*, vol. lx (1945), p. 398.
[11] Ch.Ch. letters, vol. ii, No. 257.
[12] E.S. Roll No. 272; Shadwell MS. 4; C. Ant. A. 205.
[13] Lambeth MS. 244.    [14] *Winchelsey* (C.Y. Soc.), pp. 104, and 1056.
[15] Churchill.    [16] Reg. G, f. 26.    [17] Churchill.
[18] Reg. G, f. 128b.    [19] Reg. I, f. 64b.
[20] Reg. Islip, f. 294; county not identified.    [21] Ibid., f. 289.
[22] Churchill.    [23] Reg. Sudbury, f. 9.    [24] Ibid., f. 120b.
[25] Churchill.    [26] Churchill.
[27] Reg. Sudbury, f. 12b.    [28] Reg. Langham, f. 144.

THOMAS LAUKE. Acting in 1414–15.[1]

M. JAMES BURBAYCH, B.C. and CAN.L. Acting 1415 till after 1428.[2] Successively R. of Elmley 1422 and R. of Lebourne 1423. Also R. of Chalvington, Sussex, 1426. V. of St. Dunstan's, Canterbury, 1431. V. of St. Clement's, Sandwich, 1432.[3]

M. RICHARD RAYNHILL. Acting in Mar. 1453–4.[4] Had been commissary general Jan. 1451/2 (q.v.). V. of St. Mary's, Sandwich, adm. 1447, till death.[5] V. of Chislet, adm. 1449, till death.[6] Canon and prebendary, S. Malling, till death.[7] D. 1462.[8]

M. SIMON HOGGES, B.C.L. (Oxon.). Adm. 1450. Fellow of All Souls, 1441. Acting in 1467[9] and from 1476 to 1482,[10] and probably until 1488.[11] V. of Smarden, adm. 1444,[12] vac. before 23 Mar. 1472/3.[13] R. of Newchurch, coll. 18 March 1472/3,[14] vac. before 27 June 1482.[15] V. of Hackington, adm. 21 Feb. 1473/4.[16] R. of Great Mongeham, coll. 27 June 1482, till death.[17] D. 1491.[18]

M. JOHN CHARNOK, D.C. and CAN.L. by 1483. Acting (temporarily) May 1483.[19] R. of All Saints, Bread St., London, in 1483.[20]

M. JOHN WILLIAMSON, B.CAN.L. (Cambr.). Acting 1495[21] and 1496.[22] Commissary general 1500–4 (S.V.).

M. CLEMENT HARDING, LL.B. (Oxon., New College). Acting 1493–4[23] and Apr. 1495;[24] still acting 1504–6.[25] Ord. pr., 29 Mar. 1494.[26] V. of St. Dunstan's, Canterbury, adm. 12 May 1495.[27] V. of Holy Cross, Westgate, Canterbury, adm. 6 Apr. 1507.[28] Memorial quoted in *Arch. Cant.* vol. xxx, p. 238.

M. RICHARD WILLEFORDS, LL.B. (Oxon.). Acting 1502.[29] R. of Dymchurch, adm. 1473.[30]

M. NICHOLAS HILLYNGTON, LL.B. Acting 1507[31] until 1514.[32] Official, exempt jurisdiction of Wingham in 1509.[33] V. of Sutton Valence, adm. 27 Dec. 1502, till death.[34] V. of St. Clement's, Sandwich, adm. 1509.[35] R. of Easling, adm. 1510, vac. 1514.[36] R. of Snave in 1514[37]–17.[38] V. of Chart in 1515, till death.[39] V. of Lenham, adm. 1517, till death.[40] D. 1518.

M. EDWARD BROUGHTON, B.C. and CAN.L. Acting from 1520 until 1524.[41] R.

1 Churchill.
2 *Chichele* (C.Y. Soc.), vol. i, p. 96.
3 Ibid., vol. iv (Index), p. 433.
4 Churchill.
5 Reg. Bourchier, f. 85b.
6 Reg. Jo. Stafford, f. 93.
7 Ibid., f. 100.
8 Reg. Bourchier, f. 85.
9 Ibid., f. 97b.
10 Y. 1. 9.
11 Y. 1. 14 (10 June).
12 Reg. Jo. Stafford, f. 79b.
13 Reg. Bourchier, f. 107.
14 Ibid.
15 Ibid., f. 130b.
16 Ibid., f. 109.
17 Ibid.
18 Reg. Morton, ii, f. 148.
19 Y. 1. 9.
20 Reg. Bourchier, ff. 157 and 159b.
21 Maidstone, P.R.C. 3. 1.
22 Y. 1. 17.
23 Maidstone, P.R.C. 3. 1, f. 44.
24 Y. 4. 2.
25 Z. 3. 22.
26 Reg. Morton, ii, f. 142b.
27 Ibid., f. 158.
28 Reg. Warham, f. 330.
29 Y. 4. 3.
30 Reg. Bourchier, f. 108b.
31 Z. 3. 22.
32 Maidstone, P.R.C. 3. 4.
33 Y. 2. 5, f. 8b.
34 Reg. Morton, ii. f. 170b.
35 Reg. Warham, f. 335.
36 Ibid., ff. 354b, 357.
37 Z. 3. 3, f. 20b.
38 Reg. Warham, f. 363.
39 Ibid., ff. 365b, 366b.
40 Ibid., ff. 362b, 365b.
41 Maidstone, P.R.C. 3. 5.

of Wormshill, ind. 1516,[1] till death.[2] V. of Brookland, adm. 1521, till death.[3] R. of St. George's, Canterbury, adm. 1522, till death.[4] D. 1524.[5]
ROBERT COLYNS, B.C.L. Acting from 1524 until after 1536.[6] V. of Lympne, adm. 1524.[7]

## (iii) REGISTRARS OF THE CONSISTORY COURT

ELYAS OF WESTGATE. Acting 1259.[8]

ROBERT. Monk of Ch.Ch. Acting S.V. 1292–4.[9]

M. JOHN CRANEBOURNE. Acting 1364[10] and 1372–5,[11] still acting 1396.[12] R. of Hope, in 1361, till death.[13] Warden of Hospital of Poor Priests, Canterbury, in 1393.[14]

M. ADAM BODY. Acting 1397;[15] still acting 1402/3.[16] Later practised as proctor 1415–25 (q.v.).

M. JOHN LOVELYCH (Oxon.). Acting 1411/12;[17] still acting in 1425.[18] Had been at Rome in 1406 as proctor for prior and chapter of Ch.Ch.[19] R. of Newington, Surrey, in 1419.[20] R. of St. Martin's without Canterbury, inst. 1420.[21] R. of St. Alphege, Canterbury, inst. 1428.[22] Ord. dcn.[23] and pr. 1420.[24] D. 1438, leaving legal works to All Souls College, Oxford.[25]

WILLIAM BOLD. App. 25 May 1442.[26]

HENRY TREWONWALL (Oxon.). App. 23 Oct. 1459.[27] Chaplain of free chapel of 'Botehaut' in Wighton, Norfolk, app. 1451.[28]

M. JOHN COLMAN. App. 1 Jan. 1483/4;[29] re-app. of John Colman and Thomas Barrett, 25 Aug. 1527,[30] but John Colman recorded the acts until Oct. 1534, when his hand finally disappears.[31] He was a churchwarden of All Saints parish, Canterbury, 1498,[32] and still acted as such in 1515.[33]

JOHN DRAPER. First noticed as registrar, 17 Jan. 1535/6, but probably succeeded John Colman in Oct. 1534.[34]

## (iv) REGISTRARS OF THE ARCHDEACON'S COURT

M. JOHN PENWORTHAM. App. 15 Aug. 1442,[35] and also as apparitor general.
M. JOHN COLMAN, registrar of the Consistory Court, and
M. JOHN KNYGHT, a proctor, acted temporarily as joint registrars during 1494.[36]

[1] Z. 3. 22, f. 42b.   [2] Reg. Warham, f. 381b.   [3] Ibid., ff. 371, 376, 381b.
[4] Ibid., ff. 374, 377.   [5] Ibid., f. 382.   [6] Y. 2. 7.
[7] Reg. Warham, f. 383b.   [8] C. Ant. A. 7b.
[9] S.V. 2, p. 56, and S.V. 3, p. 38.   [10] X. 1. 19.
[11] X. 1. 1.   [12] Maidstone, P.R.C. 32. 1, f. 2.   [13] Reg. Islip, f. 319.
[14] Reg. Courtenay (in Reg. Merton), f. 182b.   [15] Y. 1. 2, f. 58.
[16] Maidstone, P.R.C. 32. 1, f. 15.   [17] X. 10. 1 and X. 1. 3.
[18] X. 1. 4.   [19] Eastry Letters VI, letter from John Hale.
[20] Chichele (C.Y. Soc.), vol. i, p. 192.   [21] Ibid., vol. i, p. 178.
[22] Ibid., vol. i, p. 251.   [23] Ibid., vol. iv, p. 338.
[24] Ibid., vol. iv, p. 341.   [25] Ibid., vol. ii, pp. 560–2; cf. p. lvii.
[26] Reg. S, f. 149b.   [27] Ibid., f. 205.   [28] C.P.R. 1446–52, 412.
[29] Reg. S, f. 331.   [30] Reg. T, f. 293.   [31] Y. 2. 13.
[32] X. 8. 2.   [33] Z. 3. 3.   [34] Ibid.
[35] Reg. S, f. 151.   [36] Maidstone, P.R.C. 3. 1, ff. 45 and 46b.

M. Thomas Laurence. App. 30 June 1494;[1] still acting during 1533.[2] Involved in the Elizabeth Barton case.[3] D. before 18 Nov. 1536 (Testament of M. Thomas Laurence.)[4]

### (v) Lists of Proctors

If the proctors are specifically described as public notaries, P.N. is added after their names.

### Consistory Court, 1372–75

John Bedel; Adam Clerk.

### Consistory Court, 1397–98

M. Nicholas Archer; M. John Wilmington; M. William Warrene; Thomas Webb; William Segrym; John Petham; Richard Fischer; Thomas Borne; Simon Ornebrake.

### Consistory Court, 1415–25

M. Adam Body (P.N.), registrar in 1397 and 1401 (q.v.); M. David Mareys (P.N.); John Egerden; M. Thomas Fen; M. James Burbaych (after 1421), Official of the archdeacon (q.v.).

### Both Courts, 1474–1535

| Proctor | Consistory Court | Archdeacon's Court |
| --- | --- | --- |
| M. James Ganton (P.N.). | Before 1474–1513 | Before 1500–13 |
| M. Thomas Notyngham (P.N.). | Before 1474–1501 | Before 1481–1500 |
| M. James Das (P.N.). | Before 1474–98 | Before 1477–probably after 1495 |
| M. Thomas Ramsey (P.N.). | Before 1474–93 | |
| M. John Richardson, ll.b.(P.N.). | 1483–1512/13 | 1482/3–1512/13 |
| M. John Williamson, b.can.l. Later, archdeacon's Official and commissary general (q.v.). | 1486–93 | |
| M. John Warde. At Bologna in 1494/5?[5] | 1485/6–1492/3 | |
| Mercer. | 1486–7 | |
| M. Thomas Colman, b.c. and can.l. (P.N.). Acted as registrar, Consistory Court, May and June 1486. V. of Herne Hill, vac. 1514.[6] V. of St. Nicholas, Thanet, adm. 1514[7] till death. D. 1517.[8] | 1487–1517 | 1502–9 |

[1] Reg. S, f. 389b.
[2] Y. 4. 4.
[3] *L.P. Henry VIII*, vi. 1460 n.
[4] Maidstone, P.R.C. 3. 8, f. 82b.
[5] R. J. Mitchell, 'English Law Students at Bologna in the Fifteenth Century', *E.H.R.*, vol. li (1936), p. 282.
[6] Reg. Warham, f. 356.
[7] Ibid., f. 356b.
[8] Ibid., f. 362b.

| Proctor | Consistory Court | Archdeacon's Court |
|---|---|---|
| M. Henry Woods (P.N.). | 1489–1501 | 1489–1501 |
| Coyn. | 1493 | 1493?–1500 |
| M. William Mody, ll.b. (P.N.). V. of St. Mary de Castro, Canterbury, adm. 4 July 1498,[1] then adm. as R.[2] V. of Bredgar, adm. 1508.[3] | 1493–5 | 1493?–1500 and 1505–8 |
| M. John Knyght, m.a. (P.N.). R. of Wittersham, adm. 1512.[4] | 1497/8–1524/5 | From before 1500–1507 |
| Talbot. | 1502–3 | |
| M. Stephen Galle. R. of St. Mildred's, Canterbury, in 1508.[5] | 1504–8 | 1504–6 and 1510–1511 |
| 'Dominus' Richard Knepe. R. of All Saints, Canterbury, in 1512.[6] | 1511–25/6 | 1512–21 |
| Grey. | 1513–14 | |
| 'Dominus' John Swan. Chaplain of St. Peter's, Thanet, in 1515.[7] | 1514–18 | 1514–17 |
| M. John Some. Noted as apparitor general in 1520, also as V. of Harbledown.[8] | 1516–28 | 1516–after 1523 |
| M. William Wigmore, b.c.l. | 1517–after 1535 | 1517–after 1523 |
| Ralph White. | 1520–2 | 1520 |
| Fairbairn (P.N.). | 1522 | |
| M. Thomas Laurence (junior) | 1523–after 1535 | 1521– after 1535 |
| Robert Colyns, b.c.l. V. of Lympne, adm. 1524.[9] | 1524 | |
| M. John Webbe, m.a. V. of Elham in 1506,[10] elected dean of Elham 1521.[11] R. of Alkham, adm. 1518.[12] | 1524 | 1514 |
| M. John Cokkes (Oxon.). | 1525–after 1535 | |
| M. Thomas Cokkes, b.can.l. Chantry chaplain, Brenchley Chantry, Canterbury Cathedral, in 1533.[13] R. of Little Mongeham, adm. 1528, vac. 1530.[14] | 1527–after 1535 | 1527–after 1535 |
| John Hay, ll.b. | 1528–32 | |
| Trott. | 1533–after 1535 | |
| Percy. | 1533–after 1535 | |

[1] Reg. Morton, ii, f. 159b.  [2] Ibid., f. 165b.  [3] Reg. Warham, f. 333.
[4] Reg. Warham, f. 374b.  [5] Z. 3. 22, f. 7.  [6] Z. 3. 4, f. 87.  [7] Z. 3. 3.
[8] Z. 3. 4.  [9] Reg. Warham, f. 383b.  [10] Z. 3. 2.  [11] Z. 3. 4, f. 35b.
[12] Reg. Warham, f. 366b.  [13] Y. 2. 13, f. 130.  [14] Reg. Warham, ff. 397 and 401b.

*Proctors found practising in Archdeacon's Court only,* 1477–1535

| Proctors | Archdeacon's Court |
|---|---|
| M. RICHARD WILLEFORDS, LL.B. Later, archdeacon's official in 1502 (q.v.). | Before 1477 until ? |
| COLYN. | 1479–84 |
| DIXON. | 1508–10 |
| JOHN MILLET, D.CAN.L. (Oxon.). R. of Chadwood, adm. 1494.[1] | 1509–11 |
| VERTUE. | 1513–14 |
| ADAM. | 1517 |
| M. RICHARD HEWES, alias ap. HOWELL, B.CAN.L. (Oxon.). V. of Thornham, ind. 1516/17.[2] Elected dean of Sutton 1521.[3] V. of Stockbury, ind. 29 March 1522.[4] | 1515–after 1522 |
| BROKER. | 1520/1–1522 |
| STONE. | 1525–9 |

# II. COMMISSION OF REGISTRAR OF CONSISTORY COURT (*see* Text, p. 39)

*Archbishop Chichele appoints William Bold, 1442*

*Reg. S, f. 149b*

Henricus permissione divina Cantuar' Archiepiscopus totius Anglie primas et apostolice sedis legatus dilecto in Christo filio Willelmo Bolde clerico salutem, gratiam et benedictionem. De tuis fidelitate et industria plene confidentes officium ac custodiam registrorum consistorii nostri Cantuar' tibi committimus et conferimus ac te registrarium dicti nostri Consistorii deputamus et preficimus per presentes habendum et tenendum et exercendum dictum officium ac custodiam eiusdem ad terminum vite tue cum proficiis et commoditatibus eiusdem officii et custodie ex antiquo debitis et consuetis. In cuius rei testimonium sigillum meum presentibus apposuimus. Datum in manerio nostro de Croydon vicesimo quinto die mensis Maii anno domini millesimo cccc[mo] xlii et nostre translationis anno xxix[mo].

---

[1] Reg. Morton, ii, f. 156; place not identified.
[2] Z. 3. 22, f. 47b.        [3] Z. 3. 4, f. 25b.        [4] Ibid., f. 56b.

## III. *SEDE VACANTE* COMMISSION OF APPARITOR GENERAL OF CITY AND DIOCESE (*see* Text, p. 47)

*The prior and chapter appoint John Taylor, 1500*

*Reg. R, f. 41b*

[Margin] Commissio generalis apparitoris
in diocesi Cant'

Thomas permissione divina prior ecclesie Christi Cant' et eiusdem loci capitulum ad quos omnis et omnimodo iurisdictio spiritualis et ecclesiastica que ad Archiepiscopum Cant' pertinet sede plena ipsa sede iam vacante dinoscitur notorie pertinere dilecto nobis in Christo filio Johanni Taylor literato salutem in domino. De tua fidelitate plenius confidentes te in apparitorem nostrum generalem iuratum preficimus per presentes tibique ad citandum quascumque personas ecclesiasticas religiosos seu seculares tam clericos quam laicos cuiuscunque preeminencie condicionis seu status existant civitatis et diocesis Cant' ad apparendum coram nobis vel loca nostra tenentibus Auditoribus aut Commissariis in quibuscumque causis negociis et litibus ex officio nostro mero seu promoto vel ad partis instanciam motis et movendis necnon quibuscumque excessibus criminibus et delictis cuiuscunque persone vel quarumcunque personarum huiusmodi commissis et committendis quorum cognicio diffinicio et punicio ad forum ecclesiasticum et nos seu nostram iurisdiccionem durante vacacione predicta pertinent seu quousmodo debeant aut poterint pertinere de consuetudine vel de iure responsura ac insuper bona quorumcumque ex testamento vel ab intestato decedencium infra civitatem et diocesim Cant' tempore mortis sive obtinencium sequestrandum ac eciam ad citandum quoscumque administratores seu huiusmodi bonorum occupatores ad comparendum coram nobis aut nostro in hac parte Commissario sive Commissariis de et super administracione et occupacione bonorum huiusmodi responsura testamenta et ultimas voluntates defunctorum huiusmodi realiter exhibitura nosque et loca nostra tenentes causarumque et negociorum auditores et Commissarios quoscumque in ea parte fideliter certificandos ac omnia et singula pro te vel sufficienter deputatum tuum vel deputatos exercendumque in premissis vel circa ea necessaria fuerunt vel oportuna atque ad officium apparitoris huiusmodi pertinere noscuntur pleno tenore presencium committimus potestatem donec eam ad nos duxerimus revocandam. Datum Cant' sub sigillo nostro communi ad causas vicesimo die mensis Septembris anno domini millesimo quingentesimo.

## IV. DISPOSAL OF INSTANCE CASES: CONSISTORY COURT (*see* Text, p. 59)

| Year | Total No. of cases introduced | Libel ordered in | Assignation to hear sentence in | Witnesses produced in |
|---|---|---|---|---|
| 1416 | 195 | 51 | 4 | 17 |
| 1482 | 636 | 152 | 12 | 15 |
| 1486 | 693 | 189 | 7 | 19 |
| 1499 | 350 | 132 | 19 | 16 |
| 1511 | 198 | 76 | 4 | 12 |
| 1522 | 223 | 68 | 7 | 18 |
| 1535 | 93 | 36 | 5 | 9 |

## V. *ACTA* OF A CASE HEARD IN THE CONSISTORY COURT 1497, AND BILL OF COSTS IN SAME SUIT (*see* Text, p. 61)

*Y. 1. 17, f. 118b*, under date Tuesday 18 May

[Margin] Executores Forde contra Bounse.

In causa testamentaria Ricardi a Forde mota per Willelmum a Forde executorem etc Johannis a Forde contra Rogerum Bounsse de Molyshe citatum litteratorie actrice per Knyght ut in actis reo per Ganton in actis ad libellandum in proximo et taxate expense certificatorii ad viii d, xxviii° Maii Knyght dedit libellum ad respondendum in proximo, xix^{mo} Iunii. Ganton' contestatus est libellus negative. Ad primo producendum in proximo, x^{mo} Iulii datum ad secundo producendum in proximo et repetito libello reo Iudex decrevit partem principalem erga proximum, ultimo Iulii Ingram' certificavit et Iudex taxavit expensas certificatorii ad vi d. et datum ad tercio producendum in proximum, reus non comparuit, suspensus, xviii° Septembris comparuit pars principalis et iuravit de fide iuris posita viii° Octobris datum ad proponendum omnia in proximum, penultimo Octobris Knyght exhibuit omnia acta etc. in presencia Ganton' nihil exhibentis, ad concludendum in proximo, xx^{imo} Novembris Colman substitutus Knyght concludebat in dies in presencia Ganton tacentis, ad sentenciandum in proximo xviii^{mo} Decembris lata fuit sentencia diffinitiva in prefata causa a qua Ganton appellavit et datum ei ad recipiendum apostolos in proximo v^{to} Februarii Iudex ad peticionem Knyght decrevit partem vocandam fore ad dicendum causam quare sentencie non debet execucio demandari et ad audiendum taxationem expensarum in proximo etc. xix^mo Februarii taxavit expensas omnium ad xx s. solvendos in festa annunciationis beate Marie sancti Johannis Baptiste et sancti Michaelis per equales porciones. xxiiii^to Octobris anno domini millesimo cccc° Knyght peciit processum in presentia Ganton allegantis suspensionem iudicii per arbitrium et habet ad probandum in proximo xiiii Novembris, reus non paret, excommunicatus est.

*Y. 1. 17, at f. 48b*

## Bill of Costs 1498

[Slip of vellum, 10 in. by 3 in.]

Expense facte in quadam causa testamentaria mota ex parte executoris Ricardi a Forde defuncti contra Rogerum Bunse de Molassh.

| | |
|---|---:|
| In primis pro littera citacionis in scriptis | iiii d |
| Item pro certificatorio eiusdem | viii d |
| Item pro introduccione et dimissione cause | vi d |
| Item pro libellis | ii s. i d |
| Item pro decreto pro parte principali | viii d |
| Item pro certificatorio eiusdem | vi d |
| Item pro littera suspensionis | iiii d |
| Item pro examinacione partis principalis | xii d |
| Item pro copiis eiusdem | xii d |
| Item pro sententia diffinitiva in dicta causa | vii s. viii d |
| Item pro littera execucionis eiusdem sententie | viii d |
| Item pro certificatorio eiusdem | viii d |
| Item pro salario procuratoris pro xii diebus | vi s |
| Item pro scriptura cedule taxacionis expensarum | iii d |
| Summa—xxii s. v d. | |

xix Februarii Iudex taxavit expensas ad xx s solvendas in festis annunciationis beate Marie sancti Johannis et sancti Michaelis proximis per equales porciones.

## VI. DOCUMENTS IN TUITORIAL APPEAL
### (*see* Text, p. 65)

This appendix contains the complete 'process' of a case between the rector of the Canterbury 'schools' and the rector of St. Martin's concerning the number of scholars that the latter could maintain in his own establishment.[1]

[1] Cf. the account in C. E. Woodruff and H. T. Cape, *History of the King's School, Canterbury*, pp. 28–29. Some of the documents in this case are printed in Somner, Part 1, Appendix, pp. 33–35.

This appendix illustrates (*a*) the operation of the preliminary *provocatio* of a tuitorial appeal, and (*b*) the 'inhibition' dispatched from the provincial court to the inferior court. The documents in this case have been rearranged in a more logical order.

## Reg. I, f. 397*b*[1]

Acta et processus super statu scolarum ecclesie Sancti Martini iuxta Cantuar' coram magistro Roberto de Mallingg generali Commissario Cant' primo viva voce et postea per specialem commissionem domini W. Archiepiscopi A.D. 1321 inter magistrum Radulphum de Waltham Rectorem scolarum civitatis Cant' et magistrum Robertum de Henneye Rectorem ecclesie Sancti Martini iuxta Cantuariam.

## Commissio

Walterus permissione divina Cant' Archiepiscopus tocius Anglie Primas dilecto filio Commissario nostro Cant' salutem, graciam et benediccionem. Cum nuper tibi precepimus viva voce ut in negocio tangente magistrum Radulphum rectorem scolarum grammaticalium civitatis nostre Cant' et magistrum Robertum rectorem ecclesie Sancti Martini iuxta Cantuariam ac eiusdem loci rectorem scolarum ex officio auctoritate nostra procederes, et inquisita veritate idem negocium debito fine terminares, dictum negocium de quo miramur adhuc coram te pendet indecisum. Quocirca tibi committimus et mandamus quatinus ulterius in dicto negocio auctoritate predicta procedere et finem sentenciando previa racione celeritate qua poteris inponere non omittas. Dat' Cantuar'. iii° Non. Januar' A.D. 1321/2 (3 Jan.)

## Inquisicio

Dominus Ricardus Rector ecclesie de Moncketone
Dominus Galfridus Vicarius ecclesie de Chyleham
Dominus Stephanus de Wyk
Dominus Nicholaus capellanus Sancti Sepulcri
Dominus Theobaldus Vicarius ecclesie Sancti Pauli
Dominus Simon Rector ecclesie Sancte Marie de Castro
Dominus Thomas Rector ecclesie Sancti Petri
Dominus Johannes Rector ecclesie Omnium Sanctorum
Dominus Johannes Rector ecclesie Sancti Michaelis
Magister Robertus de Honynton
Alexander de elemosinaria
Johannes le taillour
Symon ate Fermerie

1 Transcribed by the late W. P. Blore, who translated the dates into Arabic figures.

Johannes de Stablegate
Johannes de Strode
Robertus de Sancto Martino.

The verdict is written at the right hand of the list of names:

Iurati dicunt quod non debent esse plures grammatici in scolis Sancti Martini nisi xiii et hoc se dicunt scire ex relatu bonorum et fide dignorum ab antiquo et dicunt quod semper consuevit Rector scolarum Cantuar' scolas Sancti Martini per se vel suos propter numerum scolarium visitare. Dicunt eciam quod quando hostiarius vel submonitor scolarium Cantuar' propter numerum scolarium scolas Sancti Martini visitavit, scolares Sancti Martini absconderunt se usque ad numerum xiii et hoc se dicunt scire ex relatu fide dignorum ab antiquo. De aliis scolaribus in scolis Sancti Martini, alphabetum, psalterium et cantum addiscentibus: non est certus numerus limitatus ut dicunt.

Now follows the definitive sentence of the commissary general:

*f. 398.* Sentencia diffinitiva.

In dei nomine amen. Cum nuper inter magistrum Radulphum rectorem scolarum Civitatis Cantuar' ad collacionem venerabilis patris domini W. dei gracia Cant' Archiepiscopi tocius Anglie primatis spectancium, et Magistrum Robertum de Henneye rectorem ecclesie Sancti Martini iuxta Cant' et eiusdem loci scolarum rectorem ad dictam ecclesiam Sancti Martini de patronatu eiusdem existencium pertinencium, super eo quod idem magister Radulphus pretendebat dictum magistrum scolarum Sancti Martini habere deberet in scolis suis xiii scolares in grammatica erudiendos dumtaxat idemque magister scolarum Sancti Martini omnes indistincte ad scolas confluentes in preiudicium scolarum civitatis predicte et contra consuetudinem admittere et in suis scolis tenere et docere in grammatica presumpsit orta fuisset materia questionis, tandem dictus venerabilis pater utriusque loci patronus et diocesanus nobis commissario suo Cant' generali, tam vive vocis oraculo quam subsequenter litteratorie huiusmodi questionem seu negocium per viam inquisicionis ex officio commisit fine debito terminandum. Nos igitur Commissarius predictus magistros utrarumque scolarum predictarum et Rectorem ecclesie Sancti Martini predicte coram nobis fecimus evocari, et super dicto negocio viros fidedignos clericos specialiter iuratos inquiri fecimus diligenter.

Qua inquisicione facta publicata et dictis magistris et Rectori copia decreta nichil dicto contra inquisicionem vel probato, set ad audiendam pronunciacionem nostram die eisdem prefixo, quia nos Commissarius antedictus invenimus quod magister scolarum Sancti Martini xiii scolares dumtaxat in grammatica per ipsarum scolarum magistrum

quicumque fuerit docendos habere et tenere ac docere debet ex consuetudine ab antiquo; illam consuetudinem auctoritate nobis in hac
parte commissa decernimus observandam, inhibentes magistro scolarum Sancti Martini ne plures scolares ultra numerum predictum in
suis scolis in grammatica docendos admittat decetero, nec consuetudinem predictam infringere presumat quoquo modo.

Ab ista sentencia predictus magister Robertus appellavit ad sedem
apostolicam et pro tuicione Curie Cantuar'. Et quia pars appellans
appellacionem suam prefate Curie Cant' suggestam sufficienter prout
debuit non probavit, pars appellata dimissa fuit ab examine dicte Curie
Cant' per litteram subscriptam.

But, first, the Appeal (recited in the Inhibition from the Court of
Canterbury):

*f. 393b.* Appellacio Suggestio et Citacio in causa scolarum Cantuar'
et Sancti Martini.

Officialis Curie Cant' discreto viro magistro Roberto de Malling
Commissario Cant' generali salutem in auctore salutis. Ex parte
magistri Roberti de Henneye Rectoris [*f. 394*] ecclesie Sancti Martini
Cant' nobis extitit intimatum quod cum ipse ac predecessores seu predecessores sui Rectores in ecclesia predicta omnes et singuli temporibus
suis a tempore cuius contrarii memoria non existit fuerint et adhuc sit
idem magister Robertus de Hanneye nomine suo et ecclesie sue predicte in possessione vel quasi iuris habendi scolas grammaticales in
dicta ecclesia Sancti Martini, seu infra septa eiusdem, magistrosque ad
informandum et instruendum in arte grammaticali quoscumque illuc
ea de causa accedentes ibidem preficiendi seu deputandi et eos libere
admittendi informandi et instruendi in arte grammaticali predicta. Ex
parte magistri Roberti de Henneye in possessione vel quasi iuris huiusmodi ut premittitur existentis, ac metuentis ex quibusdam causis
probabilibus et verisimilibus coniecturis grave sibi et ecclesie sue predicte circa premissa preiudicium posse generari in futurum, ne quis
circa premissa vel eorum aliquod quicquam in ipsius vel ecclesie sue
predicte preiudicium attemptaret seu faceret aliqualiter attemptari; ad
sedem apostolicam et pro tuicione Curie Cant' extitit ut asseritur palam
et publice ac legitime provocatum. Set vos ad instanciam seu procura-
ciones cuiusdam Radulfi magistri scolarum Cant' se pretendentis
provocacione predicta que vos verisimiliter non latebat non obstante,
post et contra eam, predictum magistrum Robertum de Henneye
quominus possessione sua huiusmodi libere gaudere potuit, contra
iusticiam molestastis inquietastis ac multipliciter perturbastis, ac tresdecim scolares dumtaxat in dictis scolis ecclesie Sancti Martini et non
plures admitti debere minus veraciter pretendentes, cuidam magistro

Johanni de Bucwell Magistro scolarum huiusmodi per dictum magistrum Robertum de Henneye prefecto seu deputato ne ultra tresdecim scolares huiusmodi inhiberi admitteret seu haberet inhibuistis minus iuste in ipsius magistri Roberti de Henneye et ecclesie sue predicte preiudicium dampnum non modicum et gravamen. Unde ex parte eiusdem magistri Roberti sencientis se et ecclesiam suam predictam ex hiis et eorum quolibet per vos indebite pregravari ad dictas sedem et curiam extitit ut asseritur legitime appellatum. Quare vobis inhibemus et per vos omnibus et singulis quibus ius exigit inhiberi, volumus et mandamus ut pendente in Curia Cant' huiusmodi tuitorie appellacionis negocio quicquam hac occasione in dicte partis appellantis preiudicium attemptetis vel attemptent faciatis aut faciant aliqualiter attemptari quominus liberam habeat appellacionis sue prosecucionem prout iustum fuerit utriusque. Citetis eciam seu citari faciatis peremptorie dictum Radulphum partem ut premittitur appellatam quod compareat coram nobis vel nostro commissario in ecclesia beate Marie de Aldermani cherche London' sexto die iuridico post festum (f. 394*b*) Sancti Martini yemalis in dicto tuitorie appellacionis negocio processurus facturus et recepturus quod iusticia sua debebit. De die vero recepcionis presencium et quid in premissis feceritis nos vel nostrum commissarium dictis die et loco certificetis per litteras vestras patentes harum seriem continentes. Dat' London' xii° Kalen' Novembr' A.D. 1323 (21 Oct.).

Then follows the letter of Remission, following the failure of the Appeal.

*f. 395.* Littera dimissionis Decani de Arcubus London' in causa tuitoria et appellacionis inter magistrum Robertam Rectorem ecclesie Sancti Martini et magistrum Radulphum magistrum scolarum Civitatis Cantuar'.

Thomas de Chereministr' Curie Cant' examinator generalis, domini officialis eiusdem Curie in ipsius et domini . . . Decani ecclesie beate Marie de Arcubus London Commissar' sui general' absencia Commissar' discreto viro magistro Roberto de Mallingg' Commissario Cant' generali salutem in auctore salutis. Cum nos in tuitorie appellacionis negocio quod in dicta curia vertebatur inter magistrum Robertum de Henneye Rectorem ecclesie Sancti Martini partem ut suggeritur appellantem ex parte una et magistrum Radulfum magistrum scolarum Cantuar' partem appellatam ex altera legitime procedent' dictam partem appellatam eo quod pars appellans predictam appellacionem suam prefate curie in hac parte suggest' prout debuit non probavit, ab examine dicte curie duxerimus dimittendam tenore presencium vobis intimamus quod inhibicione quacumque sub dat' London' xii

Kalen' Novembr' A.D. 1323 a Curia Cantuar' in hac parte impetrata, et vobis directa non obstante libere poteritis exequi quod est vestrum. Dat' London' xiii Kalen' Aprilis, anno domini supradicto (20 March 1323/4).

A further document concludes the material relating to this case:

*S.V. 3,p. 40*, Confirmation, dated Charing, 2 Ides November, 1326 (12 Nov.), of sentence by the archbishop, who confirms report of case by commissary, the latter dated 6 Ides August 1324 (8 August).

## VII. A GENERAL *PROVOCATIO* (See Text, p. 67)

*The prior and chapter publish a general 'provocatio' to uphold their 'Sede Vacante' jurisdiction as soon as they hear of the death of Archbishop Pecham, 1292*

*Reg. Q. f. 1*[1]

Provocacio generalis de iurisdiccione, sede vacante. In dei nomine amen. Cum sancta Cant' ecclesia inter alia sue nobilitatis insignia prerogativa gaudeat speciali quod omnibus ecclesiis tam cathedralibus quam aliis Cant' provincie ac dyocesis preesse iure metropolitico dinoscitur, ac primatibus ipsius ecclesie Cant' prelati et alii dictarum dyocesis et provincie subesse debeant prout hactenus subfuerunt, iurisdiccionemque omnimodum in subditos tam dyocesis quam provincie Archiepiscopi qui pro tempore fuerint exercuerint et exerceant sede plena racione ipsius ecclesie seu faciant exerceri, necnon Prior et Capitulum ipsius ecclesie Cant' ipsa ecclesia pastoris solacio destituta exercuerint et exerceant racione ipsius ecclesie seu faciant exerceri in casibus in quibus iurisdiccio ad dictam Cant' ecclesiam in subditos provincie et dyocesis racione sue metropolitice potestatis tam de consuetudine quam de iure dinoscitur pertinere. In cuiuscumque possessione exercicii iurisdiccionis antedicte tam venerabiles patres qui pro tempore fuerint sede plena ac eciam prefati Prior et Capitulum ipsius ecclesie nomine dum vacaret fuerunt et sunt a tempore cuius non existit memoria pacifice et quiete, sintque violatores libertatum ipsius ecclesie maioris excommunicacionis sentencia a diversis patribus tam ipsius ecclesie quam aliis in ipsos lata canonice innodati, quidam tamen qui ipsam ecclesiam deberent filiali affeccione prosequi tamquam matrem in prefatam excommunicacionis sentenciam in sue salutis dispendium incidere non verendo spiritum rebellionis et audaciam malignandi perperam contra memoratam ecclesiam metropoliticam assumentes quod ipsam ecclesiam et priorem et capitulum ipsius nomine

[1] Transcript by the late W. P. Blore.

sede Cant' vacante intendunt gravare circa iurisdiccionem antedictam,
et eius exercicium ac possessionem exercicii iurisdiccionis antedicte
sint publice sepius comminati, conventiculas illicitas de advocatis et
aliis Lond' et alibi facientes et procurantes conspirationesque excogitantes cordaque et voluntates quorundam qui dictam ecclesiam
proposuerunt prout de iure ad hoc tenentur pro viribus defensare suis
persuasionibus illicitis pervertere non omittentes aliosque modos diver-
sos in dies excogitantes per quos dictam ecclesiam in suis iuribus et
libertatibus ledere valeant ac gravare, licet publicum sit et notorium
apud sedem apostolicam litem adhuc pendere indecisam dictis priore
et capitulo semper existentibus in possessione pacifica iurisdiccionis
exercicii antedicte, non attendentes quod lite pendente nichil debeat
innovari et quod litigantes in ipsa sede apostolica pendente lite inibi
indecisa sub proteccione ipsius sedis existentes in personis capi non
debeant sive rebus; hinc est quod ego[1] procurator religiosorum virorum
prioris et capituli Cant' ecclesie coniiciens ex premissis et ex aliis verisimilibus et probabilibus coniecturis posse prefatis dominis meis ecclesie
Cant' circa premissa et alia fieri preiudicium in futurum quod tales
iniquitatis filii contra dictos dominos meos et eorum ecclesiam insur-
gant fortius in gravamen, ne quis cuiuscunque dignitatis condicionis
aut ordinis existat per se vel alium vel alios eiusdem nomine vice vel
mandato super predictis iuribus iurisdiccione et possessione dominos
meos predictos quoquo modo molestare turbare vel inquietare, aut ipsos
aut eorum officiales seu ministeriales sede Cant' vacante super premissis impedire presumat seu facere attemptet vel procuret circa premissa
seu eorum aliquid (*f. 1b*) seu quovis alio modo quod in dictorum
dominorum meorum preiudicium ledere valeat sive dampnum aliqualiter attemptare, sacrosanctam sedem apostolicam et pro tuicione
Curie Cant' sive ipsam sedem apostolicam directe prout in prosecucione
michi seu dictis dominis meis videbitur oportunum nomine eorundem
et cuiuslibet eorum in hiis scriptis provoco et appello et apostolos peto
quantum ad presens incumbet michi eorundem peticio in hac parte.
Et ne quis in me seu eosdem dominos meos ecclesiam predictam iura
iurisdiccionem libertates possessiones ac statum eorundem clericos
advocatos procuratores consiliarios et eisdem assistentes adherentes et
faventes terras redditus seu loca eorundem suspensionis excommunicacionis seu interdicti sentencias proferre presumat aut procuret preferri
memoratam sedem apostolicam ut supra appello protestans me velle
nomine dominorum meorum premissas provocaciones seu appellaciones
innovare ac eciam de novo si necesse fuerit appellare nec non apostolos
petere congruis loco et tempore coram personis coram quibus ius
premissa fieri exiget et requirit. Supponens dictos dominos meos et

---

[1] The name is not filled in.

ecclesiam Cant' iura et libertates ipsius advocatos procuratores nec non omnes alios eisdem aliqualiter adherentes pro quibus omnibus sub forma prius annotata provoco et appello bonaque eorundem et eisdem adherencium proteccioni et defensioni predictarum sedium seu sedis apostolice antedicte.

The register continues:

Publicatis vero provocacionibus seu appellacionibus predictis statim fratrem Robertum monachum ecclesie predicte Officialem Curie Cant' constituerunt per litteras suas patentes tenorem qui sequitur continentes.

## VIII. INSTRUCTIONS FOR EX OFFICIO CITATION, *circa* 1509 (*See* Text, p. 70)

*Maidstone, P.R.C. 3. 3, inserted at f. 58*

Cranebroke.

Cyte a woman with child in the house of Thomas Low
 Also cite Robert Donke dwellyng with John Brad
 Cite Thomas Barrow which is defamed with
 many women\Johanna Edwards (          )[1] Marley/
 Cite Stephyn Elys\notatur cum Johanna Offore (          )/
 Cite Agnes Sympson Wedow
 Cite William Reade\and a woman/[2]
 Cite John Albon of benynden
 Cite the wiff of one Doksowte
 Cite Thomas Taylour
          Benynden
 Cite the Vicar of Benynden
 Cite John Rolf
          Cite John Mills

## IX. EXERCISE OF THE PREROGATIVE JURISDICTION (*See* Text, p. 74)

*'Sede Vacante' commission to commissary general, A.D.1500, indicating his exercise of the archbishop's prerogative jurisdiction within the diocese. The prior and chapter appoint John Williamson, 22 Sept. 1500.*

*Reg. R., f. 41*

[Margin] Commissio Commisariatus Cant' generalis

Thomas permissione divina Prior ecclesie Christi Cant' et eiusdem loci Capitulum ad quos omnis et omnimodo iurisdiccio spiritualis et ecclesiastica que ad Archiepiscopum Cant' pertinuit sede plena ipsa

---

[1] Round brackets indicate word illegible.     [2] This line is crossed through.

sede iam vacante dinoscitur notorie pertinere dilecto nobis in Christo
magistro Johanni Williamson in decretis bacallario salutem in domino.
Ad cognoscendum et procedendum in quibuscumque causis beneficiali-
bus matrimonialibus et divorciis et nullitatis matrimonii necnon in
omnibus causis et negociis ecclesiasticis inter seu contra subditos nostros
nostrarum civitatis et diocesis Cantuar' qualitercumque motis seu
movendis aut in Consistorio Cant' indecisis pendentibus eas et ea fine
debito et canonico terminandum et finiendum necnon ad inquirendum
et corrigendum puniendum et debito restrinandum crimina excessus
et defectus quorumcumque subditorum civitatis et diocesis antedictarum
ac pro huiusmodi criminibus defectibus et excessibus penas et peniten-
tias canonicas infligendum et iniungendum ac insuper ad confirman-
dum et approbandum testamenta et ultimas voluntates quarumcumque
personarum dicte civitatis et diocesis et aliarum eciam habencium bona
in diversis diocesibus Cant' provincie ita quod diocesis Cant' sit una in
quibus bona huiusmodi existunt et ibidem decedant probationesque
legitimas de et super eisdem recipiendum et admittendum admini-
strationemque bonorum huiusmodi eciam ab intestato decedentium
committendum ac bona et debita huiusmodi auctoritate ordinaria si
oporteat in casibus a iure permissis sequestrandum ac compotum calcu-
lum sive ratiocinium administrationis bonorum huiusmodi recipiendum
et audiendum ac administratores huiusmodi bonorum dimittendum,
Archidiacono et eius Officiali ac aliis quibuscumque qui nostram
iurisdiccionem violare perturbare impugnare seu impedire presument
inhibendum inhiberi ve faciendum ac per censuras ecclesiasticas coher-
cendum et compellendum. Necnon ad faciendum et expediendum omnia
alia et singula que ad cognicionem et officium Commissarii Generalis
civitatis et diocesis Cant' de iure vel consuetudine spectare et pertinere
noscuntur et que in premissis et circa ea necessaria fuerunt vel eciam
oportuna vobis vices nostras committimus cum cuiuslibet censure eccle-
siastice potestate donec eam ad nos duxerimus revocandam. Datum in
domo nostro capitulari sub sigillo nostro de communi ad causas vicesimo
secundo die mensis Septembris anno domini millesimo quingentesimo.

## X. DOCUMENTS IN DEFAMATION SUIT (See p. 88)

ARCHDEACON'S COURT, 1517, 'JOHN BULL v. WILLIAM FLAWNE'

(i) *Y. 2. 7, f. 115*, under date 18 June 1517, the court in session at
Sittingbourne.

In causa diffamatoria Iohannis Bull de Newenton contra Willelmum Flawne de eadem citatum per Gilis actum per Some iudicialiter
rea personaliter ad libellandum in proximo et rea constituit Hews et
Wigmore iudicialiter xxix Julii Some in presencia Hewes et Wigmore

dedit libellum ad respondendum in proximo xxiii Sept. Wigmore con-
testavit litem negative protestans de ineptia libelli ad primo producendum in proximo vii Oct. ad secundo producendum in proximo; quarta
Novembris Some in presencia Wigmore et Hews produxit Johannem
Strongbow et Johannem Godard in testes admissos iuratos Hews protestante et ad tercio producendum in proximo et Hews ministravit
interrogatoria tercia Decembris dismissa per partes.

(ii) *Letter* written on behalf of John Bull by Henry Fynche an under-
sheriff (loose, preserved in Act book Y. 2. 7).

To the Ryght Wurshepfull Maister Officiall this be deliveryd.
After all dew recomendacion had etc. besecheyng youe to be gud
maister to the berer of this bill in suche causes as hee sewyth byfore
youe for I dare depose uppon a boke those persons that hee hathe in
sewte wold have hanged hym on this day yf I had nott been undersheryff this yere for they had indited him of felony and that ipocrite
with hys swete tonge William Flawnne sewyd hym for steling of a
beste of hys and had hym condempned and when hee was payde for
his boloke then hyt was founden in Byngley and so hee hath the money
and the beste also I knowell this John Bull has been in sewte some
tyme butt yff youe knewe howe he hathe been delte wyth youe wold
marveyle, hee ys a pooer kynsman of my wyff and if hee schulde be
overlede wyth wronge I wold be sory wherfore I beseche youe at my
pooer instance to be gud maister to hym in hys Rygth for ther ys
neyther Sir William Croumer neyther Sir John Norton[1] butt they
know the diffimacion of that William Flawnne very well as knowyth
god whoo ever kepe youe. Scribillyd at Milton the iiide day of November in hast.

Your own
Henry fynche
Undersheryff.

## XI. AN EXPENSE ACCOUNT (*See* Text, p. 106)

'*Acta*' of a case brought by the churchwardens of St. Dunstan's into the
Consistory Court, 5 July 1490, and their account of the expenses

*Y. 1. 15, f. 257b*

[Margin] Vicarius ac iconomi Sancti Dunstani
Cantuar' contra Johannam Baker.
Warde
Richardson[2]

In causa subtractionis iuris ecclesie mota per dominum Ricardum
Long vicarium ac Ricardum Denyse et Johannem Long iconomos

---

[1] Probably Justices of the Peace.　　　　　　　　　[2] The proctors.

ecclesie parochie Sancti Dunstani Cant' contra Johannam Baker relictâm Willelmi Belsyr nuper de eadem citatam litteratorie actore per Warde iudicialiter constitutum reo per Richardson ut in actis, ad libellandum datur in proximo. xxvi$^{to}$ Iulii Warde in presencia Richardson dedit libellum, ad respondendum in proximo, xx$^{mo}$ Septembris Richardson in presencia Warde in ecclesia sancti Gregorii protestavit de ineptissimo libello etc. et contesta est litis negative, ad primo producendum in proximo, et in productione etiam termini Warde in presencia Richardson produxit Johannem Luton Willelmum Ball Johannem Cowper Johannem Sprotte et Johannem Thomas quos dominus admisit et iurare fecit, Richardson protestante si etc. xi$^{mo}$ Octobris Iudex publicavit de consensu parcium dicta testium et decrevit partibus copias ad contradicendum in proximo. Primo Decembris Richardson in presencia Warde dedit exceptiones contra testes quas petit admitti, quibus admissis, datur ad primo producendum in proximo.

*[Here the entry breaks off.]*

J. M. Cowper, 'Accounts of the Churchwardens of St. Dunstan's Canterbury', *Arch. Cant.*, vol. xvi, p. 299.

This is the ple of Jeffery Peke for his rent of a howse in Croker lane di. li. wax be yere.

| | |
|---|---|
| In primis for the somonyng of him | iiii d. |
| Item payde for the playnt entryng | iii d.[1] |
| Item payde for the recorde of the torney | ii d.[2] |
| Item to owr proctor of the Corte for ii days | xii d. |
| Item payde the nonsute of the Corte | iii d.[3] |

So the seyde Jeffere yeld hym to the Courte to pay the duty of vi yeris behynde.[4]

This is the ple of Wyllyam Belsers lone for iii kene that he had of the stocke of the Churche

| | |
|---|---|
| In primis for entryng of the playnt | iii d. |
| Item payde for the copy of the ple and the makyng of the byll to Master Fenex | vi d. |
| Item for the sytyng of her to the somner | x d. |
| Also we gave Master Ramsey a potell of wyne | vi d. |
| Item in expensis among the proctoris of the Cort for counseyle of the lybellis makyng serteyn times | viii d. |
| Item payde for the lybellis makyng | ii s. i d. |

---

[1] The *introductio*.  [2] The *constitutio procuratoris*?  [3] The *dimissio*.
[4] This case was probably heard in the Archdeacon's Court. No trace in contemporary Consistory Act books.

Item payde in the Cort to Colman[1]                                    i d.
Item payde to Master Veker a parte of the costis
that he made to the Comessary the proctoris of
Cort and the records for their dener                            ii s. iiii d.
Item payde the Cort day after All Hallown to
Mr. Colman                                                     ix s. iiii d.[2]
Item payde for sytyng of her ageyne                                 xvi d.
Item payde to owr proctowre of Cort for his
laboure                                                                v s.
Item payde for owr expensis vi Cort days                            viii d.
Item payde for the proxe that went to London                     ii s. i d.
Item payde to our proctowre at London                          iii s. iiii d.
Item payde for the coppy of the ple                                   vi d.
Item payde for myne expensis and my labor to London  iii s. iiii d.[3]
Item spent on Master Commyssary and offycyall                     iiii d.
                    S'm both pleys xxxvs ii d

[At end of the account for 1490/1]

xxx s is of the money recovered from executors of
Wyllyam Belser e.g. stocke of iii kene

1  The registrar of the Consistory Court.
2  Probably for the copy of the *attestationes* or depositions of the witnesses.
3  The business in London may have been to collect witnesses.

# BIBLIOGRAPHY

## I. MS. SOURCES (GENERAL)[1]

### DEAN AND CHAPTER LIBRARY, CANTERBURY

Descriptions of the collections contained in the Dean and Chapter Library are to be found in Hist. MSS. Commission, Reports, No. 5 (pp. 427–62), No. 8 (pp. 315–55), and No. 9 (pp. 72–129) by J. B. Sheppard; and *Various Collections*, i (pp. 205–81), by R. L. Poole. Catalogues and indexes to the collections are to be found in the Library.

### Collections consulted

Chartae Antiquae, particularly C. Ant. A 7*b* (the 'Boniface Roll' of 1259).
Christchurch Letters, 2 volumes.
Eastry Letters.
Shadwell MSS.
Scrapbooks A, B, and C.
Sede Vacante Scrapbooks 1, 2, and 3.
Portfolio 'Z'. (The contents of this do not figure in any printed report or description. The portfolio contains some early thirteenth-century documents in suits.)
Ecclesiastical Suit Rolls. Mostly thirteenth-century rolls of *acta* and 'processes' of suits heard in the Court of Canterbury. There are over 300 of these. They have not been noticed in any printed report or description.

Thirteenth-century documents of suits heard in the Consistory Court are scattered among the above eight collections, an unfortunate consequence of the piecemeal 'discovery' of the 'sede vacante' material during the nineteenth century. While the collections cannot now be rearranged, an index of papers in suits heard in both the Consistory Court and the Court of Canterbury is desirable. The Sede Vacante Scrapbooks are particularly rich in documents in ecclesiastical suits. No Act books survive for these vacancies.

### The Registers of the Prior and Chapter

All the pre-Reformation Registers were consulted, but particularly valuable for commissions of officials were those registers containing *sede vacante* material: Registers G, I, Q, R, S, T, and T2. Register Q is particularly valuable for the business of vacancies from 1292 to 1348. A complete transcript of this register by the late W. P. Blore has been deposited in the library.

### 'Literary' MSS.

Among this collection is MS. D. 8, a quarto vellum book which contains among other items:

(1) Forms of Procedure in Canon Law with table of contents (50 ff. and a further 7 ff. at the end).
(2) Customs of the Court of Canterbury (24 ff.).
The date of these two items is probably *c*. 1315.

---

[1] Excluding Act book series of both courts, *infra*, pp. 139–42.

LAMBETH PALACE LIBRARY. ARCHBISHOPS' REGISTERS

Unpublished Archbishops' Registers were consulted to ascertain details of appointments, benefices, &c., of the personnel of the courts. No pre-Reformation material relating to the diocesan courts survives at Lambeth.

PUBLIC RECORD OFFICE

Chancery (C. 85). Significations of Excommunications.

## II. MS. ACT BOOKS AND LOOSE PAPERS

RECORDS OF THE CONSISTORY AND ARCHDEACONRY COURTS

### (i) Dean and Chapter Library

Many of the Act books have been in the Dean and Chapter Library since the last years of the nineteenth century, but a large quantity of material was transferred from the Christchurch Gateway (employed as a depository by the Diocesan Registrar) in 1928. For a summary description of this material see C. E. Woodruff, 'Records of the Courts of the Archdeaconry and Consistory of Canterbury', *Archaeologia Cantiana*, vol. xli, pp. 89–105.

The records of the Consistory Court do not seem to have suffered any major losses since they were in the custody of William Somner, the Canterbury historian, who was registrar in the seventeenth century. He attributed the absence of records previous to the late fourteenth century to the destruction wrought by the rebels of 1381.[1] It was probably William Somner who went through the Act books noting interesting cases and writing notes in the margins.

### (ii) Kent County Record Office

Although the great bulk of the records of the old Canterbury Probate Registry, deposited in the Kenty County Record Office, concern the Probate and Administration of Wills, much non-probate material of the Archdeacon's Court is to be found among it, either as separate items or as entries in multi-purpose Act books. The Registers of Wills often provide information about officials of the courts. An accurate list of this material, compiled while the records were deposited at the Public Record Office, is available at the Kent County Record Office.

CHRONOLOGICAL SURVEY OF ACT BOOKS

Happy is the archivist who receives the contents of a diocesan registry in any kind of formal order. The Act books contained in the Dean and Chapter Library at Canterbury were given references as they came to hand and placed on shelves which vanished during the blitz of 1942. They defy any detailed kind of classification based on the type of business recorded in them. One book may contain only Instance *acta*. Another may contain a variety of *acta* recorded on different sessions of one or, sometimes, the two courts. The task

[1] Somner, p. 174.

of indexing and calendaring these books and the drawing up of lists of officials, proctors, witnesses, &c., would take a trained archivist ten years.

All modern scholars will be dead before a thousandth part of the *acta* of English ecclesiastical courts can be printed, so vast is their bulk. The printing of these records *in extenso* would be folly and the work of editing them for current use must of necessity be highly selective in character. This work would be greatly eased by the drawing up of *chronological* surveys of books and papers. The over-classification of this type of record according to preconceived ideas of ideal categories of ecclesiastical records is dangerous and liable to result in considerable delays in printing and editing. The documents of particular cases should be kept as integrated as possible, so that hunts through several classes of documents for beginnings and ends may be avoided. In this respect it is important that loose papers, which sometimes can be found bulging in great profusion from between the leaves of Act books, should not be 'tidied up'. It would be best to file them in boxes and to give the boxes and papers detailed cross-references to the pages of the parent Act book from which the papers came.

The following chart contains information regarding the Act books of pre-Reformation date surviving both at Canterbury and in the Kent County Record Office at Maidstone. In a chart of this character particular Act books may be found in more than one category. Loose papers still remain between the leaves of many of the Act books and have not been classified here. All the volumes are of paper except the Registers of Wills, which are of vellum. Unless under the heading 'Maidstone', the Act books are to be found in the Dean and Chapter Library at Canterbury.

## Consistory Court Act Books 1364–1536

| Canterbury Sessions Instance | Canterbury Sessions Ex Officio | Hythe, Romney, Dover Sessions | Maidstone, Register of Wills |
|---|---|---|---|
| Y. 1. 1<br>1372–5<br>(includes Sentences) | X. 1. 19<br>Fragments 1364 | | |
| Y. 1. 2<br>1398–9<br>(includes some Ex Officio) | X. 8. 1<br>1395–1410<br>(badly mutilated) | | P.R.C. 32. 1<br>1396–1455 |
| Y. 1. 4<br>1419–25 | | | |
| Y. 1. 3 (fair copy of Y. 1. 4 in part)<br>1415/6–1423 | | | |
| Y. 1. 5<br>1453/4–1457<br>(includes some Ex Officio and some Depositions) | X. 1. 1<br>1449–57<br>(includes Depositions) | | |

| *Canterbury Sessions Instance* | *Canterbury Sessions Ex Officio* | *Hythe, Romney, Dover Sessions* | *Maidstone, Register of Wills* |
|---|---|---|---|
| *Υ. 1. 7* | | | P.R.C. *32. 2* |
| 1459–63 | | | 1459–84 |
| *Υ. 1. 6* | | *X. 8. 3* | |
| 1463–68 | | 1462–8 | |
| | | (Instance, Ex Officio, and Probate) | |
| *Υ. 1. 8* | *Υ. 1. 11* | *Υ. 1. 10* | |
| 1468–74 | 1468–74 | 1468–78 | |
| | | (Instance, Ex Officio, and Probate) | |
| *Υ. 1. 12* | | | P.R.C. *32. 3* |
| 1474–9 | | | 1484–93 |
| *Υ. 1. 13* | | | |
| 1479–84/5 | | | |
| *Υ. 1. 14* | | | |
| 1484/5–1487/8 | | | |
| *Υ. 1. 15* | | | |
| 1487/8–1492 | | | |
| *Υ. 1. 16* | | Instance 'Acta' for | P.R.C. *32. 4* |
| 1492–6 | | 1494 included in | 1494–8 |
| | | *Υ. 2. 2* | |
| *Υ. 1. 17* | | | |
| 1496–8/9 | | | |
| *Υ. 1. 18* | | | P.R.C. *32. 5* |
| 1498/9–1500 | | | 1499–1500 |
| *Υ. 2. 2* | | | P.R.C. *32. 6* |
| 1500/1–1502/3 | | | 1500–1 |
| *Υ. 2. 1* | | | P.R.C. *32. 7* |
| 1503–5 | | | 1501–3 |
| *Υ. 2. 9* | | *Υ. 2. 8* | P.R.C. *32. 8* |
| 1505/6–8 | | 1504–9 | 1503–6 |
| | | (Instance only) | |
| *Υ. 2. 5* | | | P.R.C. *32. 10* |
| 1509–15 | | | 1509–11 |
| | | | P.R.C. *32. 11* |
| | | | 1511–15 |
| *Υ. 2. 6* | | *Υ. 2. 10* | P.R.C. *32. 12* |
| 1516–1520/1 | | 1515–1523/4 | 1515–20 |
| | | (Ex Officio, Instance, and Probate) | |
| *Υ. 2. 11* | | | P.R.C. *32. 13* |
| 1521 | | | 1519–23 |
| *Υ. 2. 12* | | | P.R.C. *32. 14* |
| 1521/2–1528 | | | 1524–27 |
| *Υ. 2. 13* | | | P.R.C. *32. 15* |
| 1528/9–1536 | | | 1527–37 |
| | | | P.R.C. *32. 16* |
| | | | 1533–4 |

*Other books, &c.*

Instance Depositions, 1410–21. *x. 10. 1.*
Maidstone, Wills in boxes, covering period 1450 to 1538: P.R.C. 16. 1; 2; 3; and 4.

### *Archdeacon's Court Act Books, 1476–1536*

| Canterbury Sessions. Instance | Canterbury Sessions. Ex Officio | Western Deaneries. Instance | Western Deaneries. Ex Officio and Probate | Deanery of Sandwich. Ex Officio, Probate, and Instance | Visitation Books |
|---|---|---|---|---|---|
| | (*All at* Maidstone) | *Y. 4. 2* 1476–84 (mutilated) | (*All at* Maidstone) | *Y. 4. 2* 1487–95 | Part of *X. 8. 2* for 1498 |
| *Y. 4. 3* 1499–1511 | *P.R.C. 3. 1* 1487–1503 | | | | |
| | *P.R.C. 3. 2* 1503–11 *P.R.C. 3. 4* 1511–21 | | *P.R.C. 3. 3* 1505–12 | | *Z. 3. 1* 1499 *Z. 3. 2*[1] 1501–8 |
| *Y. 2. 4* 1511–24 | *P.R.C. 3. 6* 1523–31 *P.R.C. 3. 8* 1531–9 | *Y. 2. 7* 1520–5 | *P.R.C. 3. 5* 1520–4 *P.R.C. 3. 7* 1524–31 | *Y. 4. 4* 1521–36 | *Z. 3. 3* 1514–16 *Z. 3. 4* 1520–3 |

1 Some of this has been printed by C. E. Woodruff, 'An Archidiaconal Visitation of 1502', *Arch. Cant.*, vol. xlvii (1935), pp. 13–54.

*Other books, &c.*

*Z. 3. 22.* Account Book of the Archdeacon's Receiver and Registrar, 1504–17.

P.R.C. 33. 1 (Maidstone), 'Register Wingham' for wills proved in exempt jurisdiction of Wingham, 1471–1546.

P.R.C. 17. 1–21 (Maidstone), Registers of Wills, continuous series, 1449–1538.

## III. PRINTED SOURCES

### (i) RELATING TO CANTERBURY AND TO KENT

*Eadmeri Historia*, Rolls Series, ed. M. Rule (1884).

GERVASE OF CANTERBURY, *Opera*, Rolls Series, ed. W. Stubbs, 2 vols. (1879–80).

*Registrum Epistolarum Johannis Peckham, Archiepiscopi Cantuariensis*, Rolls Series, ed. C. T. Martin, 3 vols. (1882–85).

*Register of Archbishop Winchelsey*, Canterbury and York Society, ed. R. Graham (1917–  ).

*Register of Archbishop Chichele*, Canterbury and York Society, ed. E. F. Jacob, 4 vols. (1937–47).

COTTON, C. 'Churchwardens' Accounts of the Parish of St. Andrew, Canterbury, 1485–1625', *Archaeologia Cantiana*, vol. xxxii (1917), pp. 181–246.

COWPER, J. M. 'Accounts of the Churchwardens of St. Dunstan's, Canterbury', ibid., vol. xvi (1904), pp. 299–303.

DAVIS, A. H. *Chronicle of St. Augustine's Abbey*, W. Thorne (1934).

WOODRUFF, C. E. 'Some Early Visitation Rolls preserved at Canterbury', *Archaeologia Cantiana*, vol. xxxii (1917), pp. 143–80; and vol. xxxiii (1918), pp. 153–71.

—— 'An Archidiaconal Visitation of 1502', ibid., vol. xlvii (1935), pp. 13–54.

(ii) GENERAL

BRACTON, HENRY DE. *De Legibus et Consuetudinibus Angliae*, ed. G. E. Woodbine (Yale Historical Manuscripts III, 1915–  ).

*Calendar of Letters and Papers, Foreign and Domestic, Henry VIII* (1864–1932).

*Calendar of Papal Letters* (1894–  ).

*Calendar of Patent Rolls* (1891–  ).

*Concilia Magnae Britanniae et Hiberniae*, ed. D. Wilkins (London, 1737).

Fitzherbert's *Natura Brevium* (London, 1677).

*Rotuli Parliamentorum* (1771–83).

*Statutes of the Realm* (1810–28).

# IV. GENERAL BIBLIOGRAPHY

## A. TREATISES ON ECCLESIASTICAL LAW AND PRACTICE

Post-Reformation works have to be used with care. Later practice must be continually checked against the medieval practice of the courts as it appears in the Act books.

The best short survey of Court Practice is that of F. S. Hockaday, 'The Consistory Court of the Diocese of Gloucester', *Transactions, Bristol and Gloucester Archaeological Society*, vol. xlvi (1924), pp. 195–287.

### General

LYNDWOOD, W. *Provinciale* (Oxford, 1679).

GIBSON, E. *Codex Iuris Ecclesiastici Anglicani*, 2 vols. (Oxford, 1761).

*Quellen zur Geschichte des römisch-kanonischen Processes im Mittelalter.* Herausgegeben von Dr. Ludwig Warhmund. (Innsbruck, 1907–28).

### More particular (in chronological order)

CONSET, H. *The Practice of the Spiritual or Ecclesiastical Courts, etc.* (London, 1708).

BURN, R. *Ecclesiastical Law*, ed. R. Phillimore, 4 vols. (London, 1842).

# 144 BIBLIOGRAPHY

LAW, J. T. *Forms of Ecclesiastical Law* (London, 1851).
PHILLIMORE, R. *Ecclesiastical Law of the Church of England*, 2 vols. (London, 1895).

**B. WORKS AND ARTICLES RELATING TO KENT AND CANTERBURY**

HAINES, C. R. *Dover Priory* (1930).
HASTED, E. *History of Kent*, 12 vols. (Canterbury, 1797–1801).
JACOB, E. F. 'Chichele and Canterbury', in *Studies in Medieval History presented to F. M. Powicke* (1948), pp. 386–404.
MORGAN, M. 'Early Canterbury Jurisdiction', *English Historical Review*, vol. lx (1945), pp. 392–9.
MURRAY, K. M. E. *The Constitutional History of the Cinque Ports* (1935).
NEILSON, N. *Cartulary and Terrier of Bilsington Priory*, British Academy Records, vi (1928).
SMITH, R. A. L. *Canterbury Cathedral Priory* (1943).
SOMNER, W. *Antiquities of Canterbury*, ed. N. Battely (1703).
Victoria County History, *Kent*, ed. W. Page, vols. ii and iii (1926–32).
WOODRUFF, C. E., and DANKS, W. *Memorials of Canterbury Cathedral* (1912).

**C. GENERAL**

The indispensable foundation of any study of ecclesiastical jurisdictions within the province of Canterbury is:
CHURCHILL, I. J., *Canterbury Administration*, 2 vols. (1933).

*Other Works*

ADAMS, N. 'The Judicial Conflict over Tithes', *English Historical Review*, vol. lii (1937), pp. 1–22.
BATESON, M. *Borough Customs*, 2 vols., Selden Society (1904, 1906).
BRINKWORTH, E. R. 'The Study and Use of Archdeacons' Court Records: illustrated from the Oxford Records (1566–1759)', *Transactions of the Royal Historical Society*, Fourth Series, vol. xxv (1943), pp. 93–119.
BROWNE, A. L. 'Medieval Officials Principal of Rochester', *Archaeologia Cantiana*, vol. xliii (1941), pp. 29–61.
CHENEY, C. R. *English Bishops' Chanceries 1100–1250* (1950).
*Dictionary of National Biography*.
FELTOE, C. L., and MINNS, E. H. *Vetus Liber Archidiaconi Eliensis*, Cambridge Antiquarian Society, No. xlviii (Cambridge, 1917).
FLAHIFF, G. B. 'Use of Prohibitions by Clerics against Ecclesiastical Courts in England', *Medieval Studies of the Pontifical Institute of Toronto*, vol. iii (1941), pp. 101–16.
—— 'Writ of Prohibition to the Court Christian in the thirteenth century', ibid., vol. vi (1944), pp. 251–313.
FOURNIER, P. *Les Officialités au Moyen Âge* (Paris, 1880).
FOWLER, R. C. 'Secular Aid for Excommunication', *Transactions of the Royal Historical Society*, Third Series, vol. viii (1914), pp. 113–17.
GAIRDNER, J. *Lollardy and the Reformation in England*, 4 vols. (1908–13).
GRAHAM, R. *English Ecclesiastical Studies* (1929).

HALE, W. H. *Precedents in Criminal Causes* (London, 1847).

HALL, H. *Select Cases concerning the Law Merchant*, 3 vols., Selden Society (1908–32).

HASELMAYER, L. A. 'The Apparitor and Chaucer's Summoner', *Speculum*, vol. xii (1937), pp. 43–57.

HOLDSWORTH, W. S. *History of English Law*, 13 vols. (1922–38).

HUNT, R. W. 'The Abbot and Convent of Merevale *v.* The Rector of Halsall, A Tuitorial Appeal in the Fourteenth Century before the Court of the Arches', *Transactions of the Historical Society of Lancashire and Cheshire*, vol. ci, pp. 47–61.

JENKINS, C. 'Cardinal Morton's Register', in *Tudor Studies*, ed. R. W. Seton Watson (1924), pp. 26–74.

KNOWLES, M. D. *The Monastic Order in England* (1940).

LE NEVE, J. *Fasti Ecclesiae Anglicanae, etc.*, 3 vols. (Oxford, 1854).

LLOYD, A. H. 'Notes on Cambridge Clerks petitioning for Benefices 1370–1399', *Bulletin of the Institute of Historical Research*, vol. xx (1943–5), pp. 75 and 192.

MAITLAND, F. W. *Roman Canon Law in the Church of England* (1898).
—— *English Law and the Renaissance* (1901).

MAJOR, K. 'The Office of Chapter Clerk at Lincoln in the Middle Ages', in *Medieval Studies presented to Rose Graham*, ed. V. Ruffer and A. J. Taylor (1950), pp. 163–88.

MAKOWER, F. *The Constitutional History and Constitution of the Church of England* (1895).

MITCHELL, R. J. 'English Law Students at Bologna in the Fifteenth Century', *English Historical Review*, vol. li (1936), pp. 270–87.

PLUCKNETT, T. F. T. *Concise History of the Common Law* (1948).

RIDLEY, T. *A View of the Civil and Ecclesiastical Law* (Oxford, 1675).

ROGERS, J. E. THOROLD. *Six Centuries of Work and Wages* (1894)

ST. GERMAIN, C. *Dyalogue Betwixt a Doctor of Dyvynyte and a Student in the Lawes of England* (1530).

STUBBS, W. 'Report on Ecclesiastical Courts, 1883', Historical Appendix No. 1 to vol. 1 (*Parliamentary Papers*, 1883, vol. xxiv).

THOMPSON, A. HAMILTON. *The English Clergy and their Organisation in the Later Middle Ages* (1947).

# INDEX

All place-names are in Kent unless otherwise indicated.

M. is used as an abbreviation for *Magister.*

Benefices and offices held by personnel of the ecclesiastical courts are not mentioned under their names (although cross-references are made from the benefices, &c.) because they are listed in Appendix I in the careers of the individuals concerned.

Abergwilly (Carmarthen), prebend of Llandysilio in collegiate church of, 116.

Absolution, 97, 101; cost of, 97; post-mortem, 94 n. 3; private, 112; procedure of, 97.

Acrise, Achiryse, rector of, *see* Moonie, Thomas.

— Walter de, commissary general, 14; his career, 113.

Act books, Ex Officio, probate *acta* in, *see* Probate; extent of survival of, in Canterbury and Maidstone, 3.

Adam, proctor, 123.

Adisham, 32.

— rector of, 22; *see also* Blodwell, David; Cooper, Henry; Parmenter, John; Warmington, Richard de; Woodward, Robert.

Advocates, 11, 42.

Albon, John, 133.

Alcham, Christopher, 109.

Aldington, rector of, *see* Warmington, Richard de; Wymbourne, John de.

Alkham, rector of, *see* Webbe, John.

Allen, William, 49 n. 4.

Ames, Robert, 57 n. 3.

Apostacy, 79.

*Apostolos, see* Appeals.

Apparitors, 29 n., 45–49, 50, 51, 73 n. 1, 79, 81, 93, 94 n. 1, 102, 104; abuse of powers by, 48; appointment of, 45; costs of, 61, 62, 136; differentiation of, between courts, 48; incomes of, 77; inquisitorial activity of, 69; numbers of, 48 and n. 1, 112; as originators of business, 49; term *preco* for, 45.

— general, 19, 46, 47.

—— *Sede Vacante* commission of, 124.

Appeals, 10, 12; Act in Restraint of (1553), 13; *apostolos* in, definition and use of, 64–65; to Court of Canterbury, 17, 28, 129; direct, 64; in Instance

cases, 63–67; jurisdiction in, 12; numbers of, 63; provincial machinery of, 6; *provocatio* in, 66–67, 67 n. 2, 94 n. 3, 131–3; *suggestio* in, 65; *remissio* in, 65; to Rome, 14, 17; tuitorial, 64–67, 126–33.

Appledore, Apuldore, 73.

Archer, M. Nicholas, proctor, 41 n. 1, 121.

Arches, court of, 7; *see also* Canterbury, court of; dean of, 7, 11; commissary of, 130; deanery of, archbishop's exempt, 7, 9.

Archier, William le, rector of Saltwood, 95.

Ash, 25 and n. 4.

Ashert, John, 101 n. 3.

Ashford, 35, 36, 90.

Assheton, M. Matthew, commissary general, 56; his career, 115.

Audience, court of, 6, 12, 13, 28 and n. 4, 48, 63, 80.

— as court of first instance, 64.

— records of, 28 n. 4.

Auditors of Causes, 28, 37, 124; *see also* Malling, Robert de.

Austin, Henry, 68.

Austyn, John, 26 and n. 2.

—Thomas, 88.

Aylonds, James, 43, 105.

Bachelor, William, 90 n. 3.

Baker, apparitor, 48.

— Joan, 135, 136.

Baldock, William, 48 n. 3.

Baldwin, archbishop of Canterbury, 20.

Baldwyn, William, 57 n. 3.

Ball, William, 136.

Barber, John, 64 n. 3.

Barfreston, 17 n. 4, 99 n. 2.

Barjona, Simon, archdeacon of Canterbury, 18.

Barrett, Thomas, registrar, 120.

Barrow, Thomas, 133.
Barton, Elizabeth, 112, 121.
— Richard, 99 n. 2.
Basset, M. Roger, commissary general, 115.
Bath and Wells, diocese of, 37, 114; see also Malling, Robert de.
Beccles, John de, proctor, 11 n. 3.
Becket, Thomas, archbishop of Canterbury, 94 n. 6.
Bedel, John, proctor, 40 n. 9, 121.
Beke, John, 112 n. 1.
Bellynger, James, apparitor, 105 n. 1.
Belser, Belsers, Belsyr, William, 107, 136, 137.
Benefices, collation to, 16, 24, 76; held by proctors, 42; vacancies of, 75.
Benenden, Benynden, 64 n. 2, 133.
— vicar of, 133.
Benger, M. Richard, commissary general, his career, 118.
Benyngton, John, 96.
Bergrove, Thomas, 56 n. 1.
Bernard the goldsmith, 109 n. 2.
Berrewic, Henry de, proctor, 11 n. 3.
Bert, Thomas, 54 n. 3.
Bertram, Thomas, 58 n. 1.
Biddenden, 35, 54 n. 4.
— rector of, see Bradegare, Robert; Menesse, William.
Birchington, 54 n. 1.
Bishopsbourne, commendarius of, see Moonie, Thomas.
Blechynden, Ralph, 62 n. 3.
Blodwell, M. David, commissary general, his career, 116.
Bocher, Geoffrey, 98.
— John, 59 n. 1.
— Thomas, 59 n. 1.
Bocking, dean of, see Parmenter, John.
— deanery of, 8 n. 1.
Bodewell, Richard, 111.
Body, Adam, registrar, 39, 41 n. 2, 52 n. 1, 121; his career, 120.
Bold, William, registrar, 39, 123; his career, 120.
Bolney, Agnes, 56 n. 1.
Bologna (Italy), 43, 121.
— James, canon of, auditor of papal curia, 17 n. 8.
Bona notabilia, 26, 74.
Boniface, archbishop of Canterbury, 11, 13, 14, 45.

Borne, Thomas, proctor, 41 n. 1, 121.
Borough court, 110.
'Bothaut' (in Wighton, Norfolk), free chapel in, chaplain of, see Trewonwall, Henry.
Bounsse, Bunse, Roger, 61 n. 1, 76, 125, 126.
Bourne, M. Robert de, commissary general, 21, 37; his career, 114, 118.
Bowman, Joan, 85 n. 1.
Bracton, Henry, 1, 95 n. 5.
Brad, John, 133.
Bradegare, M. Robert, commissary general, his career, 115.
Breche, Christopher, sergeant ad clavem of Canterbury, 108 n. 3.
Bredgar, college at, 115.
— vicar of, see Mody, William.
Brent, Roger, 107.
Breto, Bernard Etil de la, 20 and n. 5.
Bridge, 80 n. 4; dean of, 17 n. 3; deanery of, 35.
Broc, de, family of, 94 n. 6; see also Brokhele.
Broker, proctor, 123.
Brokhele, Sir William, 94.
Brookland, rector of, see Canterbury, Thomas of.
— vicar of, see Broughton, Edward.
Broughton, M. Edward, his career, 119.
Brygge, William, 80.
Brynchele, John, 54 n. 4.
Buckingham rebellion, 109.
Bucwell, Bukwell, M. John de, 56 n. 1, 130.
Bull, John, 88, 134, 135.
Bunse, see Bounsse.
Burbaych, M. James, official, his career, 119, 121.
Burmarsh, rector of, 90.
Burnoth, John, 12 n. 5, 63 n. 2.
Byngley, 135.
Byrchet, apparitor, 77.

Cade, Jack, rebellion of, 109.
Calais, commissary of, see Redesheaf, Adam; Williamson, John; Woodward, Robert.
Cambio, John de, proctor, 11 n. 3.
Cambridge, university of, 42 n. 5.
Canon law, 42, 57.

INDEX

CANTERBURY, 33, 34, 35, 54, 55 n. 4, 91, 124, 127.
— archbishop of, 14 n. 4, 15; *see also* Baldwin; Becket, Thomas; Boniface; Chichele, Henry; Kilwardby, Robert; Lanfranc; Langton, Stephen; Morton, John; Pecham, John; Reynolds, Walter; Rich, Edmund; Richard; Stratford, John; Sudbury, Simon; Walter, Hubert; Warham, William; Winchelsey, Robert.
— — almoner of, 99.
— — as metropolitan, 14.
— — diocesan consistory court of, *see* Consistory.
— — diocesan jurisdiction of, 6–14, 124.
— — manors of, *see* Charing, Croydon, Saltwood, Teynham.
— — prerogative jurisdiction of, *see* Prerogative.
— archdeacon of, 10, 14 n. 4, 15–18, 19–21, 26, 134; *see also* Barjona, Simon; Clifforde, Richard; Ferringes, Robert de; Gernemuth, Richard de; Langton, Simon; Mortimer, Hugh de; Valerius.
— — court of, 13, 27, 28, 45, 48, 73, 79, 88, 90, 92, 100, 107, 134, 136 n. 4; appeals from, 28, 63; persons using, 104–5; records of, 26 n. 4, 34, 142; sessions of, 34–36, 100.
— — income of, 75.
— — jurisdiction of, 19–21, 29 n., 103.
— — official of, *see* Official.
— — privileges of, 13.
— — rights of signification of, 95.
— — vice, 19; *see also* Everard; Ralph; Robert.
— archdeaconry of, 73.
— churches and parishes of:
All Saints, 34, 52 n. 1, 52 n. 2, 56, 116; churchwarden of, *see* Colman, John; rector of, 116; *see also* John; Knepe, Richard.
Cathedral, 7, 33; Brenchley chantry in, chaplain of, *see* Cokkes, Thomas.
Holy Cross, Westgate, 34, 69 n. 2; vicar of, *see* Harding, Clement.
St. Alphege, 33; rector of, *see* Lovelych, John.
St. Andrew's, 56 n. 1; churchwardens of, 107; rector of, *see* Cokke, John.
St. Dunstan's, 54 n. 4, 105; churchwardens of, 106–7, 136–7; *see also* Denyse, Richard; Long, John; vicar of, *see* Burbaych, James; Harding, Clement; Long, Richard; Roper.
St. George's, 34; vicar of, *see* Broughton, Edward; Payne, Edward; Williamson, John.
St. Margaret's, 96 n. 1.
St. Martin's, school of, 127–9; rector of, 24; *see also* Henneye, Robert de; Lovelych, John.
St. Mary Bredman, rector of, *see* Goldwell, James; vicar of, *see* Robert.
St. Mary de Castro, rector of, 96 n. 1. vicar of, *see* Mody, William; Simon.
St. Mary Magdalen, rector of, *see* Woodward, Robert.
St. Mary Northgate, 99; vicar of, *see* Gerard, Walter.
St. Michael's, rector of, *see* John.
St. Mildred's, 111 n. 4; rector of, *see* Galle, Stephen; Petham, John de.
St. Paul's, vicar of, *see* Theobald.
St. Peter's, rector of, *see* Thomas.
— Court of, *Curia Cantuariensis*, 6–14, 22, 24, 28, 29, 42, 48, 63, 64, 96, 130, 131; appeal to, 17, 95, 129, 132; establishment in London, 7, 9–12; examiner general of, *see* Chereminstr', Thomas de; Swanton, William de; official of, 83 n. 2; records of, 11; statutes regulating, 42.
— Croker Lane, 136.
— Dean and Chapter Library, 3, 139.
— dean of Christianity of, 9.
— diocese of, 103, 108, 124, 131.
— Guildhall (speche house) of, 91.
— jurisdiction in, 6–14.
— inns of:
Cardinal's Hat, 82 n. 1; inn of Roger Dyer, 52 n. 2; Fleur de Lys (Flor de Lis), 52 n. 1.
— mayors of, 105.
— province of, 14 n. 4, 74, 131, 134.
— religious houses of:
Christ Church, monks of, 13–15; *see also* Godmersham, Richard; Robert; Woodnesburghe, John; prior of, 23, 31, 56 n. 1, 76, 90 n. 3; *see also* Chillenden, Thomas;

CANTERBURY, religious houses of (*contd.*):
Eastry, Henry; prior of, seal *ad causas*, 124, 134; prior and chapter of, 8 n. 1, 9, 14–16, 19, 20, 22, 29 n., 38, 42, 47, 59 n. 1, 63, 74, 82, 83; advocate of, 17 n. 9; auditors of, 47; commissaries of, 11; *see also* Selseya, Robert de; prerogative jurisdiction of, 133; proctors of, 11; *see also* Lovelych, John; records of, 2, 39; *Sede Vacante* jurisdiction of, 11, 15–19, 133–4.
Dominicans, chapter house of, 56.
Poor Priests' hospital, 34; warden of, 120.
St. Augustine's abbey, 23; almoner of abbot of, *see* William.
St. Gregory's priory by Northgate, 33, 109, 136.
St. Sepulchre's priory, chaplain of, *see* Nicholas; prioress of, 85 n. 1.
St. Thomas's hospital, Eastbridge, 32; master of, *see* Ligham, Peter.
— schools of, 126–33; rector of, *see* Waltham, Ralph de.
— sergeant *ad clavem* of, *see* Breche, Christopher.
— Thomas of, commissary general, his career, 114.
Capel le Ferne, parishioners of, 57 n. 1.
Caption, letter of, *see* Signification.
Cary, apparitor, 48.
Castlyn, John, 62 and n. 3.
Celeseye, *see* Selseya.
Cely, John, 53 n. 2.
Chadwood, rector of, *see* Millet, John.
Challock, 28 n. 3.
Chalvington (Sussex), rector of, *see* Burbaych, James.
Chancery, 93, 95–97; *see also* Signification.
Chantry, revenues of, 107.
Chapleyne, Margaret, 102 n. 2.
Chapman, John, 52 n. 1, 116.
Charing, dean of, 17; deanery of, 35, 48; manor of, archiepiscopal, 21, 22 n. 1, 131; rector of, 24.
Charlton, rector of, *see* Sellyng, Richard.
Charnok, M. John, official, his career, 119.
Chart, vicar of, *see* Hillyngton, Nicholas.
— Magna, rector of, *see* Malberthorp, Robert de.
— Parva, 59 n. 1.

Chartham, 12 n. 5, 58 n. 2, 63 n. 2.
— rector of, *see* Chartham, Thomas de.
— Thomas de, commissary general, 21; his career, 114, 118.
Chelmyngton, Nicholas, 96.
Cheltenham, M. Walter, commissary general, his career, 115.
Chereminstr', Thomas de, examiner general of Court of Canterbury, 130.
Cheriton, rector of, *see* Goldwell, James.
Cheseman, 34 n. 1.
Cheyne, Robert, 89 n. 2.
Chichele, Henry, archbishop of Canterbury, 39, 72 n. 3, 76, 116, 123.
Chichester, diocese of, *see* Malling, Robert de.
Chilham, Chylham, 28 n. 3, 49 n. 2, 61 n. 1.
— vicar of, 94 n. 3; *see also* Geoffrey.
Chillenden, M. Thomas, commissary general and prior of Christ Church, 124, 133; his career, 115.
Chislet, vicar of, *see* Raynhill, Richard.
Churches, appropriated, 23.
Churchwardens, 1, 68, 86, 105; accounts of, 86, 106, 136–7.
Cinque Ports, 92, 105.
Clergy, married, 39.
Clerk, Adam, proctor, 40 n. 9, 121.
Clerke, Joan, 57 n. 2.
Clerks, parish, wages of, 87.
Clifforde, Richard, archdeacon of Canterbury, 29 n.
Clyffords, Margaret, 97 n. 3.
Clyve, Richard de, commissary general, 10, 14, 16, 17, 18, 22, 24, 31, 45, 83 n. 2, 95, 98, 108; his career, 113.
Cokelyn, Richard, 58 n. 2.
Cokke, M. John, rector of St. Andrew's, Canterbury, 56 n. 1.
— Robert, 55 n. 3.
Cokkes, M. John, proctor, his career, 122.
— Thomas, proctor, 42 n. 1; his career, 122.
Colman, M. John, registrar, 39, 59 n. 2; his career, 120, 121.
— — his wife Elizabeth, 39.
— Thomas, proctor, 41 n. 4, 43, 125, 137.

Colonia, Hans de, 52 n. 1.

Colyn, proctor, 123.

Colyns, Robert, official, his career, 120, 122.

Commissaries general, 7–10, 12, 16, 18, 20, 21, 24–28, 29 n., 37–38, 42, 56, 63 n. 1, 73, 74, 95, 96, 98, 101–3, 107, 134; benefices of, 76; list of names and careers of, 113–18; of prior and chapter of Christ Church, 9; payment of, 62, 136.

'Conscience', courts of, 92, 110.

Consistory court, diocesan, of archbishop, 6–8, 12, 13, 14, 18, 23–25, 27, 28, 37, 39, 41, 45–51, 56, 59, 80, 85–88, 90, 96, 99, 100, 101, 105–11, 123, 125, 134, 135; appeals from, 63; expenses of, 76, 77; persons using, 104–5; prerogative jurisdiction in, 74; provincial business in, 12; records of, 12, 13, 140–2; sessions of, 31–34; see also Lincoln, bishop of; London, bishop of.

Cooper, M. Henry, commissary general, his career, 117.

Cophurst, John, 91.

Copyn, John, 54 n. 1.

Correction, letters of, 27.

Costs, 60–62, 106; awarding of, 97; bills of, 61, 106; of litigation, 70, 136–7.

Court, contempt of, 51, 101.

Courts, ecclesiastical, see. Audience; Canterbury, archdeacon of; Canterbury, Court of; Consistory.

— business of: Ex Officio, 27, 30; Instance, 27, 30; Probate, 30; see also Suits; Probate.

— finance of, 75–78, 106.

— personnel of, 37–49; see also Advocates; Apparitors; Apparitors general; Commissaries general; Officials; Proctors; Registrars.

— records of, 18, 19, 21, 25, 139–42.

— sessions of, 100.

— secular, 1, 104, 110; see also Borough; Exchequer; Chancery; 'Conscience'; King's Bench; Pie-powder.

— Litigation in, in cases of debt, 90.

— — in cases of defamation, 88–89.

Cowper, John, 136.

Coyn, proctor, 122.

Cranbrook, 35, 36, 64 n. 2.

— chaplain of, see Wylkys, Nicholas.

Cranebourne, M. John, registrar, 32, 33, 58 n. 4; his career, 120.

Crawley, North (Bucks.), rector of, see Hunden, William.

Cressfelds, William, 62 n. 4.

Cristiane, William, 81 n. 6.

Croumer, Sir William, 135.

Croydon, dean of, see Canterbury, Thomas of; manor of, archiepiscopal, 123.

Crundale, William of, 26.

Cudworth, Robert, chaplain of Faversham, 88 n. 1.

Curdy, John, 83 n. 3.

Curia Cantuariensis, see Canterbury, Court of.

Custos Spiritualitatis, see Mortimer, Hugh de.

Dane, William a, apparitor general, 47.

Darrell, John, 59 n. 1.

Das, M. James, proctor, 41 n. 4, 121.

Dawndelyon, John, 96 n. 2.

Deal, 34.

— rector of, 24; see also Moonie, Thomas.

Deans, rural, 17, 45, 50.

Denton, rector of, see Wymbourne, John de.

Denyse, Richard, churchwarden of St. Dunstan's, Canterbury, 107, 135.

Depham, Henry of, commissary general, 9.

Derbye, Thomas, 98 n. 2.

Dewer, 34 n. 1.

Dixon, proctor, 123.

Doctor's Commons, 111.

Doksowte, 133.

Donke, Robert, 133.

Doule, Richard le, proctor, 11 n. 3.

Dover, 34, 44 n. 1, 64 n. 3; St. Martin's monastery, 9 n. 2, 33; St. Radegund's, archives of monastery of, 57 n. 1.

Downe, William atte, 57 n. 4.

Draper, John, registrar, 40 n. 3; his career, 120.

Dublin, bishop of, see Ferringes, Richard.

Dunham, Muriel of, 12 n. 5, 63 n. 2.

Dwyt, M. John, official, his career, 118.

Dyer, Roger, 52 n. 2.
Dymchurch, rector of, *see* Canterbury, Thomas of; Willefords, Richard.
Dyne, Joan, 56 n. 1.

Easling, vicar of, *see* Hillyngton, Nicholas.
Eastry, 53 n. 2.
— Anselm of, rector of Eastry, 22, 24, 83.
— rector of, *see also* Malling, Robert de.
Ebony, 81 n. 6.
Edinton, William, churchwarden of Westwell, 68.
Edwards, Joan, 133.
Egerden, John, proctor, 41 n. 2, 51 n. 3, 121.
Elemosinaria, Alexander de, 127.
Elham, 51 n. 3.
— dean of, 17 n. 3; *see also* Webbe, John.
— deanery of, 35.
Elmley, rector of, *see* Burbaych, James.
Ely, archdeacon of, his official, *see* Parmenter, John.
Elys, Stephen, 133.
Essex, archdeacon of, *see* Goldwell, James.
— County Record Office, records at, 2 n. 3.
Essexia, William de, proctor, 11 n. 3.
Eston, Elizabeth, 85 n. 1.
Estwell, Thomas, 90 n. 3.
Everard, Master, vice archdeacon of Canterbury, 19, 118.
Ewell, parish clerk of, *see* William.
Exchequer, 90.
Excommunicates, signification to Chancery of, 16.
Excommunication, 54 n. 1, 62, 70, 83, 90, 99–102; *ab homine*, 94 n. 4; *aggravatio* of, 93; for contumacy, 45, 51, 94; decline in, 102; *ipso facto*, 94 n. 4; letters of, 38, 97, 102; secular disabilities of, 94.
Executors of wills, 28, 47, 72, 85.
Exempt deaneries, 12; parishes, 19, 26, 27, 103; jurisdiction in, 21–25, 29 n.
Exeter, chancellor of, *see* Hunden, William.
Expenses, bill of, 136–7.
Eyre, justices in, 94.
Eythorne, 34.

Fairbairn, proctor, 122.
Fauconbridge rising, 109.
Faversham, 27 n. 2, 35, 36, 54 n. 3; abbot of, 57 n. 1; chaplain of, *see* Cudworth, Robert; St. Mary's church, 56 n. 2.
Fayrewey, Richard, 99 n. 3.
Fees, 38, 112.
— mortuary, 86.
— in probate business, 72.
Fen, M. Thomas, proctor, 53 n. 1, 121.
Fenex, Master, 136.
Fermerie, Symon ate, 127.
Ferringes, Richard de, archdeacon of Canterbury and bishop of Dublin, 17, 18, 20.
Fines of money, 59, 83.
Fischer, Richard, proctor, 121.
Flawne, William, 88, 134, 135.
Fleta, 1.
Folkestone, 34.
Forde, John a, 125.
— Richard a, 61 n. 1, 76, 125.
— William a, 125.
Forsham, M. Hugh de, commissary general, his career, 113.
Forster, Thomas, 81 n. 9.
Fower, Roger, 48 n. 3.
Freckenham (Norfolk), rector of, *see* Bourne, Robert de.
Freysel, William, proctor, 11 n. 3.
Frittenden, 62 and n. 3.
— rector of, *see* Raulyn, Robert.
Frognal, Sir Richard, 112 n. 2.
Frogynhale, Richard de, 52 n. 1.
Frost, Thomas, 51 n. 2.
Furneus, John de, proctor, 11 n. 3.
Fynche, Henry, under-sheriff, 135.

Galle, Stephen, proctor, 42; his career, 122.
Ganton, M. James, proctor, 41 n. 4, 43, 89 n. 2, 105 n. 1, 125, 126; his career, 122.
Garter, Order of the, registrar of, *see* Goldwell, James.
Gavelonde, John, 55 n. 4.
Gerard, Walter, vicar of St. Mary Northgate, Canterbury, 38.
Gernemuth (Yarmouth), Robert de, archdeacon of Canterbury, 17.
Gilis, 134.
Godard, John, 135.

Godfrey, John, 26 n. 2.
Godmersham, exempt parish of, 26, 49 n. 2.
— rector of, *see* Warmington, Richard de.
— Richard, commissary general, his career, 116.
Goodhewe, Richard, 112 n. 2.
Goodnestone, 25.
Goods, administration of, 47; *see also Bona notabilia*: Executors.
Gore, Denise, 59 n. 2.
Graf, Henry, 49 n. 3.
Gray, John, 101.
Grey, proctor, 122.
— Richard, 108 n. 3.
Gryme, Sampson, 93 n. 2.
Gylys, John, 51 n. 2.

Hackington, 20.
— vicar of, *see* Hogges, Simon; Moonie, Thomas.
Hadstock (Essex), rector of, *see* Hunden, William.
Hakenyman, William, 27 n. 2.
Hale, John, 85 n. 1.
Halke, 61 n. 1.
Ham, churchwardens of, 53 n. 2.
Hampton, M. Martin de, commissary general, 8, 10, 12, 18; his career, 113.
Harbledown, vicar of, *see* Some, John.
Harding, M. Clement, official, his career, 119.
Harrietsham, 35, 83 n. 3.
— rector of, *see* Goldwell, James.
Harry, Thomas, 98 n. 4.
Harvy, Richard, 81 n. 6.
Hawker, Stephen, 28 n. 3.
Hawte, John, 59 n. 1.
— Sir William, 56 n. 1.
Hay, John, proctor, 122.
Headcom, 62 n. 3.
Henneye, Robert de, rector of St. Martin's schools, Canterbury, 127–30.
Heresy, 29, 80–81.
Heretics, 80.
Herford, Richard, 49 n. 2.
Herne, 68.
— Hill, vicar of, *see* Colman, Thomas; Payne, Edward.
Hewes, Hews, 134, 135.
— *alias* Holwell, M. Richard, proctor, his career, 123.

Hillyngton, M. Nicholas, official, 25; his career, 119.
Hogges, M. Simon, 96 n. 1; his career, 119.
Hokbourne, John, 102 n. 3.
Hokerygge, Thomas, 64 n. 2.
Hollingbourne, rector of, *see* Bradegare, Robert.
Honynton, M. Robert de, 127.
Hope, rector of, *see* Cranbourne, John.
Horlanston, Robert de, official, 118.
Horton, 98.
Howell, M. Richard, *see* Hewes.
Hunden, M. William, commissary general, his career, 115.
Hunt, John, apparitor general, 48.
Hurst, William, 59 n. 1.
Hythe, 25, 33, 34, 44 n. 1, 83 n. 3; St. Leonard's church, 33.

Ickham, rector of, 24.
Induction, 17; fees of, 75.
Ingram, 125.
Inhibition, 24, 64 n. 3; of inferior jurisdictions, 72; from superior to inferior court, 127.
Inquisitions, 38, 49, 69, 127.
Institutions, powers of archdeacon in, 16.
Intestates, 72; sequestration of goods of, 47.
Inventories of goods in probate, 72.
Ivychurch, rector of, *see* Assheton, Matthew.

John, apparitor of Sutton, 45.
— rector of All Saints, Canterbury, 127.
— rector of St. Michael's, Canterbury, 127.
— le taillour, 127.
Judges delegate, 6, 17.
Jurisdictions, *see* Appeal; Canterbury, archdeacon of; Canterbury, archbishop of; exempt parishes; Suits, Instance, matrimonial; Prerogative; Provincial; *Sede Vacante*.

Kelsam, William, 108 n. 3.
Kempe, John, 55 n. 3.
Kent, undersheriff of, 88, 89.
Kibbeworth, William, 101 n. 4.
Kilwardby, Robert, archbishop of Canterbury, 11.

King's Bench, court of, 91.
'Kingswode' (unident.), rector of, see Menesse, William.
Knepe, Richard, proctor, 42; his career, 122.
Knokke, William, 88 n. 1.
Knyght, apparitor, 125, 126.
— M. John, registrar, 120, 122.
Kynge, Alice, 62 n. 4.

Lacey, Edmund, 101 n. 1.
Lambeth Palace, archiepiscopal registers at, 3.
Lanfranc, archbishop of Canterbury, 19, 82.
Langdon, East, 81.
Langton, Simon, archdeacon of Canterbury, 16, 20, 82, 95.
— Stephen, archbishop of Canterbury, 16, 19, 20.
Lauke, Thomas, official, 119.
Laurence, M. Thomas, registrar, 59 n. 2, 112, 122; his career, 121.
Laybrooke, Isabella, 88.
Lebourne, rector of, see Burbaych, James.
Leeds, 35.
Leicester Museum, records at, 2 n. 3.
Lenham, 24, 35, 57 n. 4, 62 n. 4, 111.
— vicar of, see Hillyngton, Nicholas.
Lenna, Michael de, proctor, 11 n. 3.
Ligham, M. Peter, his career, 117.
Lincoln, canon of, see Hunden, William.
— consistory of bishop of, 4.
— dean and chapter of, clerk of, see Pakyngton, John.
— Record Office, records at, 2 n. 3.
Littlebourne, 80.
Llandysilio, see Abergwilly.
Londiniis, J. de, official, 19.
London, 55 n. 4, 130, 131, 137.
— bishop of, 14 n. 4, 15; consistory of, 92 n. 2.
— churches of:
    All Saints, Bread Street, rector of, see Charnok, John.
    Bow Church (St. Mary de Arcubus), 7; see also Arches.
    St. Dunstan by the Tower, rector of, see Basset, Roger.
    St. Mary 'Aldermanicherche', 130.
    St. Paul's, canon of, see Bradegare, Robert; Goldwell, James.

London, Court of Canterbury in, see Canterbury, Court of.
— court of 'Conscience', in Guildhall, 92.
— court of province in, 111.
— diocese of, 69.
— Joan, 96 n. 1.
Long, John, churchwarden of St. Dunstan's, Canterbury, 107, 135.
—, Richard, vicar of St. Dunstan's, Canterbury, 135.
Lovelych, M. John, registrar, 39, 56, 116; his career, 120.
Low, Thomas, 133.
Lucas, Agnes, 54 n. 4.
— Godeleva, 64 n. 2.
Lustyntone, Angelina de, 98 n. 1.
— Ivona de, 98 n. 1.
— Walter de, 98 n. 1.
Luton, John, 136.
Lyminge, 54 n. 3.
— vicar of, 24.
Lympne, deanery of, 35.
— vicar of, 17; see also Colyns, Robert.
Lyndsay, brother, 93 n. 2.
Lyndwood, 4, 50, 73, 93 n. 1, 94 n. 4.
Lynton, M. John, commissary general, his career, 115.

Maidstone, 22 n. 1, 29 n., 98 n. 4; records at, 73, 140–2; rector of, 24.
Malberthorp, M. William de, commissary general, 21; his career, 115.
Malling, M. Robert de, commissary general, 21, 37, 127, 129, 130; his career, 114, 118.
—, South, canon and prebendary of, see Raynhill, Richard.
Mareys, David, proctor, 41 n. 2, 52 n. 2, 53 n. 2, 68, 116, 121.
Marley, 133.
— Margaret, 61 n. 1.
Marshall, Robert, 58 n. 1.
— William, 69 n. 2.
Marten, Robert, 96 n. 1.
Matthew, apparitor, 48.
Mattie, Thomas, 62 n. 2.
Mennesse, M. William, official, his career, 118.
Mercer, proctor, 41 n. 4, 121.
Millet, John, proctor, his career, 123.

Mills, John, 133.
Milstead, 89 n. 2.
Milton, 36, 135.
— curate of, 97 n. 3.
Minster (in Thanet), 24.
— vicar of, see Ligham, Peter; Sellyng, Richard; Williamson, John.
Mocock, James, 70 n. 3.
Mody, M. William, proctor, his career, 122.
Molash, Molassh, Molyshe, 61 n.1, 125, 126.
Mongeham, Great, rector of, see Cooper, Henry; Hogges, Simon.
— Little, rector of, see Cokkes, Thomas; Woodward, Robert.
Monkton, Monckton, 24, 31, 81.
— rector of, 25; see also Richard.
— vicar of, see Payne, Edward.
Moonie, M. Thomas, commissary general, his career, 116.
More, Margaret, 105 n. 3.
Mores, Joan, 81.
Mortimer, Hugh de, archdeacon of Canterbury, official and custos spiritualitatis, 14, 16, 95.
Morton, John, archbishop of Canterbury, 117.

Nash, Juliana atte, 111.
Nethersole, Robert, 57 n. 2.
— — Alice his wife, 57 n. 2.
Nevinson, Christopher, commission of, 74 n. 3.
Newchurch, rector of, see Hogges, Simon; Parmenter, John.
Newenham, Katherine de, 83 n. 2.
Newington, Newenton, 88, 134.
— (Surrey), rector of, see Lovelych, John.
Nicholas, chaplain of St. Sepulchre's, Canterbury, 127.
Nobyll, William, 102 n. 3.
Nonington, 25.
Non-residence, 79.
Norton, John, 27 n. 2.
Norwich, archdeacon of, 116.
— bishop of, see Goldwell, James.
— diocese of, 102.
Notaries public, proctors as, 42, 43, 110, 121–3.
Notyngham, M. Thomas, proctor, 41 n. 4, 43, 77, 121.

Obstruction of ecclesiastical jurisdiction, 79.
Odyerne, Simon, 53 n. 1.
Officials, archbishops', 9, 103; presiding over Court of Canterbury, 14, 95.
— archdeacons', 10, 15, 17, 19–21, 24, 26–28, 35, 38, 42, 62, 68, 69, 73, 95, 129, 134, 135, 137; deputies of, 9, 38; list of names and careers of, 118–20; salary of, 75, 76.
— of provost of Wingham college, 25.
Offore, Joan, 133.
Olyver, Joan, 54 n. 3.
— Robert, 48.
Omer, Master, official, 19; his career, 118.
— Laurence, 25 n. 4.
Ordinary, bishop as, 3.
Ordination, letters of, 79.
Ornebrake, Simon, proctor, 121.
Orpington, 95 n. 4.
Ospringe, 35.
— deanery of, 35, 48.
Otes, Robert, apparitor general, 46.
Otho, constitutions of, 52 n. 4.
Otterden, 81.
Ovynden, Thomas, 57 n. 2.
Oxene, brother James de, 114.
Oxford, university of, 42 n. 5.
— All Souls College, 120; fellow of, see Hogges, Simon.
— Bodleian Library, records at, 2 n. 3.

Pagham, rector of, 24.
Pakyngton, John, clerk of dean and chapter of Lincoln, 39 n. 6.
Pancake, Lucas, 81.
Papacy: appeal to, 14, 17, 129; archdeacons, papal nomination of, 20; bull, papal, 24, 57 n. 1.
Papal curia, auditor of, see Bologna, James, canon of; suits in, 22 n. 1.
Park, William a, 89 n. 1.
Parmantory, Master, see Parmenter, John.
Parmenter, alias Parmantory, M. John, commissary general, 37, 107, 109; his career, 117.
Payne, Christine, 25 n. 4.
— M. Edward, commissary general, his career, 117.
Peasants' Revolt, 109.
Pecham, John, archbishop of Canterbury, 8, 10, 11, 18, 23, 64, 103, 131.

Peke, Jeffrey, 136.
Penance, 80, 90, 97–99, 102.
— commutations of, 75, 98, 99, 102.
Pensions, 75, 86.
Penwortham, M. John, registrar and apparitor general, 39, 47; his career, 120.
Peraune, Richard, 94 n. 1.
Percy, proctor, 122.
Peter's Pence, 75.
Petham, 26, 93 n. 2.
— M. John de, official, 21; his career, 118, 121.
Piepowder courts, 91.
Piers, Richard, 85 n. 1.
Pilgrim Trust, report on ecclesiastical archives, 2.
Plott, Francis, 85 n. 1.
Poole, John, 57 n. 3.
Poverty, pleas in forma pauperis, 62, 105.
Preco, see Apparitors.
Prerogative jurisdiction, 27, 29 n., 73, 74, 133–4.
Probate, 1, 23, 26, 72–75, 85; see also Suits.
— acta entered in Ex Officio Act books, 72.
— in exempt and non-exempt parishes, 28, 29 n.
Procedure in suits in ecclesiastical courts, see Suits.
Proctors, 11, 14, 28, 36, 40–45, 107, 111, 112; appointment of, 52; business of, 43–44, 77; constitutio of, 52; cautione de rato in, 52; incomes of, 61, 77, 78, 126, 136–7; list of names of, 121–3; numbers of, 40, 41, 44; as public notaries, see Notaries; substitution of, 52; table of cases handled by, 44.
Procurations, 68, 75.
Prohibitions, 62, 88, 92, 108.
'Proof' in canon law, 57.
Provincial jurisdiction, 10–11; see also Canterbury, Court of.
Provocatio, see Appeals.
Prowde, James, 61 n. 1.
Purgation, letters of, 27; of criminous clerks, 29.

Quynt, Thomas, 97 n. 3.

Rainham, 48, 49.
Ralph, vice archdeacon of Canterbury, 19, 118.

Ramsey, M. Thomas, proctor, 41 n. 4, 105, 121, 136.
Raulyn, M. Robert, commissary general, his career, 116.
Raveningham, Ravenigham, Ravingham, M. John de, commissary general, 8, 37; his career, 113.
Ravenisdale, Richard, 57 n. 4.
Ravyn, John, 81.
Raynhill, M. Richard, commissary general, his career, 116, 119.
Reade, William, 133.
Rectors, in exempt parishes, autonomous powers of, 21–24, 103; commissions of, 82 n. 4.
Reculver, Recolver, 34, 54 n. 2, 56 n. 1, 114.
— rector of, 24.
Redesheaf, Adam, commissary of Calais, 117.
Registrars, of Consistory and archdeacons' courts, 14, 32, 38, 39, 50, 57, 68–70, 75, 80, 93 n. 2, 102, 104, 107, 112, 137; assistants of, 40; commissions of, 39, 123; duties of, 38; income of, 39, 76–78, 123; life grants of office to, 39, 104; list of names and careers of, 120–1; practise as public notaries, 76; payment of, 62; as receivers of the archdeacon, 34, 98.
Reynolds, Walter, archbishop of Canterbury, 18, 21, 24, 127, 128.
Rich, Edmund, archbishop of Canterbury, 16, 82.
Richard, archbishop of Canterbury, 19.
— preco consistorii, 45.
— rector of Monkton, 127.
Richardson, M. John, proctor, 41 nn. 3, 4, 57 n. 1, 121, 135, 136.
Ringwold, Rinwould, 51 n. 2, 80.
Robert, apparitor, 45.
— registrar, 120.
— vicar of St. Mary Bredman, Canterbury, 82.
— vice archdeacon of Canterbury, 19, 118, 133.
Robertson, 81.
Roche, Aymer de la, 21.
Rochester, archdeacon of, see Hunden, William.
— diocese of, official principal of, see Bourne, Robert de.
— vicar general of, see Assheton, Matthew.

Rodmersham, 89 n. 2.

Rodyng, Matilda, 83 n. 5.

Rolf, John, 133.

Romney, 25, 33, 34, 35, 44 n. 1; exempt rural deanery, dean of, 25; St. Mary's church, 116; St. Nicholas's church, 33.

Roper, family, 105.

— John, 107.

— Master, vicar of St. Dunstan's, Canterbury, 107.

Rosseley, rector of, see Raulyn, Robert.

Ruckinge, rector of, see Moonie, Thomas.

Rusyll, John, churchwarden of Westwell, 68.

Ruxley, rector of, see Hunden, William.

St. Alban's, abbey of, 23.

St. Asaph, dean of, see Blodwell, David.

St. David's, bishop of, 116; clerk of the household of, see Raulyn, Robert.

— canon of, Clyde prebend, and vicar general of, see Raulyn, Robert.

St. Margaret, Hugh de, commissary general, 113.

St. Martin's, Winfred de, proctor, 11 n. 3.

Salisbury, dean of, 38; see also Goldwell, James.

Salkyn, apparitor, 48 n. 3.

Saltwood, archiepiscopal manor of, 21, 22 n. 1; castle and chapel of, 94 n. 6; rector of, 24, 94; see also Archier, William le; Ligham, Peter.

Samson, Thomas, 80.

Sandwich, 73, 92.

— churches of:

St. Clement's, 35; vicar of, see Burbaych, James; Hillyngton, Nicholas; Payne, Edward.

St. Mary's, 35; vicar of, see Raynhill, Richard.

St. Peter's, 35.

— customs of, 92 n. 1.

— dean of, 17 n. 3.

— deanery of, 34, 35, 41.

Saukyn, William, 55 n. 3.

Scott, Henry, 90 n. 3.

Seal ad causas of prior of Christ Church, 124, 134.

— of Statute Merchant, 91 n. 3.

— of rural dean, 52 n. 3.

Sede Vacante jurisdiction, 15–19, 133–4; provocatio to uphold, 131–3; records of, 11, 31; see also Canterbury, Christ Church, prior and chapter of.

Segrym, William, proctor, 121.

Selseya, Celeseye, Selsey, Robert de, commissary of prior and chapter of Christ Church, 8, 9, 12, 14, 16, 17; his career, 113.

Sellyng, M. Richard, official, his career, 118.

Selveston, John de, official, 10, 14.

Sequestration of women, during matrimonial suits, 83.

Sheffields, John, apparitor general, 47.

Sheldwich, 59 n. 2.

Shoreham, dean of, see Canterbury, Thomas de; Forsham, Hugh de.

Signification (letter of caption), 93, 95–97, 100–1.

Simon, vicar of St. Mary de Castro, Canterbury, 127.

Sittingbourne, 35, 134; deanery of, 35; apparitor of, see Baker.

Skell, John, 73 n. 1.

Skome, John, 111.

Skynner, John, 83 n. 3.

Slapton, rector of, see Assheton, Matthew.

Smallwode, Margaret, 83 n. 3.

Smardon, parishioners of, 87.

— vicar of, see Hogges, Simon.

Smeeth, 26.

Smyth, Alice, 52 n. 1.

— apparitor, 48.

Snave, rector of, see Hillyngton, Nicholas.

Some, M. John, proctor, 134, 135; his career, 122.

Sone, William, 52 n. 2, 101 n. 2.

Southfleet, rector of, see Bourne, Robert de.

Sparows, John, 62 n. 2.

Spender, John, 83 n. 5.

Sprat, John, 80.

Sprotte, John, 136.

Stablegate, John de, 128.

Staplehurst, 27 n. 2.

Statute Merchant, 91, 92; seal of, 91 n. 3.

— Staple, 91.

Stevenys, Crispina, 54 n. 1.

Stockbury, vicar of, *see* Hewes, Richard.
Stodmarsh, 55 n. 3.
Stokbury, John de, 83 n. 2.
Stoks, William, 89 n. 1.
Stone, 53 n. 1.
— proctor, 123.
Stratford, John, archbishop of Canterbury, 47, 70.
— R. de, official, 14.
Strode, John de, 127.
Strongbow, John, 135.
Studle, John, 94 n. 1.
Sturry, 23, 57 n. 3.
Stylman, Joan, 64 n. 3.
Suits in ecclesiastical courts:
— *Ex Officio mero*, 68.
— — *promoto*, 68–71.
— — summary treatment of, 70.
— — types of :
  Administration of goods, temerarious, 79; ambushes, set for apparitors, 48; begging on false pretences, 81; brawling, 81, 82; clergy, offences of 79, 82; communion, reception of, by excommunicates, 101 n. 3, 101 n. 4; criticism of sermon, 70 n. 3; defamation of apparitors, 49 n. 2; disturbance of ecclesiastical law and discipline, 55 n. 3, 79, 80, 81; fast breaking, 81; heresy, 80–81; non-performance of duties by churchwardens, 68; obstruction of ecclesiastical jurisdiction, 79; perjury, 79; sabbath breaking, 80; sexual offences, 79; sorcery, 81; surgery, illegal practice of, 81; unlawful exercise of office of apparitor, 49 n. 3.
— Instance, adjourned, 60.
— — disposal of, table showing, 125.
— — numbers of, 60, 82–92.
— — plenary, 59.
— — types of:
  Adultery, 27 n. 2, 61 n. 1; debt, recovery of, 85, 89–90, 102, 106–7, 109, 110; defamation 1, 55 nn. 3, 4, 56 n. 1, 58 n. 1, 79, 87–89, 94 n. 1., 106, 134–5; dues, ecclesiastical, non-payment of, 86; fees, recovery of, 42 and n. 4; litigation, vexatious, 87; matrimony, 12 n. 5, 24, 25 n. 4, 54 n. 3, 56 n. 1, 62 n. 4, 64, 64 n. 3, 83 nn. 2–5, 98 n. 1, 106,

jurisdiction over, 19, 20, 23, 26, 82–85, 103; muniments, illegal detention of, 57 n. 3; perjury, 1, 26 n. 2, 48 n. 3, 54 n. 1, 62 n. 1, 63 n. 3, 78, 89, 90 n. 3, 90–93, 96 n. 2, 97 n. 2, 101 n. 2, 102, 105, 112 n. 1; rent, recovery of, 106–7, 135–7; sacrilege, 87; testamentary, 28 n. 3, 34 n. 1, 51 n. 2, 53 n. 1, 54 n. 4, 57 n. 2, 59 n. 1, 59 n. 2, 61 n. 1, 85–86, 102 nn. 2, 3, 125; tithe, 1, 57 n. 1, 86, 96 n. 1; usury, 87.
— procedure in (both types of business): acts, propounding of, 53.
  arbitration, 59.
  citation 50–51; certificated, 50; cost of mandates of, 61, 136; 'exception' to, 51; mandates of, 9, 50; primary, 50–51; peremptory, in Ex Officio business, 69–70; *viis et modis*, 51, 96.
  compurgation, in Ex Officio suits, 70; in Instance suits, 57, 58, 99 n. 1.
  depositions of witnesses, 56, 57, 61, 137.
  *dimissio*, 136 n. 1.
  execution, letter of, 61.
  *gravamen*, 64.
  interrogatories, 56, 57.
  *introductio*, 136 n. 1.
  libel, 44, 53, 135; 'articulated', 53; cost of, 61, 126, 136.
  oath *de calumpnia*, 55, 55 n. 1.
  plenary procedure, 53.
  presentments (*billae detectionis*), 69.
  probatory terms, 53, 54, 58.
  proofs, 55–58.
  remission, letter of, 12, 130.
  sentence, 126, 128; confirmation of, 131; cost of, 61, 126; definitive, 58, 83, 128; interlocutory, 58.
  summary hearing, 53.
  summons for delay (*temeraria fatigatio*), 54.
  *see also* Appeals; Excommunication; Inhibitions; Penances; Probate; Signification; Suspension.
Sudbury, Simon, archbishop of Canterbury, 25.
Suspension, letters of, 38, 70, 93, 97; numbers of persons sentenced to, 99–101.

Sutton, apparitor of, *see* John; dean of, *see* Hewes, Richard; deanery of, 35.
— 'Bery' of, 51.
— Valence, 35.
— — vicar of, *see* Hillyngton, Nicholas.
Swalecliff, rector of, *see* Williamson, John.
Swan, John, proctor, 122.
— Ralph, 55 n. 3.
Swanton, M. William de, official, 118.
Swetman, Thomas, 99.
Sympson, Agnes, 133.

Talbot, proctor, 122.
Tarring, East (Sussex), rector of, *see* Basset, Roger.
Taylor, John, apparitor general, 19, 47, 124.
Taylour, Thomas, 133.
Tenterden, 35, 62 n. 3.
Teynham, archiepiscopal manor, 14, 20.
Thanet, 81, 96 n. 2; St. Laurence, 58 n. 2; St. Nicholas, vicar of, *see* Colman, Thomas; St. Peter's, 80; chaplain of, *see* Swan, John; *see also* Minster, Monkton.
Theobald, vicar of St. Paul's, Canterbury, 127.
Thomas, dompnus, 25.
—John, 136.
— rector of St. Peter's, Canterbury, 127.
Thomson, Robert, 81 n. 8.
Thornham, vicar of, *see* Hewes, Richard.
Tithability, 86 n. 1.
Tody, Hamo, 96 n. 2.
Tong, 112 n. 2.
Torner, 61 n. 1.
Totnes, archdeacon of, *see* Hunden, William.
Trewonwall, Henry, registrar, his career, 120.
Tropham, William, 58 n. 2.
Trott, proctor, 122.
Tur, Alice, 83 n. 4.
Turner, Richard, 102 n. 2.

Ulcombe, 62 n. 4.

Vacancy, archiepiscopal, *see* Sede Vacante jurisdiction.
Valerius, archdeacon of Canterbury, 19.
Veker, Master, 137.

Verich, William, 58 n. 2.
Vertue, proctor, 123.
Vicars, in appropriated churches, 23.
Visitation, 69, 72, 101; by official of the archdeacon, 26, 68; diocesan, 30; provincial, 30.
Vyan, Richard, 88 n. 1.

Waltham, M. Ralph de, rector of the schools of Canterbury, 127–30.
Warde, John, proctor, 41 n. 4, 43, 121, 135, 136.
Warham, William, archbishop of Canterbury, 72, 80, 101.
Warmington, M. Richard de, commissary general, his career, 114.
Warrene, William, proctor, 41 n. 1, 121.
Webb, Thomas, proctor, 121.
Webbe, M. John, proctor, 122.
Westbere, deanery of, 35, 56 n. 1.
Westgate, Elyas de, registrar, 40, 120.
Westwell, 59 n. 1.
— churchwardens of, *see* Edinton, William; Rusyll, John.
— parishioners of, 68.
— rector of, *see* Wymbourne, John.
White, Ralph, proctor, 122.
— Robert, 28 n. 3.
— Stephen, 90.
Whitstable, 54 n. 1.
Whyte, Juliana, 55 n. 4.
— Thomas, 80.
Widerley, Thomas, 80.
Wigmore, M. William, proctor, 122, 134, 135.
Willefords, M. Richard, official, 38, 108 n. 3; his career, 119.
Willesborough, 80.
— vicar of, *see* Williamson, John.
William, almoner of St. Augustine's, Canterbury, 24.
— official, 17 n. 2.
— parish clerk of Ewell, 70.
Williamson, M. John, commissary general, 37, 41 n. 4, 42, 74, 134; his career, 117, 119, 121.
Wills, 57; registers of, 142; *see also* Executors.
Wilmington, M. John, proctor, 41 n. 1, 121.
Winchelsey, Robert, archbishop of Canterbury, 18, 23, 24, 28 n. 4, 29 n., 103.

Wingham, college of:
canon of, *see* Bradegare, Robert; Cooper, Henry; Parmenter, John; Warmington, Richard de; Woodward, Robert; prebendaries, of, 76; *see also* Williamson, John; provost of, 25, 76; *see also* Assheton, Matthew; Moonie, Thomas.
— exempt jurisdiction of, 29 n.; official of, *see* Hillyngton, Nicholas; register of wills of, 25, 142.
Witnesses, attendance of, 55.
— examination of, 38, 57.
Wittersham, 53 n. 1, 70 n. 3.
— rector of, *see* Hampton, Martin; Knyght, John; Wymbourne, John de.
Wode, John, 112 n. 2.
'Woldham' (unident.), rector of, *see* Bourne, Robert de.
Wormshill, rector of, *see* Broughton, Edward.
Woodchurch, rector of, 22 n. 1.

Woodnysburghe, John, commissary general, his career, 116.
Woods, M. Henry, proctor, 41 n. 4, 122.
Woodward, M. Robert, commissary general, 32; his career, 117.
Writ *de admittenda cautione*, 97 n. 1; *de excommunicato capiendo*, 95, 97.
Wyk, Stephen de, 127.
Wykham, Stephen, 98 n. 2.
Wyldington, Emma de, 45.
Wylkys, Nicholas, chaplain of Cranbrook, 99 n. 3.
Wylmot, John, 53 n. 1.
Wymbourne, M. John de, commissary general, his career, 114.
Wythot, John, 83 n. 4.
'Wythyndon' (unident.), rector of, *see* Cheltenham, Walter.

Yarmouth, *see* Gernemuth.
York, diocesan archives of, 2 n. 3.
Ystele, Ysteley, Nicholas de, official, 38; his career, 118.

PRINTED IN GREAT BRITAIN
AT THE UNIVERSITY PRESS, OXFORD
BY CHARLES BATEY, PRINTER TO THE UNIVERSITY